Syntactic Theory

a unified approach

Robert D Borsley

Lecturer, School of English and Linguistics, University of Wales, Bangor

Edward Arnold
A member of the Hodder Headline Group
LONDON NEW YORK MELBOURNE AUCKLAND

© 1991 Robert D Borsley

First published in Great Britain 1991
Reprinted 1992, 1994

Distributed in the USA by Routledge Inc.
29 West 35th Street, New York, NY 10001

British Library Cataloguing in Publication Data
Borsley, Robert D.
  Syntactic theory: A unified approach.
  I. Title
  415

  ISBN 0-7131-6543-X

Typeset in Linotron Times by Rowland Phototypesetting Limited,
Bury St Edmunds, Suffolk
Printed and bound in Great Britain for Edward Arnold,
a division of Hodder Headline PLC,
338 Euston Road, London NW1 3BH
by Biddles Limited, Guildford and King's Lynn

for Ewa and Stefan

Contents

Preface

Why do we need a new textbook on syntactic theory? One answer is that new textbooks are always necessary in a field that is alive and developing, and syntactic theory is undoubtedly such a field. There is, however, a more specific answer that can be given in the present context. This is that there are no textbooks of the kind that I have tried to produce here. In this book, I attempt to introduce a body of ideas that are at the heart of more or less all approaches to syntax and to consider how they have been developed within two broad frameworks: the Government-Binding theory (GB) and Phrase Structure Grammar (PSG), by which I mean Generalized Phrase Structure Grammar and Head-driven Phrase Structure Grammar. The book introduces the two approaches more or less simultaneously. Each chapter focusses on a specific theoretical topic, and considers what both GB and PSG have to say about it. Other textbooks are either concerned with just one approach, or they look at a number of approaches, one at a time. The first type is unsatisfactory if one thinks that there is more than one approach that merits the student's attention. The second type is likely to make the various approaches seem more different than they really are and to give the impression that they are neat self-contained packages of ideas which you have to 'buy' in toto or not at all.

The book is an introduction to current syntactic theory and refers extensively to the recent literature. It places considerable emphasis, however, on ideas which antedate the emergence of current approaches and which are likely to remain when current approaches have been revised in major ways or abandoned. The organization of the book is designed to highlight these ideas. Most of the chapters focus on one of them. For example, chapter 10 highlights the idea that there is a class of raising sentences with a specific array of properties. This idea is unlikely to be abandoned even if both GB and PSG analyses of such sentences prove to be untenable.

I say little here about the history of the ideas that I am concerned with. The history of syntactic theory is a topic of considerable interest, but I do not think that knowing how the ideas developed necessarily makes it any easier to understand them. Moreover, there are good discussions of the history elsewhere, notably Newmeyer (1986). I do, however, make a point of indicating when and where various ideas emerged. I think it is important to give some sense that syntactic theory has a history, and that it did not appear fully formed the day before yesterday. Of course, readers who are not interested in these matters can ignore all references to them.

Each chapter in the book includes notes and exercises. The notes are not just an adornment to the basic text. They qualify and elaborate on the discussion in the text, provide further information and raise further issues, and give relevant references. Many of the references are not at all easy to read. I make a point, however, of referring to other textbooks – I do not assume that this is the only syntax textbook that anyone could wish to read. The exercises reinforce the points made in the text and in some cases raise various questions. The book also includes a glossary bringing together the most important terms used.

The book introduces a lot of ideas in a relatively small space, and is therefore quite demanding. However, it presupposes very little knowledge of syntax. Essentially, all I assume is that the reader understands that linguistics is concerned with description and not prescription, and that she or he has some acquaintance with the traditional parts of speech. Of course, the book will be more accessible for readers with more extensive knowledge of syntax, but further knowledge is not strictly necessary.

I am grateful to a number of people for the help that they have given me in connection with this book. I am particularly grateful to Dick Hudson (University College London), who provided detailed comments on a draft of the book, and to Andrew Radford (University of Essex), who commented at length on most of the chapters. I have also had valuable comments from Geoff Horrocks (University of Cambridge). The comments that I have received have led to many improvements in the text. All remaining shortcomings are my responsibility. I am also grateful to the staff of Edward Arnold for their assistance, encouragement and patience. Finally, I am grateful to my wife, Ewa Jaworska, for encouragement and for various kinds of assistance.

1

Preliminaries

1.1 Introduction

There are many aspects of language that one might be interested in. One might study the systems of sounds that they employ, the way language reflects the structure of society, or the way it is used in literature or in propaganda of various kinds. Syntactic theory is concerned with the ways words are combined to form sentences. This might sound like a dry and unglamorous study and it has to be admitted that some people find it so. It is clear, however, that it is full of intellectual challenges. It is also a potential source of insight into the human mind. It is even potentially useful. In this chapter, we will consider a number of preliminary matters, and then in the next chapter, we will begin the real work.

1.2 The Goals of syntactic theory

Syntactic theory, as the term is used here, has its origins in Noam Chomsky's 1957 book *Syntactic Structures* and is widely seen as the heart of modern theoretical linguistics. It can be said to have two goals. On the one hand, it is concerned to develop grammars, i.e. precise descriptions of the syntax of various languages, the ways in which they combine words to form sentences. On the other hand, it aims to develop a general framework for specifying what languages have in common in this area and how they can vary. This is often known as a theory of universal grammar.

One point that should be stressed immediately is that the two goals are not pursued separately. It is not a matter of first describing individual languages and then developing a theory of universal grammar. Rather, syntacticians are always concerned both with individual languages and with language in general. Investigations of individual languages are guided by ideas about what languages are like and how they should be described and in turn contribute towards the evaluation and refinement of these ideas.

The second of these aims entails a rejection of the view expressed by one linguist in the 50s that 'languages can vary without limit.' (Joos, 1957). If languages really could vary without limit, there could be no theory of universal grammar. We could have a theory of English syntax, a theory of Welsh syntax, and so on, but no general theory. It is in fact fairly clear that languages do not vary without limit in their syntax. Differences between languages which seem massive to the learner of foreign language can be seen to be rather minor when one has a sophisticated descriptive framework that can identify all the similarities.

One thing that is clear is that there are all sorts of situations that do not occur in languages. For example, it is clear that there are no languages in which questions are formed from statements by turning the whole statement back to front. In other words, there are no languages where the question related to (1) would be (2).

(1) The boy ate the beefburger.
(2) Beefburger the ate boy the?

Perhaps more interestingly, it is fairly clear that there are no languages where questions are formed from statements by moving the second word of the statement to the front. English might seem to be such a language if one looks at a pair of sentences like the following:

(3) Stefan will be here.
(4) Will Stefan be here?

Notice, however, that the question related to (5) is (7) not (6).

(5) The boy will be here.
(6) * Boy the will be here?
(7) Will the boy be here?

Following standard practice, I use an asterisk in (6) to mark an ungrammatical string.

Of course, it sometimes happens that things that were thought to be impossible do in fact occur. For example, it was widely assumed in the 70's that there are no languages whose normal order is object-verb-subject or object-subject-verb, no languages, that is, where the meaning of (1) is expressed by a sentence like (8) or a sentence like (9).

(8) The beefburger ate the boy.
(9) The beefburger the boy ate.

In the late 70s, however, it became clear that there are languages with these word orders, especially in the Amazon basin.

There is perhaps a moral here. In general, it seems likely that proposed universals which relate to relatively concrete and superficial features of languages are unlikely to be tenable. Viable universals are likely to be rather abstract. The various concepts and principles discussed in the following chapters are plausible candidates for universals. It may be, however, that they take a somewhat different form in different languages. Hence, as Chomsky has stressed, syntactic theory should not just seek a body of universal principles but should also try to identify the parameters within which these principles can vary.

A final point that we should note here is that the following pages will largely ignore languages other than English. The ideas that we will be concerned with will generally be illustrated with data from English. This is simply because English examples will be more accessible to most readers than examples in other languages.

1.3 Languages

We have used the term 'language' a number of times in the preceding discussion. It is appropriate, then, to ask what exactly a language is. When we use the term in ordinary conversation, we normally think of something that is shared by a group of people, possibly a very large group. This concept is quite problematic, however. Suppose we say we want to describe the English language using this term in its ordinary sense. What exactly do we describe? The English spoken by a Yorkshire miner is not the same as the English spoken by a Surrey stockbroker. Similarly, the English spoken in the West Indies is different from the English spoken in Australia. If we say we are interested in all varieties of English, what exactly do we count as a variety of English? Did Chaucer speak a variety of English or a variety of something else, say Middle English?

Because of problems like these, many linguists prefer to see a language as something essentially individual. Individuals have languages and in all probability no two individuals have exactly the same language if only because no two individuals use exactly the same set of words. We still need, however, to say what a language is. In *Syntactic Structures*, Chomsky defines a language as a set of sentences. Building on this, we might suggest the following:

(10) A language is the set of sentences that some speaker uses.

There is, however, no fixed set of sentences that an individual uses over and over again. Speakers regularly use new sentences that they have never used before. We might, then, replace (10) by the following:

(11) A language is the set of sentences that some speaker could use.

There are, however, many sentences which a speaker, for non-linguistic reasons, could never use. Presumably, no one is going to use a sentence over a thousand words long. That, however, is not a linguistic matter. Rather, it has to do with the limitations of human powers of concentration, which are seen in all sorts of human behaviour and not just in the use of language. In view of this, we might revise (11) as follows:

(12) A language is the set of sentences that some speaker could use if no non-linguistic factors were operative.

This is probably a definition that many syntacticians would be happy with. Chomsky, however, has advanced a rather different conception of language in recent work. We can formulate this conception as follows:

(13) A language is the set of rules and principles in the mind of a speaker specifying the set of sentences which he/she could use if non-linguistic factors were operative.

Chomsky (1985) calls language as defined in (12) E-language (externalized language) and language as defined in (13) I-langauge (internalized language) and argues that it is the latter that syntacticians should study. In his earlier work, particularly Chomsky (1965), he uses the term linguistic competence in essentially the same sense as I-language.

On the face of it, these are two very different conceptions of language. It is not clear, however, that it really matters as far as the practice of syntactic theory is concerned which conception one assumes. Chomsky and his critics disagree on many details of syntactic theory, but it is doubtful whether any of these differences stem from the fact that they subscribe to different conceptions of language.

One point to note about Chomsky's conception of a language is that it makes syntactic theory a branch of psychology, and especially of cognitive psychology, the psychology of systems of knowledge and belief. Chomsky in fact argues not just that a language is a body of rules and principles in the mind of the speaker, but also that universal grammar is a body of principles and parameters which is an innate component of the mind. Thus, for Chomsky, what syntactic theory is ultimately about is the human mind. But even if one isn't prepared to go all the way with Chomsky, it is reasonable to assume that syntactic theory can offer some insight into the workings of the human mind. For many people, this is a major attraction of syntactic theory.

1.4 Acceptability and Grammaticality

Whichever view of language we adopt, it is necessary to specify what sentences a speaker could use if no non-linguistic factors were operative, or, as we will say, what sentences are grammatical for the speaker. We do this by eliciting speaker's judgements or intuitions about sentences. These intuitions establish that certain sentences are acceptable for unacceptable. Acceptability, however, is not the same thing as grammaticality. This is mainly because sentences can be unacceptable for a variety of reasons.

Sentences can be unacceptable because they cause problems for the perceptual mechanisms. We can look first at the following example:

(14) The horse raced past the barn fell.

This is unacceptable, but it is clear that this is because it leads the perceptual mechanisms astray. To use the standard terminology, it is a 'garden path' sentence. This view is supported by the fact that the very similar sentence (15) is perfectly acceptable.

(15) The horse ridden past the barn fell.

Notice also that (14) is a reduced version of (16) in essentially the same way as (15) is a reduced version of (17).

(16) The horse which was raced past the barn fell.
(17) The horse which was ridden past the barn fell.

We can also consider the following:

(18) The man the girl the boy knows likes is here.

This too is unacceptable, but it is clear that this is because it is just too complex for the perceptual mechanisms. This view is supported by the fact that the related sentences in (19) and (20) are perfectly acceptable.

(19) The man the girl likes is here.
(20) The girl the boy knows likes the man.

Sentences can also be unacceptable because they involve contradictions or because they conflict with our views of how the world is, (21) illustrate the first of these possibilities and (22) the second.

(21) Stefan succeeded in seeing Maja but he didn't see her.
(22) My lawnmover thinks that I don't like it.

Thus, there are a variety of ways in which sentences can be unacceptable without being ungrammatical.

All the unacceptable examples that we will consider in subsequent discussion will be ones which as far as anyone knows are unacceptable because they are ungrammatical. It is important, however, to remember when looking at data that sentences can be unacceptable without being ungrammatical.

A natural question to ask here is whether sentences can be acceptable when they are ungrammatical. It is questionable whether there are any such sentences. It has been suggested, however, that the phrase in (23) is ungrammatical although it is acceptable.

(23) a not unintelligent person

Not cannot generally combine with a pre-nominal adjective, but it can combine with the adverb *very*, as the following illustrate:

(24) * a not intelligent person
(25) a not very intelligent person

It is suggested that speakers hear an example like (23) as if it involved an adverb like *very* and not the prefix -*un* and find it acceptable although it violates the rules they have internalized.

1.5 Syntactic theory and traditional grammar

Although syntactic theory, as the term is used here, dates from 1957, this does not mean that it is completely unlike earlier work on syntax – what we might call 'traditional grammar'. There are, however, some important differences. It is appropriate to look briefly at these differences here. Subsequent chapters will flesh out the picture.

Firstly, syntactic theory places great emphasis on the precise specification of analyses. It is often referred to as 'generative', which means precise and explicit. In this it is quite different from traditional grammar, which is characterized by a general lack of precision. The stress on precision is really just a matter of good scientific practice. If an analysis is not precisely formulated, we cannot determine what exactly it says. And if we cannot determine what exactly it says, we cannot evaluate it. In practice, the stress on precision means that syntacticians use various kinds of formalism, something largely absent from traditional grammar. For example, instead of the statement in (26), a syntactician might use the formula in (27).

(26) A sentence can consist of a noun phrase followed by a verb phrase.
(27) S → NP VP

As a result, work in syntactic theory has a somewhat mathematical appearance – at least to those with little background in mathematics.

Secondly, there is a stress in syntactic theory on the justification of analyses. This means that syntacticians seek to demonstrate that their analyses work well and especially that they work better than the obvious alternatives. In contrast, in traditional grammar, constructions are often analyzed in a particular way for no better reason than that they have always been analyzed that way.

Finally, as we have already indicated, syntactic theory is unlike traditional grammar in being concerned not just to describe specific languages but also to develop a general theory. It means that other languages are always potentially relevant when one is describing a particular language.

1.6 The usefulness of syntactic theory

It is probably true to say that most syntacticians are interested in syntax for its own sake and not because of any practical applications that an understanding of syntax might have. It has sometimes been suggested that syntactic theory is of no practical use. In fact, this has never been true. It has always been potentially useful in a number of areas. In particular, it has always had considerable potential in connection with language teaching (although attempts to exploit this potential have not always been very successful). Over the last ten years, however, an important development has made it much clearer than it once was that syntactic theory is useful. This is a major expansion in attempts to get computers to use ordinary language. Precise descriptions of languages are essential here because computers, unlike people, will not tolerate imprecision.

Among the things that it would be useful if computers could do are recognizing and producing speech. By the former we mean converting speech into writing, and by the latter we mean converting writing into speech. Getting computers to do these things is very difficult, and current achievements are quite limited. It is easy to show, however, that syntactic information is important in both cases.

We can look first at speech recognition. An obvious source of problems here is that different words with different spellings sometimes have the same pronunciation. Consider, for example, the verb *meet* and the noun *meat*. How can a computer know that it is the former in (28) and the latter in (29)?

(28) Can you meet me tomorrow?
(29) I bought some meat.

The answer is that it needs to have access to the following information:

(30) Only the basic form of a verb is possible in the context: *Can you — me.*
(31) Only a noun is possible in the context: *I bought some —*

Only if it incorporates a precise analysis of the relevant aspects of English syntax will this be the case. There are many other pairs of words that we might mention. One is the verb *write* and the adjective *right*. The computer needs syntactic information to know that it is the former in (32) and the latter in (33).

(32) I made him write a letter.
(33) I gave him the right letter.

Other examples will be found in the exercises.

Problems may also arise where pairs of expressions have similar pronunciations. Consider, for example, the verb *oil* and the determiner *all*. Although
they have distinct pronunciations, the computer may be unable to decide on the
basis of the acoustic evidence which word has actually been produced. If so, it
will need syntactic information to work out that it is the former in (34) and the
latter in (35).

(34) I tried to oil the wheels.
(35) I talked to all the girls.

Specifically, it will need to know that the verb *tried* combines with what is
known as an infinitive whereas the very *talked* combines with what is known as
a prepositional phrase. Again, it is only if the computer incorporates a precise
analysis of the relevant aspects of English syntax that this will be the case. A
similar pair of words are the verb *reach* and the adjective *rich*, illustrated in the
following examples:

(36) I saw her rich aunt.
(37) I saw her reach out.

Here again, if the computer is unable to decide on the basis of the acoustic
evidence which word has been produced, it will need syntactic information to
reach a decision.

We can turn now to speech synthesis. Here, the main problem is that
different words which are pronounced differently are sometimes spelt in the
same way. Consider, for example, *mouth*. This may be either a noun, in which
case the *th* is pronounced as in *thin*, or a verb, in which case it is pronounced as
in *then*. In (38) it is a noun, and in (39) it is a verb.

(38) I saw her mouth move. .
(39) I saw her mouth the answer.

A computer, however, will only know this if it knows something about English
syntax. *Mouth* is not a unique example. There are many similar examples. The
following illustrate just one:

(40) They made the council house filthy.
(41) They made the council house the family.

In (40), *house* is a noun and rhymes with *mouse* while in (41) it is a verb and
rhymes with *cows*. Another interesting example is *read*. This can be what can
be called the non-third person singular present tense form, the form used
where the subject is anything other than the pronouns *he*, *she* and *it* or singular
expressions like *the boy*, and it can be the past tense form. In the former case, it
is pronounced like *reed*. In the latter case, it is pronounced like *red*.

Consider now the following examples:

(42) The boy read the paper.
(43) The boys read the paper.

In (42), *read* can only be the past tense of the verb. Hence, it must be pronounced like *red*. In (43), however, it can be either the non-third person singular present tense form or the past tense form. Here, then, it can be pronounced like *red* or like *reed*. Why is this? Clearly, it is because we have the singular subject *the boy* in (42) and the plural subject *the boys* in (43). In (42) and (43), these are adjacent to *read*, but they need not be, as the following illustrate:

(44) The boy often read the paper.
(45) The boys often read the paper.

In fact, there is no real limit to how far away the crucial expression can be.

(46) Which boy do you think read the paper?
(47) Which boys do you think read the paper?
(48) Which boy did you say you thought read the paper?
(49) Which boys did you say you thought read the paper?

In (46) and (47) we have three words between *which boy* and *which boys* and *read*, and in (48) and (49) we have five. Clearly, we could construct more complex examples. We are dealing here with a particularly complex area of syntax, which we will not be looking at in any detail until Chapter 12. It is clear, then, that speech synthesis requires some complex information about syntax.

1.7 Some further background

In the final section of this chapter, we can look briefly at the history of syntactic theory and at the current scene. As we noted earlier, syntactic theory has its origins in Chomsky's *Syntactic Structures*. In that book, Chomsky introduced an approach to syntax known as transformational grammar (TG). Remarkably, Chomsky has been the dominant figure in syntactic theory ever since. In his 1965 book *Aspects of the Theory of Syntax*, he introduced what is often known as the Standard Theory or classical TG. We will use the latter term in later discussion, especially in Chapters 9 and 10. Over the last 20 years, a number of alternatives to TG have been developed. The first major alternative was Relational Grammar (RG), which appeared in the early 70s. This was followed at the end of the 70s by Lexical Functional Grammar (LFG). Both will be discussed briefly in Chapter 8.

The most prominent theory in the 80s was Chomsky's Government-binding theory (GB) first presented in detail in Chomsky's *Lectures on Government and Binding* in 1981 and revised in important ways in his *Barriers* in 1986. This is a version of TG, but one that is very different from the TG of the 50s and 60s. The 80s also saw the emergence of Phrase Structure Grammar (PSG) as a major alternative to TG. This is in fact two different though related approaches: Generalized Phrase Structure Grammar (GPSG), presented in Gazdar *et al.'s Generalized Phrase Structure Grammar* in 1985, and Head-driven Phrase Structure Grammar (HPSG), presented in Pollard and Sag's *Information-Based Syntax and Semantics, Vol. 1: Fundamentals* in 1988. The term PSG was originally applied by Chomsky to a formalization of the descriptive practices of pre-Chomskyan linguists. I will refer to this in subsequent discussion as Chomskyan PSG. PSG, as it developed in the 80s, differs in a number of ways from Chomskyan PSG.

We can summarize the preceding remarks with the following table:

Early 50s – approaches to syntax subsequently formalized as phrase structure grammar

1957 – the beginnings of modern syntactic theory and especially transformational grammar in Chomsky's *Syntactic Structures*

1965 – classical transformational grammar (the Standard Theory) introduced in Chomsky's *Aspects of the Theory of Syntax*

Early 70s – the emergence of relational grammar as a competitor to transformational grammar

Late 70s, early 80s – the emergence of the Government-binding theory, first presented in Chomsky's *Lectures on Government and Binding*, of Generalized Phrase Structure Grammar, presented in detail in Gazdar et al.'s *Generalized Phrase Structure Grammar*, and of Lexical Functional Grammar

1986 – the presentation in Chomsky's *Barriers* of some major revisions to GB

1988 – the presentation in Pollard and Sag's *Information-Based Syntax and Semantics, Vol. 1: Fundamentals* of Head-driven Phrase Structure Grammar

---

We can turn now to the current scene. As the preceding remarks indicate, there is no single approach that enjoys general acceptance. GB is the most widely assumed framework, but PSG enjoys considerable influence, and both RG and LFG have significant numbers of adherents. There are also other approaches not mentioned above. In other words, syntacticians have many disagreements. This might lead one to ask: How can we take syntacticians seriously when they disagree so much? However, this question betrays a serious misunderstanding of the nature of science. Disagreements are normal, especially in a young science. In fact, if syntacticians agreed on everything, one couldn't take them seriously. Unanimity is a characteristic of religious sects, not of sciences.

Some of the disagreements are quite important and I will try to highlight these in the following chapters. One hopes, of course, that these diagreements will eventually be resolved, but resolving them will not be a simple matter. Apart from anything else, there are a lot of languages out there and none of them, not even English, has been described in a fully satisfactory way.

It is important, however, not to exaggerate the extent of the differences. There is in fact a measure of agreement, more in fact than meets the eye. When people have disagreements they tend to exaggerate their differences, and syntacticians are no exception. The similarities are often obscured by differences of terminology and notation, and by rhetorical excesses. In fact, there is considerable agreement about what the most important phenomena are and how they are like and unlike each other and about what sorts of concepts are relevant to their description.

Although there is a measure of agreement, it remains true that there are some major disagreements among syntacticians. This makes it harder than it would otherwise be to get to grips with syntactic theory, but I hope to show that it is not as difficult as it might seem.

1.8 Summary

In this chapter, we have looked at a variety of preliminary matters. We began in 1.2 by looking at the goals of syntactic theory, stressing that it is concerned both with individual languages and with language in general. Then, in 1.3, we looked at what syntacticians mean by a language, noting that the term has two rather different meanings. Next in 1.4 we looked at the important difference between acceptability and grammatically. In 1.5 we considered the relation between syntactic theory and traditional grammar, and in 1.6 we highlighted the way that syntactic theory is useful in connection with the computer processing of ordinary language. Finally, in 1.7 we looked briefly at the history of syntactic theory and the current scene, noting that there are some important disagreements in syntactic theory, but that there is also a considerable measure of agreement.

Notes

For further discussion of the central assumptions of syntactic theory and a defence of these assumptions against various criticisms, see Newmeyer (1983). Chomsky has presented his views on the nature of language and linguistics in many places. Fairly accessible recent discussions are Chomsky (1985, 1987) and Chomsky, Huybregts and van Riemsdijk (1982). Earlier works such as Chomsky (1972, 1976a, 1980a) are also worth looking at. Botha (1989) provides a clear and detailed discussion of Chomsky's ideas and the various criticisms that have been advanced against them. Some very interesting philosophical discussion of Chomsky's ideas can be found in Pateman (1987). Various other philosophers discuss Chomsky's ideas in George (1989).

Subject-verb-object languages are exemplified by English, French and Vietnamese. Subject-object-verb languages are exemplified by Japanese, Tibetan and Korean. Examples of verb-subject-object languages are Welsh, Irish and Tongan. Malagasy is a verb-object-subject language. One of the few object-verb-subject languages is Hixkaryana. One of the few object-subject-verb languages is Apurina. Pullum (1977) argued that there are no object-verb-subject and object-subject-verb sentences. Pullum (1980) discusses how he became aware that he was wrong.

For further discussion of the difference between acceptability and grammaticality, see Newmeyer (1983, 2.2.1.) and Horrocks (1987, 1.4.). The example in (14) is from Bever (1974). Examples like (18) were first discussed in Miller and Chomsky (1963). Langendoen and Bever (1973) argue that examples like (23) are ungrammatical but acceptable.

Major examples of traditional grammar are Jespersen (1909–1949) Kruisinga (1925) and Poutsma (1926–29). Quirk *et al.* (1985) can also be seen as an example of traditional grammar.

For general discussions of the computer processing of language, see Gazdar and Mellish (1987) and Halvorsen (1988). See Pullum (1987) for some discussion of military interest in this work. For more general discussion of the usefulness of syntactic theory, see Newmeyer (1983, 5.).

For further discussion of the history of syntactic theory, see Newmeyer (1986) and Horrocks (1987, 2.1., 2.2.). For discussion of the development of GB, see van Riemsdijk and Williams (1986). Chomsky introduces and criticizes what we are calling Chomskyan Phrase Structure Grammar in Chomsky (1957). GPSG was first presented in Gazdar (1981, 1982), and HPSG was first presented in Pollard (1985). For discussion of the various senses of the term phrase structure, see Manaster-Ramer and Kac (1990).

The most important frameworks not discussed in this book are Categorial Grammar, Word Grammar and Functional Grammar. For Categorial Grammar, see the notes to Chapter 5. For Word Grammar, see the notes to Chapter 2. For Functional Grammar, see Dik (1978, 1980).

Exercises

Exercise 1

The sentences in (1) can be seen as related to the sentences in (2). Similarly, the sentences in (3) can be seen as related to the sentences in (4). Using other similar sentences, show that the statements in (5) and (6) do not provide satisfactory descriptions of these relations.

1 (a) Ben saw Debbie.
  (b) Ben gave Debbie a hard time.
  (c) Ben told Debbie to leave.
2 (a) Debbie was seen.
  (b) Debbie was given a hard time.
  (c) Debbie was told to leave.
3 (a) It is likely that Ben will be late.
  (b) It is sure that Debbie will do it.
  (c) It is certain that Debbie will be there.
4 (a) Ben is likely to be late.
  (b) Debbie is sure to do it.
  (c) Debbie is certain to be there.
5 Sentences of the kind that are illustrated in (2) can be derived from sentences of the kind that are illustrated in (1) by a number of processes including the movement of the third word into sentence-initial position.
6 Sentences of the kind that are illustrated in (4) can be derived from sentences of the kind that are illustrated in (3) by a number of processes including the movement of the fifth word into sentence-initial position.

Exercise 2

Rearrange sentences (1)–(3) so that they are as they would be if English were a language with the order verb-subject-object. Rearrange sentences (4)–(6) so that they are as they would be if English were a language with the order object-verb-subject.

1 Gentlemen prefer blondes.
2 Too many cooks spoil the broth.
3 Humpty Dumpty had a great fall.
4 Whatever he does annoys her.
5 The man she likes dislikes her.
6 The fact that he was late surprised everybody.

Exercise 3

All the following sentences are unacceptable in some way. Try to determine the nature of the unacceptability and in particular to determine whether or not the sentences are ungrammatical.

1 This is a four-sided triangle.
2 He managed to lift the rock but he couldn't lift it.
3 They am intelligent.
4 I've never known a more intelligent man than Mary.
5 Who did you talk to him?
6 I heard the smell of the cheese.
7 Three fours are thirteen.
8 She is knowing the time.
9 The book was given the book to Mary.

Exercise 4

Each of the following pairs of sentences contains two words with the same pronunciation but different spellings. In each case, indicate whether grammatical information is sufficient to ensure the right spelling, and if so indicate what sort of grammatical information is necessary using any grammatical terminology with which you are familiar.

1 (a) I think he *ate* snails.
  (b) I gave him *eight* snails.
2 (a) He was standing under the *beech*.
  (b) He was walking along the *beach*.
3 (a) I had *read* the book.
  (b) I had the *red* book.
4 (a) We told him to *wait*.
  (b) We told him the *weight*.
5 (a) The *floor* in the cottage was uneven.
  (b) The *flaw* in the argument was obvious.
6 (a) This is made of *steel*.
  (b) This made him *steal*.

Exercise 5

Each of the following pairs of sentences contains two words with the same spelling but different pronunciations. In each case, indicate whether grammatical information is sufficient to ensure the right pronunciation, and if so, indicate what sort of grammatical information is necessary using any grammatical terminology with which you are familiar.

1 (a) This is the student that *read* the book.
  (b) This is the student that must *read* the book.
2 (a) The *content* of the book was dreadful.
  (b) He was *content* with the situation.
3 (a) I saw her *protest* in the paper.
  (b) I saw her *protest* in the street.
4 (a) He has some *live* ammunition.
  (b) He wants to *live* in France.
5 (a) I'd *read* that book by the time I was ten.
  (b) I'd *read* that book if you asked me to.

2

Constituent structure

2.1 Introduction

Having dealt in the last chapter with a number of preliminary matters, we can now begin to look at the central ideas of syntactic theory. One thing that all syntacticians are agreed on is that sentences are more than just strings of words of various kinds. Rather, they have structures. Most syntacticians assume that words are grouped together to form larger units or phrases of various kinds. Such a grouping is standardly known as a constituent structure. In this chapter, we look first at the motivation for the assumption that sentences have constituent structures. Then, we consider ways of representing constituent structure. Next, we look at how the constituent structure of sentences can be investigated. Finally, we consider evidence for what we can call intermediate categories.

2.2 The motivation for constituent structure

What, then, is the motivation for the assumption that sentences have constituent structures? The most general answer is that without it it is more or less impossible to specify what is and what is not possible in a language. This soon becomes clear if we try to specify what is and what is not possible without making this assumption.

How might one specify what is and what is not possible if one assumes that sentences are just strings of words of various kinds? Consider the following sentence:

(1) The boy was angry about the girl.

Here, we have the following parts of speech or lexical categories:

(2) Determiner – Noun – Verb – Adjective – Preposition – Determiner – Noun

If one assumes that this is all there is to the sentence, one could represent it as follows, using standard abbreviations:

(3)

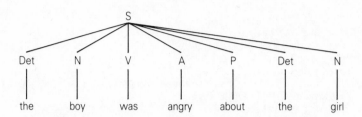

And one could specify that a sentence can take this form with the following rule:

(4) S → Det N V A P Det N

We can interpret this as saying that an S can consist of a Det, followed by a N, followed by a V, etc. If one assumes that sentences are just strings of words, one might specify what is possible with a set of rules of this kind.

It is clear, however, that this is not a satisfactory approach. If we agree that there is no longest sentence, then specifying what is possible by formulating rules of this kind is a task that would never be completed. Even if we limited ourselves to sentences of no more than thirty words, we would have a massive number of rules. It is clear too that this approach will miss numerous generalizations. In (1), we have Det + N at the beginning of the sentence and at the end. It seems, then, that there is a generalization here. However, if we have rules like (4), we are ignoring this. With such rules, we could just as easily have Det + N at the beginning of the sentence and N + Det at the end as have Det + N in both positions. It is clear, then, that we need to look for an alternative approach.

Another approach that one might consider involves specifying possible transitions, i.e. specifying for each category what categories it can be followed by. For example, one might say that Det can be followed by N, but that N cannot be followed by Det. This would allow (1), while ruling out the following:

(5) * Boy the was angry about girl the.

It is not true, however, that Det cannot follow N. The following shows this:

(6) The boy gave the girl the book.

Here, the noun *girl* is followed by the Det *the*. In fact, almost any category can follow almost any category. The following illustrate this. The crucial words are capitalized and their categories are given in brackets.

(7) a. The UNIVERSITY LIBRARY was closed. (N, N)
    b. The BOY DID it. (N, V)
    c. I did SOMETHING STUPID. (N, A)
    d. They gave the BOOK TO Maja. (N, P)
    e. I know the GIRL THE man described. (N, Det)
    f. He LIKES BEANS. (V, N)
    g. The man you SAW DID it. (V, V)

    h. They LIKE OLD cars. (V, A)
    i.   We WENT TO London. (V, P)
    j.   They SAW THE man. (V, Det)
    k. The OLD MAN was there. (A, N)
    l.   Somebody STUPID DID this. (A, V)
    m. He was a TALL DARK man. (A, A)
    n. She is AFRAID OF spiders. (A, P)
    o. He isn't as TALL A man as his brother. (A, Det)
    p. He argues WITH PEOPLE. (P, N)
    q. The man you talked TO DID it. (P, V)
    r.   He appeared FROM BEHIND the hedge. (P, P)
    s. We looked AT THE picture. (P, Det)
    t.   I saw THE MAN. (Det, N)
    u. They disturbed THE SLEEPING child. (Det, V)
    v.   THE OLD man was there. (Det, A)
    w. He had AN OVER the moon feeling. (Det, P)

Thus, this too is not a very plausible approach.

How, then, can we provide a more satisfactory account of what is and what is not possible? The answer most syntacticians would give is by assuming that words are grouped together to form phrases. We noted earlier that certain sequences recur if we list the lexical categories in sentences. In fact it is not just certain sequences that recur, but certain ranges of options. The following illustrate this:

    (8) Stefan was angry about Maja.
    (9) The old man was angry about the young girl.
  (10) Stefan and Ben were angry about Maja and Debbie.

In (8), we have a single N, a proper name, in the positions where Det + N appears in (1), in (9), we have Det + A + N in these positions, and in (10), we have N + *and* + N in these positions.

We can account for the facts by calling all these options noun phrases (NPs), and introducing NP into rules for S and specifying just once what an NP can be. Instead of (4), we can introduce the rule in (11), and we can specify the range of options with (12).

(11) S → NP V A P NP

$$(12)\ \ NP \rightarrow \begin{Bmatrix} \text{Det} & \text{N} \\ \text{N} \\ \text{Det} & \text{A} & \text{N} \\ \text{N} & and & \text{N} \end{Bmatrix}$$

The curly brackets in (12) indicate that each sequence of categories is one option. One point to note about this approach is that it involves the assumption that a phrase can consist of a single word. This approach gives us the following, more complex representation for (1):

(13)

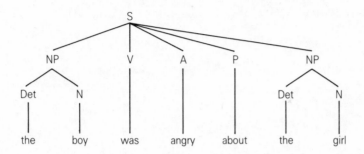

This is clearly a more satisfactory approach. (12), however, is not completely satisfactory. Any sequence of words that is an NP can be conjoined with any other sequence of words that is an NP. The following illustrate:

(14) a. Stefan and his mother
 b. Maja and her grannie
 c. the boy and the old man

We can account for this fact by reformulating (12) as follows:

(15) NP → $\begin{Bmatrix} \text{Det} & \text{N} \\ \text{N} \\ \text{Det} & \text{A} & \text{N} \\ \text{NP} & and & \text{NP} \end{Bmatrix}$

Considerations like those which support the recognition of NPs support the recognition of other types of phrase. There is evidence firstly for verb phrases (VPs). For example, the range of options that can occur after a subject, the initial NP in a simple sentence, can appear elsewhere. (16) illustrates some of the options that can appear after a subject.

(16) a. The boy slept.
 b. The boy saw the girl.
 c. The boy was angry about the girl.
 d. The boy came and went.

(17) shows that these options can appear in another position: following the modal *may*:

(17) a. The boy may sleep.
 b. The boy may see the girl.
 c. The boy may be angry about the girl.
 d. The boy may come and go.

We can account for the facts by introducing VP into rules for S and specifying just once what a VP is. We can introduce VP with the rules in (18) and specify what a VP can be with the rule in (19).

(18) a. S → NP   VP
 b. S → NP   M   VP

(19) VP →
$$
\begin{Bmatrix}
\text{V} \\
\text{V} \quad \text{NP} \\
\text{V} \quad \text{A} \quad \text{P} \quad \text{NP} \\
\text{V} \quad \textit{and} \quad \text{V}
\end{Bmatrix}
$$

This revision will give us the following representation for (1).

(20)

(19), however, is not quite satisfactory. Any VP sequence can be conjoined with any other VP sequence, as the following illustrate:

(21) a. The boy arrived and saw the girl.
       b. The boy arrived and sent the book to her.
       c. The boy saw the girl and sent the book to her.

This suggests that we should reformulate (19) as follows:

(22) VP →
$$
\begin{Bmatrix}
\text{V} \\
\text{V} \quad \text{NP} \\
\text{V} \quad \text{A} \quad \text{P} \quad \text{NP} \\
\text{VP} \quad \textit{and} \quad \text{VP}
\end{Bmatrix}
$$

There is also evidence for prepositional phrases (PPs). The following shows that the sequence P + NP, which appears in (1), can appear in a different position.

(23) It was about the girl that the boy was angry.

This is what is known as a cleft sentence. It suggests that we should analyze P + NP as a PP. It seems, then, that we should replace (22) with (24) and introduce (25) to specify what a PP can consist of.

(24) VP →
$$
\begin{Bmatrix}
\text{V} \\
\text{V} \quad \text{NP} \\
\text{V} \quad \text{A} \quad \text{PP} \\
\text{VP} \quad \textit{and} \quad \text{VP}
\end{Bmatrix}
$$

(25) PP → P   NP

With this revision, we will have the following representation for (1):

(26)

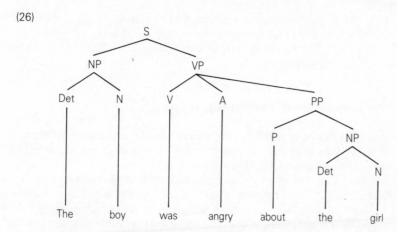

Finally, there is evidence for adjective phrases (APs). The following shows that the sequence A + PP, which appears in (1), can appear in a different position.

(27) What the boy was was angry about the girl.

This is what is known as a pseudo-cleft sentence. Such examples suggest that we should analyze A + PP as a AP. Thus, it seems that we should replace (24) with (28) and introduce (29) to specify what an AP can consist of.

(28) VP →
$$\begin{Bmatrix} V \\ V \quad NP \\ V \quad AP \\ VP \quad and \quad VP \end{Bmatrix}$$

(29) AP → A   PP

With this revision, we have the following as our final representation for (1).

(30)

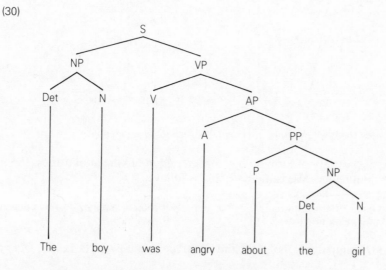

Thus, a consideration of range of sentences has led us to propose a complex constituent structure for (1). More generally, it has led us to recognize four phrasal categories: NP, VP, PP and AP. We will see in 2.5 that there is evidence for further phrasal categories.

2.3 The representation of constituent structure

We can now consider how constituent structure can be represented. We have already seen one way, but there is another that we should consider, and there are a number of related matters that we need to look at.

There are two standard ways of representing constituent structure. The first is a labelled tree diagram like those that we used in the last section. Such a diagram is a set of positions or nodes labelled by syntactic categories and related in specific ways. The second way of representing constituent structure is a labelled bracketing. For (1), we will have the following:

(31) [s [NP [Det The][N boy]][VP [V was][AP [A angry][PP [P about][NP [Det the][N girl]]]]]]

It should be stressed that these are two ways of representing the same information. Which form of representation one uses is a matter of con-venience. Both forms can be used to provide a partial representation of the structure of sentences if not all the details are important. For example, if one is not concerned with the internal structure of the NPs in (1), one could use the labelled tree diagram in (32) or the labelled bracketing in (33).

(32)

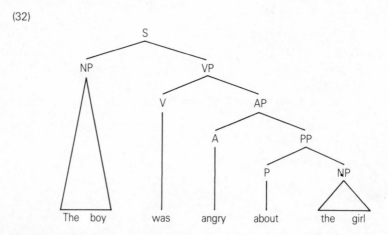

(33) [s [NP The boy][VP [V was][AP [A angry][PP [P about][NP the girl]]]]]

There is a variety of terminology that is used in talking about trees. Firstly, there is dominance. We can define this as follows:

(34) A node X dominates a node Y iff (if and only if) there is a purely downward path through the tree from X to Y.

PP in (30) dominates P, NP, Det and N, AP dominates A, PP, P, NP, Det and

N, and so on. Then, there is immediate dominance. We can define this as follows:

(35) A node X immediately dominates a node Y iff X dominates Y and there is no
 node Z such that X dominates Z and Z dominates Y.

PP in (30) immediately dominates P and NP. It does not immediately dominate Det and N because they are also dominated by NP which is dominated by PP. Next, there is constituency and immediate constituency, which we can define as follows:

(36) X is a constituent of Y, iff Y dominates X.
(37) X is an immediate constituent of Y iff Y immediately dominates X.

Finally, we have mother, daughter and sister, which can be defined as follows:

(38) X is the mother of Y iff X immediately dominates Y.
(39) X is the daughter of Y iff Y immediately dominates X.
(40) X and Y are sisters iff they have the same mother.

There are two important restrictions on constituent structures that we should note. Firstly, it is generally assumed that only adjacent expressions can form a constituent, and hence that there are no discontinuous constituents. This means that there is no branch crossing in trees, i.e. that there are no trees of the following form:

(41)

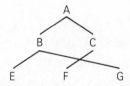

Secondly, it is generally assumed that no expression can be a constituent of two different expressions unless one is a constituent of the other. This means that no node can have more than one mother, i.e. that there are no trees like the following:

(42)

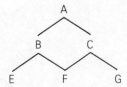

These restrictions rule out what might seem like quite plausible analysis. Consider firstly the following:

(43) He put the cat out.

There is a sense here in which *put* and *out* go together. Note that the following is an alternative form of (43):

(44) He put out the cat.

This might lead one to suggest that *put* and *out* form a constituent in (43) although they are not adjacent. In other words, one might suggest that (43) has the following structure:

(45)

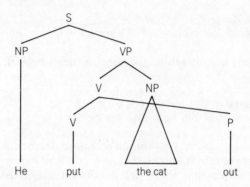

This, however, is ruled out if we do not allow discontinuous constituents. Consider next the following:

(46) Stefan seemed to like Maja.

As we will see in Chapter 7, there is a sense in which *Stefan* here is the subject both of *seemed to like Maja* and *to like Maja*. This might lead one to suggest the following structure:

(47)

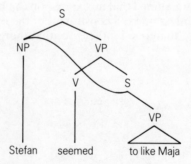

This, however, is ruled out if no node can have more than one mother.

2.4 The investigation of constituent structure

We can look now at how we can investigate the constituent structure of a sentence. There are two main matters to consider, one quite complex, one more simple
The earlier discussion suggests that we can make the following assumption:

(48) A sequence of categories is a constituent if it can appear in some other position in a sentence.

We assumed that the sequence Det + N is a constituent because it can appear both before a verb and after a preposition. This, however, is a little too simple. The problem is that it is possible for a particular sequence of categories to be a constituent in one sentence but not in another. For this reason, we need to replace (48) by the following, more complex assumption:

(49) A sequence of words is a constituent if it can appear in some other position in a related sentence.

We will consider a number of types of related sentence in the following paragraphs.
To see why we need to make the more complex assumption and how in practice we go about investigating constituent structure, we can look at the following examples:

(50) Stefan looked up Maja's nose.
(51) Stefan looked up Maja's number.

One might assume that both *up Maja's nose* and *up Maja's number* are PP's. Notice, however, that while there is a cleft sentence related to (50), there is no cleft sentence related to (51).

(52) It was up Maja's nose that Stefan looked.
(53) * It was up Maja's number that Stefan looked.

This suggests that while *up Maja's nose* is a PP, *up Maja's number* is not. Hence, it suggests that we have the following structures for (50) and (51):

(54)

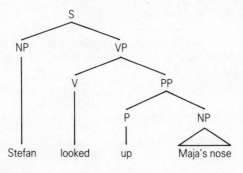

(55)

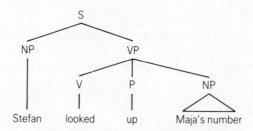

It is not hard to find pairs of sentences like (50) and (51). Consider the following:

(56) Stefan painted a picture of Maja.
(57) Stefan gave a book to Maja.

The expression *a picture of Maja* in (56) can appear in other positions in a number of related sentences, but this is not possible with the superficially similar expression *a book to Maja* of (57). Firstly, we can consider cleft sentences. Here, we have the following data:

(58) It was a picture of Maja that Stefan painted.
(59) * It was a book to Maja that Stefan gave.

Secondly, we can consider pseudo-clefts, where we have the following data:

(60) What Stefan painted was a picture of Maja.
(61) * What Stefan gave was a book to Maja.

Thirdly, we can consider passives:

(62) A picture of Maja was painted by Stefan.
(63) *A book to Maja was given by Stefan.

Finally, we can consider sentences involving what is known as topicalization, the movement of an expression to the front of a sentence for some kind of emphasis.

(64) A picture of Maja Stefan painted.
(65) * A book to Maja Stefan painted.

Thus, there is a variety of evidence that *a picture of Maja* is a constituent, but no evidence that *a book to Maja* is a constituent. Here, then, we can propose the following structures:

(66)

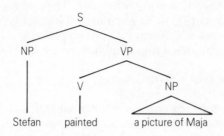

(67)

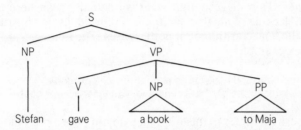

The last examples illustrate the fact that there are various kinds of related sentences to consider when investigating the constituent structure of a sentence. One point to stress is that a putative constituent need not be able to appear in some other position in the whole range of related sentences. For example, *up Maja's nose* in (50) cannot appear in a different position in a related passive sentence.

(68) * Up Maja's nose was looked by Stefan.

A second matter that we can consider when investigating the structure of a sentence is coordination. We saw earlier that wherever a particular phrasal category can appear, we can have two instances of that phrasal category combined with *and*. We can also have two instances of that phrasal category combined with *or*. The combining of categories with *and* and *or* is known as coordination. It has often been suggested that coordination always involves members of the same category. It is clear, however, from examples like the following that this is not the case:

(69) Ben is healthy and of sound mind.
(70) I am hoping to get an invitation and optimistic about my chances.

In (69) an AP *healthy* is coordinated with a PP *of sound mind*, and in (70) a VP *hoping to get an invitation* is coordinated with an AP *optimistic about my chances*. It does seem, however, that only constituents can be coordinated. Some evidence for this comes from the following examples:

(71) Stefan looked up Maja's nose and up Debbie's nose.
(72) * Stefan looked up Maja's number and up Debbie's number.

We saw earlier that there is evidence that *up Maja's nose* is a constituent, but that *up Maja's number* is not a constituent. Thus, if coordination involves constituents, we expect (71) to be grammatical but not (72).

One type of sentence which seems to pose a problem for the view that only constituents can be conjoined is exemplified by the following:

(73) Stefan likes but Maja hates the man next door.

Here, we have a sequence consisting of a subject and the following verb conjoined with another similar sequence. On standard assumptions this is not a constituent since the verb is part of a VP. There is, however, a different way of looking at this sentence. Notice that there are breaks in the intonation after *likes* and *hates*. This suggests that what we actually have here is conjoined clauses each lacking a final constituent followed by a constituent which functions as the final constituent of both clauses. The following are similar, but more complex examples:

(74) Stefan talked to and Maja talked about the man next door.
(75) Stefan seems to like but Maja seems to hate the man next door.

If we view these examples in this way, they do not pose a problem for the view that only constituents can be coordinated since they involve coordinated Ss. Sentences like these are standardly said to involve right-node raising.

There is another type of sentence that seems to pose a problem. Consider the following:

(76) Stefan painted a picture of Maja and a picture of Debbie.
(77) Stefan gave a book to Maja and a record to Debbie.

We saw earlier that there is evidence that *a picture of Maja* is a constituent, but that *a book to Maja* is not a constituent. Hence, we would expect (76) to be grammatical but not (77). Why is it grammatical? A possible answer is suggested by the following example:

(78) Stefan likes beer, and Ben wine.

Here, we have coordinated Ss with the second lacking a verb. Such sentences are said to involve gapping. It is possible that sentences like (77) are similar. It is possible, that is, that they involve coordinated VP's with the second lacking a verb. We will return to such examples briefly in Chapter 8.

It is clear, then, that the situation with coordination is rather complex. On the whole, however, it is reasonable to assume that a sequence of categories is a constituent if it can be coordinated with another similar sequence.

Thus, a consideration of various kinds of related sentences and coordination possibilities allows one to determine the constituent structure of a sentence with a considerable degree of confidence. I will not spend time in later chapters justifying the details of the constituent structures that I will assume, but the details could be justified in the way that I have justified various details here.

2.5 Some further categories

A fairly basic investigation of syntax suggests that it is necessary to recognize phrasal categories like NP and VP as well as lexical categories like N and V. A closer investigation shows that it is also necessary to recognize a class of what might be called intermediate phrasal categories to label expressions that are potentially more than a single word but less than a full phrase.

We can begin by looking at evidence for an intermediate nominal category. Consider firstly the following example:

(79) every painting of Maja and photograph of Debbie

This is an NP, as shown by the fact that it can appear in typical NP positions such as subject of a sentence.

(80) Every painting of Maja and photograph of Debbie pleased Ben.

The important point to note is that we have the N + PP sequence coordinated with another N + PP sequence. This suggests that these strings are constituents. What can we label them? We cannot label them N if lexical categories are only applied to single words. Nor, however, can we label them NP since they do not appear in positions in which NP's appear. Neither can appear as subject of a sentence:

(81) * Painting of Maja pleased Ben.
(82) * Photograph of Debbie pleased Ben.

Thus, we need some other category. We can use the category N′ (pronounced N-bar). With this category, we can assign the following structure to (79):

(83)

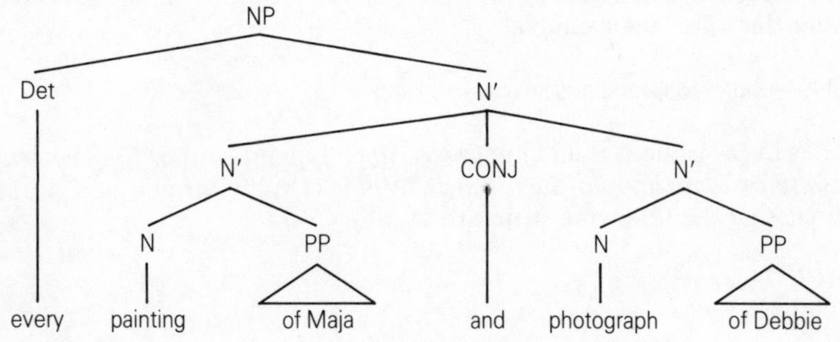

Rather like (79), but not quite the same, is the following:

(84) most paintings of Maja and photographs of Debbie

Here, there is an ambiguity. *Most* may qualify just *paintings of Maja* or to both *paintings of Maja* and *photographs of Debbie*. We can attribute this to the fact that *photographs of Debbie* can be a full NP, as shown by the following:

(85) Photographs of Debbie pleased Ben.

Thus, one possible structure for (80) is the following:

(86)

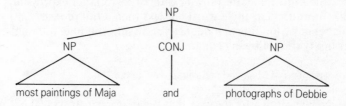

Given the N′ category, however, we can also assign the following structure to (84):

(87)

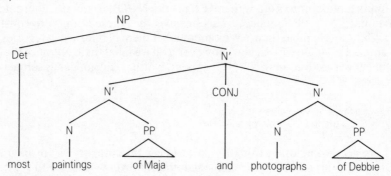

Given this structure, it is not surprising that (80) has the second interpretation.
   We can turn now to evidence for an intermediate adjectival category. We can consider the following example.

(88) so fond of Maja and hostile towards Debbie

Here, as in (84), there is an ambiguity. *So* can qualify either *fond of Maja* or both *fond of Maja* and *hostile towards Debbie*. On the former interpretation, we can assign the following structure to (88):

(89)

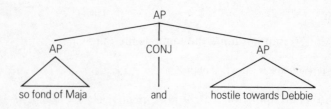

We can account for the latter interpretation if we assume an intermediate category A' (pronounced A-bar). Given this category, we will also have the following structure for (88):

(90)

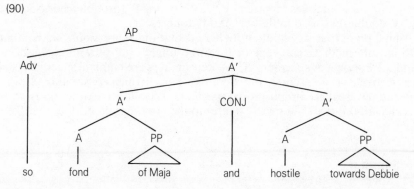

With this structure, the second interpretation of (88) is only to be expected.

Finally, we can consider evidence for an intermediate prepositional category. We can look at the following example:

(91) a mile beyond the river and towards the wood

Once more, we have an ambiguity. *A mile* can qualify just *beyond the river* or both *beyond the river* and *towards the wood*. On the former interpretation, we can assign the following structure to (91):

(92)

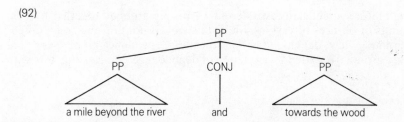

We can account for the latter interpretation if we assume a P' (pronounced P-bar). This will allow us to assign the following structure to (91).

(93)

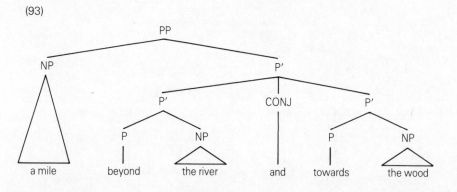

It seems, then, that coordination data provides evidence for three intermediate phrasal categories, N', A', and P'. It is generally assumed that there is also an intermediate verbal category, V'. If so, then we have intermediate categories corresponding each of the full phrasal categories, NP, VP, AP and PP. The latter are sometimes replaced by N", V", A" and P" (pronounced N-double-bar, V-double-bar, A-double-bar, and P-double-bar).

A final point that we should note here is that the expressions that combine with an intermediate category to form the related full phrasal category are standardly known as specifiers. Thus, determiners are nominal specifiers, *so* is an adjectival specifier, and expressions like *a mile* (which are sometimes called measure phrases) are prepositional specifiers. We will have little to say about specifiers in this book, but we will refer to the notion again in chapters 10 and 12.

2.6 Summary

We have been concerned in this chapter with one of the most basic assumptions of syntactic theory, the assumption that sentences have constituent structures. In 2.2, we looked at the motivation for this assumption. In 2.3, we looked at ways of representing constituent structure, considering both tree diagrams and labelled bracketings. In 2.4, we looked at how we can investigate the constituent structure of sentences. Finally, in 2.5, we considered reasons for assuming a class of what we called intermediate categories.

Notes

Although most syntacticians assume that words are grouped together to form larger units or phrases of various kinds, this view is not universally accepted. An alternative view, developed within so-called dependency grammar, is that words are grouped together by a relation of dependence. We can illustrate with (1).

(1) a book about the weather

Here, in some versions of dependency grammar the Det *a* and the P *about* will depend on the N *book*, the noun *weather* will depend on the P *about*, and the Det *the* will depend on the noun *weather*. One way of representing this is as follows:

(2)

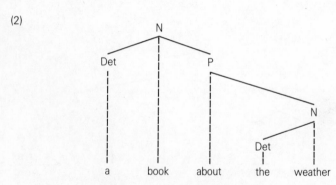

Dependency grammar has its origins in Tesniere (1959). Matthews (1981, Ch. 4) provides a textbook introduction. In recent years, dependency has played a central role in the framework known as Word Grammar developed in Hudson (1984, 1990).

As we note in Chapter 10, modals are analyzed as verbs in PSG and as members of the category I (or INFL or INFLECTION) in GB.

Although discontinuous constituency and multiple mothers have generally been rejected, there are proposals that they should be allowed. See especially McCawley (1982, 1987), Ojeda (1987, 1988). Sampson (1975) argues for an approach to pronouns which involves multiple mothers. Borsley (1980) criticizes this argument.

For further discussion of the ways in which syntactic structure can be investigated, see Radford (1988, 2.8).

The fact that different categories can be coordinated is highlighted and its implications discussed in Sag *et al.* (1985).

The assumption that there is a class of intermediate phrasal categories is commonly associated with X-bar theory, a body of ideas about syntactic structure, which originate in Chomsky (1970) and which were developed by a number of syntacticians in the 70s.

For further discussion of the structure of the main phrase types in English, see Radford (1988, 4 and 5), Huddleston (1984, 4, 6 and 8), and Baker (1989, 2, 3 and 5).

Exercises

Exercise 1

Provide a tree for (1) which embodies the information given in (2).

(1) The boy was showing the girl his scars.
(2) *The boy* is an NP. *Was* is a V. *Showing* is a V. *The girl* is an NP. *His scars* is an NP. *Showing the girl his scars* is a VP. *Was showing the girl his scars* is a VP. The boy was showing the girl his scars is an S.

Exercise 2

Give tree diagrams that are equivalent to the following labelled bracketings. Don't remove any information or add any extra information.

(1) [s [NP Ben] [VP [V is] [AP [A mad] [PP [P about] [NP Debbie]]]]]
(2) [s [NP the student] [VP [V has] [VP [V read] [NP the book]]]]
(3) [s [V did] [NP he] [VP [V talk] [PP [P to] [NP the lecturer]]]]

Exercise 3

Give labelled bracketings that are equivalent to the following tree diagrams. Don't remove or add any information.

(1)

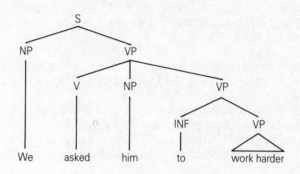

(2)

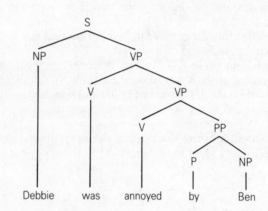

(3)

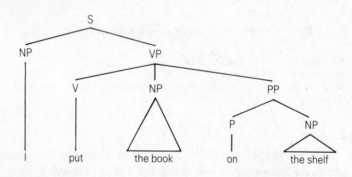

Exercise 4

Consider the tree in (1) and answer the questions that follow.

(1)

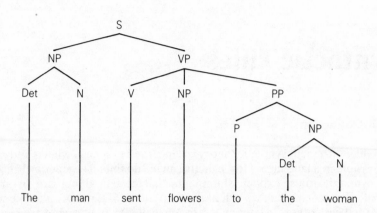

(2) Which nodes does VP dominate?
(3) Which nodes does PP immediately dominate?
(4) Which pairs of adjacent words form constituents and which do not?
(5) What are the immediate constituents of S?
(6) Which sets of nodes are sisters?
(7) What are the daughters of VP?
(8) What is the mother of each of the NP's?

Exercise 5

Try to determine the constituent structure of the following sentences making appropriate use of related examples.

(1) a. John bought a book on syntax.
    b. John put a book on the table.
(2) a. She turned down the side street.
    b. She turned down his offer.
(3) a. He looked at a book about cricket.
    b. He talked to a girl about cricket.

3

Syntactic rules

3.1 Introduction

As we have stressed, syntactic theory is concerned to specify what is and what is not possible in a language. How exactly can we do this? The standard answer is with syntactic rules: explicit statements that certain things are or are not possible. In this chapter, we will look at a number of types of rule. We will be concerned with others in later chapters. We will look first at what are known as phrase structure (PS) rules – a type of rule that we have already in fact introduced. Then we will consider the relation between rules and sentences. Next we will look at the reasons for replacing phrase structure rules with two different kinds of rule. Finally, we will consider the possibility that we need rules that are somewhat broader in their scope, what we can call non-local conditions on trees.

3.2 The nature of phrase structure rules

We introduced PS rules in the last chapter. For what we referred to in Chapter 1 as Chomskyan Phrase Structure Grammar, Chomsky's formalization of the descriptive practices of pre-Chomskyan linguists, a grammar is just a set of PS rules, and PS rules were generally assumed to be an important component of a grammar until the 80s. Both the Government-Binding theory and Phrase Structure Grammar, as it developed in the 80s, reject PS rules. Nevertheless, it is important to have a clear understanding of such rules.

PS rules are rules of the following form, where each C is a syntactic category:

(1) $C^0 \rightarrow C^1 C^2 \ldots C^n$

Such rules consist of a left hand side and a right side separated by an arrow. The left hand side is a single category and the right hand side is a sequence of one or more categories. Sometimes, they have a more complex form. For example, one might have curly brackets identifying a set of options, as we did in the last chapter. Here, however, we can restrict our attention to simple PS rules.

There are various ways in which one might view PS rules. One possibility is to see them as instructions for forming trees from top down. From this perspective, (1) means the following:

(2) A C^0 can be expanded as a C^1 followed by a C^2 followed by . . . followed by a C^n

Alternatively, one might see them as instructions for forming trees from bottom up. From this perspective, (1) has the following interpretation:

(3) A C^1 followed by a C^2 followed by . . . followed by a C^n can be combined to form a C°

There is, however, a reason for taking a rather different view of PS rules. We are concerned with what is and what is not possible, not with how speakers actually put sentences together. That is a matter for psychologists to investigate. For this reason, it has been common since McCawley (1968) to see PS rules as conditions on local trees, a local tree being a category and its daughters. As a condition on local trees, (1) can be interpreted as (4), (5) or (6).

(4) A C° can immediately dominate a C^1 followed by a C^2 followed by . . . followed by a C^n
(5) A C^1 followed by a C^2 followed by . . . followed by a C^n can be immediately dominated by a C°
(6) A local tree consisting of a C° immediately dominating a C^1 followed by a C^2 followed by . . . followed by a C^n is well-formed

These are different ways of saying the same thing.

One point that we should stress about PS rules is that they state that certain structures are possible. In other words, they allow or license certain structures. There is only one situation in which a PS rule could be said to require a particular structure. This is if there is no other rule with the same category on the left hand side. If we have the rule X → Y Z, and no other rule has X on the left hand side, an X must immediately dominate a Y followed by a Z. To take a concrete example, if a language has the rule NP → Det N and no other rule with NP on the left hand side, an NP must immediately dominate a Det followed by an N.

It has generally been accepted in syntactic theory that PS rules cannot by themselves provide a satisfactory grammar. Recently, it has been argued that they are not even a necessary component of a grammar. As we have said, they have been rejected in both GB and PSG. It is important, however, to understand such rules.

3.3 Rules and sentences

Before we look at why many syntacticians have rejected PS rules, we should look at a number of general points about the relation between rules and sentences.

The first point to note is that a set of rules on their own cannot identify any sentences as possible. To do this, we need not just rules but a set of rules combined with a set of words assigned to particular lexical categories, or a lexicon to use the standard term. We can illustrate with the rules in (7) and the lexicon in (8).

(7) a. S → NP VP
    b. NP → Det N
    c. VP → V NP
    d. VP → V S

(8) a. boy   N
    b. girl   N
    c. dog   N
    d. saw   V
    e. thought   V
    f. the   Det
    g. a   Det

Among the trees that these allow is the following:

(9)

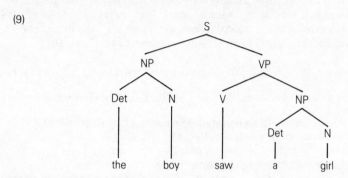

This contains the following local trees, (10)b. appearing twice:

(10)

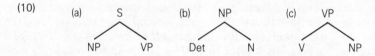

(10)a. is identified as possible or licensed by the rule in (7)a. (10)b. is licensed by (7)b. and (10)c. is licensed by (7)c. The association of lexical items with lexical categories is licensed by the lexicon. Thus, every aspect of this structure is legitimate. Therefore, our rules and lexicon identify *The boy saw the girl* as a possible sentence, or, to use the standard term, they generate this sentence.

Another tree that our rules and lexicon allow is the following:

(11)

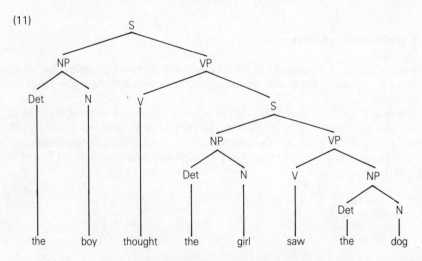

Here, we have all the local trees in (10) and the following local tree:

(12)

VP

V   S

This is licensed by (7)d. Again, then, all the local trees are licensed, and the association of lexical items and lexical categories is licensed by the lexicon. Again, therefore, every aspect of the tree is legitimate and another sentence is generated.

A natural question to ask about the rules and lexicon is: how many sentences do they generate? The answer, perhaps surprisingly, is an infinite number. This is because they allow an S to dominate another S and there is nothing to prevent the second S dominating another S, and nothing to prevent that S dominating a further S, and so on. A set of rules and a lexicon will generate an infinite number of sentences whenever the rules allow a particular category to dominate itself. When a set of rules does do this, it is said to allow recursion.

We can now consider what is involved in providing an analysis for some construction in some language. Typically, the syntactician has a number of aims. The first is to develop a set of rules, which given a suitable lexicon, would generate all and only the examples of the construction. The qualification 'and only' is crucial here. It is very easy to generate all of some set of sentences if one is happy to generate ungrammatical sequences as well. Instead of our earlier rules, we might have the following:

(13) S → Word S
     S → Word

If we assume a lexicon in which our earlier words are simply labelled word, we will allow the following structure:

(14)

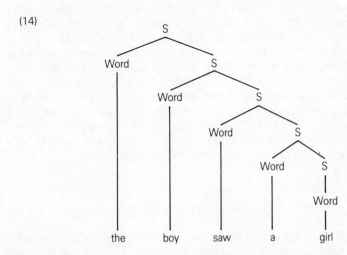

Here, we have a grammatical sentence. The problem, of course, is that these rules will generate any sequence of words at all. Hence they will generate any ungrammatical sequence. Clearly, this is not a satisfactory analysis of anything. It is important, then, to require that any analysis does not generate any ungrammatical sequence. In other words, we require that an analysis should get the facts right. An analysis which does this is conventionally said to achieve observational adequacy.

A further aim that the syntactician normally has is to achieve the simplest possible analysis. This means especially that one is concerned to capture whatever generalizations can be found in the data. For example, if a subject always follows the associated verb in some language, one wants to say this just once and not to say first that it follows one type of verb, then that it follows another type of verb, and so on. An analysis, which does capture all the available generalizations is standardly said to achieve descriptive adequacy. Of course, what the available generalizations are may not be immediately obvious. For example, it may not be obvious that there is a single generalization ruling out both (16) and (17) as alternatives to (15).

(15) Stefan talked to Maja.
(16) * Stefan to Maja talked.
(17) * Stefan talked Maja to.

This, however, is what most syntacticians would say, as we will see in the next section. Similarly, it is not obvious that there is a single generalization ruling out (20) and (21) as alternatives to (18) and (19):

(18) Stefan believes himself to be a genius.
(19) Stefan is believed to be a genius.
(20) * Stefan believes himself is a genius.
(21) * Stefan is believed is a genius.

This, however, is the view of GB, as we shall see in Chapter 9.

A final aim is to develop an analysis that is compatible with what one knows or assumes about other languages. Thus, an analysis which can be extended without difficulty to what is on the face of it the same construction in some other language is preferable to one which can't. For example, an analysis of English relative clauses that can easily be extended to relative clauses in Welsh is preferable to one that can't. Similarly, an analysis that is compatible with what one assumes that languages in general are like is preferable to one that isn't. For example, if one assumes that languages only involve certain kinds of rule, one will try to develop an analysis of any construction one is concerned with which only employs such rules. Only if it proves to be quite impossible to analyze a language in a way that is compatible with one's assumptions about what languages are like will one adopt an analysis which is incompatible with these assumptions (and in the process revise these assumptions).

3.4 Immediate dominance and linear precedence rules

We noted earlier that both GB and PSG reject PS rules. The problem with PS rules is that they miss generalizations about the order of constituents. For this reason, it is assumed in both GB and PSG that they should be replaced by two different kinds of rules.

Among the PS rules that we might have in a grammar of English are the following:

(22) a. V' → V NP
     b. V' → V PP
     c. V' → V S
     d. V' → V NP PP
     e. V' → V NP S
     f. V' → V PP S
(23) a. N' → N PP
     b. N' → N S
(24) a. A' → A PP
     b. A' → A S
(25) a. P' → P NP
     b. P' → P PP
     c. P' → P S
     d. P' → P NP PP

These rules would provide for the italicized strings in the following examples:

(26) a. Stefan *saw Maja.*
     b. Stefan *talked to Maja.*
     c. Stefan *thinks Maja likes him.*
     d. Stefan *put the book on the shelf.*
     e. Stefan *persuaded Maja that he liked her.*
     f. Stefan *said to Maja that he likes her.*
(27) a. a *picture of Maja.*
     b. the *belief that the earth is flat.*
(28) a. Stefan is *afraid of spiders.*
     b. Stefan is *afraid that there is a spider in the bath.*
(29) a. Stefan is *in the bath.*
     b. Stefan appeared *from behind the wall.*
     c. Stefan arrived *before Ben arrived.*
     d. Stefan was in charge *with Ben out of the country.*

The rules miss a number of generalizations about linear precedence. The most important one is the following:

(30) A lexical category precedes any phrasal category that is its sister.

All the rules exemplify this generalization. This is also the generalization that (16) and (17) violate. In (16) a PP precedes a V which is its sister, while in (17) an NP precedes a P which is its sister. Another important generalization is the following:

(31) An NP precedes any other phrasal category that is its sister.

This is exemplified by rules (22)d., (22)e. and (25)d. A further generalization is the following:

(32) An S follows all its sisters.

this is exemplified by (22)e. and (22)f.

The fact that PS rules miss generalizations about linear order in this way is a serious objection to them. The obvious way to avoid this problem is to assume separate immediate dominance and linear precedence statements. Following PSG, we might call the first set of statements immediate dominance (ID) rules, and we might distinguish them from PS rules by separating the right hand side categories by commas. In other words, we might have rules of the following form:

(33) $C^0 \rightarrow C^1, C^2, \ldots C^n$

We can interpret such a rule as (34) or (35).

(34) A C^0 can immediately dominate a C^1 and a C^2 and . . . and a C^n
(35) A C^1 and a C^2 and . . . and a C^n can be immediately dominated by a C^0

We might also follow PSG in calling the second set of rules linear precedence (LP) rules.

A further objection to PS rules is that they obscure similarities between different languages. Consider, for example, a language in which V', N', A' and P' allow exactly the same constituents as in English but in which the order of constituents is reversed. If we assume PS rules, we will have the following rules:

(36) a. V' → NP V
      b. V' → PP V
      c. V' → S V
      d. V' → PP NP V
      e. V' → S NP V
      f. V' → S PP V
(37) a. N' → PP N
      b. N' → S N
(38) a. A' → PP A
      b. A' → S A
(39) a. P' → NP P
      b. P' → PP P
      c. P' → S P
      d. P' → PP NP P

Given such rules, the two languages look very different. In particular, we completely miss the fact that they allow exactly the same constituents. Again, we can solve the problem by assuming separate ID and LP rules. If we do this, we will have exactly the same ID rules and just different LP rules.

If PS rules are replaced by separate ID and LP rules, whether or not a local tree is well-formed becomes a more complex matter. If the grammar is a set of PS rules, we have the following statement about local trees:

(40) A local tree is well-formed if and only if it matches a PS rule.

If the grammar consists of separate ID and LP rules, we have the following, more complex statement:

(41) A local tree is well-formed if and only if it matches an ID rule and conforms to all relevant LP rules.

We can illustrate this with the following trees.

(42)

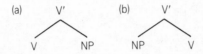

Both these trees match the following ID rule, which will replace the PS rule in (22)a.:

(43) V' → V, NP

However, only (42)a. conforms to the LP rule in (30).

A further point that we should note here is that ID and LP rules have a somewhat different status. ID rules, like PS rules, are permissive. They state that certain situations are possible. LP rules, on the other hand, impose certain requirements. They state that certain situations are necessary and thus rule out other situations.

A final point that we should note is that it is only if the order of sister categories is the same whatever their mother is that PS rules can be replaced by ID and LP rules. If two sister categories could appear in one order with one sort of mother and in the opposite order with another, it would be impossible to replace PS rules by separate ID and LP rules. Thus, we are committed to the following assumption:

(44) Sister categories have the same order whatever their mother is.

This is one of the most important assumptions that GB and PSG share.

3.5 Non-local conditions on trees

We can turn now to an important difference between GB and PSG. The rules we have considered so far are quite limited in their scope. None of them affects anything larger than a local tree. It is natural to ask whether any rules need affect anything larger than a local tree. In other words, it is natural to ask whether we need non-local conditions on trees. PSG assumes that there is no need for such conditions, but GB assumes that they are necessary.

It is not hard to find data that suggest that such conditions are necessary. We can look at the following examples containing the reflexive pronoun *himself*:

(45) Stefan scratched himself.
(46) * Himself scratched Stefan.

How can we account for this contrast? For (45) we will have the tree in (47), while if (46) were possible, it would involve the tree in (48):

(47)

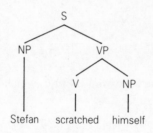

(48)

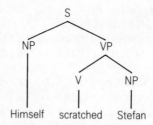

If we allow non-local conditions on trees, we can allow (47) while excluding (48) if we adopt the following condition:

(49) A reflexive must have a c-commanding antecedent.

(We will introduce a more restrictive condition in Chapter 9.) The antecedent of a reflexive is the expression that determines who or what it refers to. C-command, which derives from Reinhart (1976), can be defined as follows:

(50) A node X c-commands a node Y iff neither dominates the other and the first branching node (i.e. node with more than one daughter) above X dominates Y.

We can illustrate with the following tree:

(51)

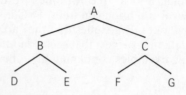

Here, A does not c-command anything because it dominates all the other nodes. B, however, c-commands C, F and G. It does not dominate and is not dominated by any of them and the first branching node above it, A, dominates all of them. In much the same way, C c-commands B, D and E. In addition D and E c-command each other, and so do F and G. Having explained (50), we can return to (47) and (48). In both trees, the first NP c-commands the second since the first branching node above the first NP is the S, which dominates the second NP. However, the second does not c-command the first because the first branching node above the second NP is the VP, which does not dominate the first NP. It follows that *Stefan* can be antecedent of *himself* in (47), but not in (48).

This approach will also account for the following contrast:

(52) Stefan talked to himself.
(53) * Stefan's mother talked to himself.

(52) will have the tree in (54), while if (53) were possible, it would involve something like the tree in (55).

(54)

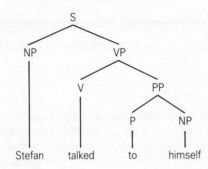

(55)

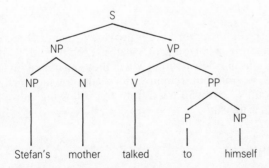

In (54), the first branching node above *Stefan* is the S, which dominates *himself*. Hence, *Stefan* c-commands *himself* and consequently can be its antecedent. In contrast, in (55), the first branching node above *Stefan* is the NP which is a daughter of S. Hence, *Stefan* does not c-command *himself* and cannot be its antecedent.

This approach to the contrasts between (45) and (46) and between (52) and (53) seems quite plausible. Thus, it looks as if there may be a need for non-local conditions on trees.

There are two further points that we should note here. Firstly, (49) has essentially the same status as an LP rule. It says that certain situations are necessary and rules out other situations. Secondly, if we assume non-local conditions like (49), a tree can be ill-formed even though every local tree that it consists of is well-formed.

Here, then, we have highlighted a major issue in syntactic theory. This is in fact one of the two main differences between GB and PSG. We will introduce the other in Chapter 7.

3.6 Summary

In this chapter, we have been concerned with a number of types of syntactic rule. We began in 3.2 by looking at the nature of phrase structure rules. Then, in 3.3, we looked more closely at the relation between rules and sentences. Next, in 3.4, we looked at a major objection to phrase structure rules – that they miss generalizations about constituent order – and saw how this objection can be avoided if phrase structure rules are replaced by separate immediate dominance and linear precedence rules. Finally, in 3.5, we looked at some data which seems to suggest that we need certain non-local conditions on trees. Here, we highlighted one of the main differences between GB and PSG.

Notes

Although PS rules are standardly viewed as conditions on local trees, they are commonly treated as instructions for forming trees from top down or from bottom up in parsing systems, computer systems that assign structures to sentences. See Gazdar and Mellish (1989, 5.), for discussion.

For further discussion of levels of adequacy, see Horrocks (1987, 1.5.) and Radford (1988, 1.6.).

Languages with very free word order provide a further objection to PS rules. Consider, for example, a language in which V', N', A' and P' allow exactly the same constituents as in English but in which they can appear in any order. If we assume PS rules, we will require many more rules for such a language than for English. For example, we will need both the following rules, where we just need the first for English:

(1)   a. V' → V NP
      b. V' → NP V

Similarly, we will need all of the following rules, where for English we just need the first.

(2)   a. V' → V NP PP
      b. V' → V PP NP
      c. V' → NP V PP
      d. V' → PP V NP
      e. V' → NP PP V
      f. V' → PP NP V

We can offer a much simpler account of such a language if we assume separate ID and LP rules. We will simply need the same ID rules as English and no LP rules.

Rather like reflexive pronouns in its behaviour is the reciprocal pronoun *each other*. Thus, parallel to (45) and (46), and (52) and (53) in the text, we have the following:

(3) The boys scratched each other.
(4) * Each other scratched the boys.
(5) The boys talked to each other.
(6) The boys' mothers talked to each other.

(6) is grammatical but only *the boys' mothers* and not *the boys* can be the antecedent of *each other*.

Other relations like c-command have been employed at various times in the history of syntactic theory. For technical discussion of the full range of relations, see Barker and Pullum (1990).

PSG analyses of reflexives which do not employ non-local conditions on trees are developed in Hukari (1989) and Pollard and Sag (1990, forthcoming).

Exercises

Exercise 1

Provide a tree diagram that uses each of the following PS rules at least once. Use any suitable lexical items. Note that 'Comp' is an abbreviation for 'complementizer', a lexical category whose most important member is *that*.

(1) S → NP M VP
S → NP VP
NP → Det N
NP → N
VP → V S'
VP → V PP
PP → P NP
S' → Comp S

Exercise 2

List all the PS rules that are needed to allow the following tree:

(1)

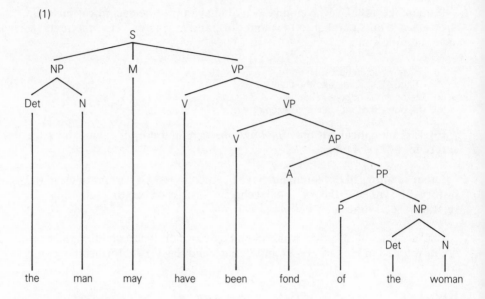

Exercise 3

If grammar (1) is just rule (1), grammar (2) rules (1) and (2), grammar (3) rules (1), (2) and (3), and so on, which of the grammars can be replaced by separate ID and LP rules?

    (1) A → B C
    (2) A → C B
    (3) B → B C
    (4) B → A C
    (5) B → C B
    (6) C → C A

Exercise 4

Which of the following examples conform to the requirement that a reflexive must have a c-commanding antecedent and which do not? Use tree diagrams to illustrate your answer.

    (1) He told Maja a story about herself.
    (2) Pictures of themselves please most people.
    (3) Most people are pleased by pictures of themselves.
    (4) We talked to Maja about herself.
    (5) Was Maja scratching herself?
    (6) The picture of herself that Maja painted was terrible.

Exercise 5

Provide trees for each of the following and show how the data can be accounted for if we assume that the expression *give a damn* must be c-commanded by a negative expression such as *didn't*. Assume that *didn't* is a verb that combines with a VP to form a larger VP.

(1) They told us they didn't give a damn.
(2) * The man you didn't like gave a damn.
(3) * That he gave a damn didn't surprise me at all.
(4) I don't think he gives a damn.
(5) * The man who gave a damn didn't see us.
(6) I don't expect any of them will give a damn.

4

Syntactic categories

4.1 Introduction

In Chapter 2 we introduced syntactic categories, and in Chapter 3 we used them in a number of types of rule. But what exactly are syntactic categories? For what we have called Chomskyan Phase Structure Grammar, Chomsky's formalization of the descriptive practices of his predecessors, syntactic categories are simple, unanalyzable entities. However, most current approaches, and in particular GB and PSG, assume that they are complex entities made up from smaller elements. In this chapter, we will consider why this is. One reason arises from the fact that we need a richer classification of expressions than that provided by the categories we have been employing, another stems from the relation between phrasal and lexical categories, and a further reason stems from similarities between different lexical or phrasal categories. We will consider each of these matters. Then, we will look at features, the basic building blocks of categories. Finally, we will look at the relation between categories in rules and the lexicon and categories in trees.

4.2 Additional information about expressions

In Chapter 2, we introduced three sets of categories to which linguistic expressions can be assigned, lexical categories, intermediate phrasal categories and full phrasal categories. In general, however, it is necessary to say more about linguistic expressions than which of these categories they are members of.

For example, we need to say of the word *man* not just that it is an N but also that it is singular. Similarly, we need to say of *sang* not just that it is a V but also that it past tense. We can include such additional information in what are known as feature specifications. We can assign *man* to the extended category in (1) and *sang* to the extended category in (2).

(1) N[+SING]
(2) V[+PAST]

In these examples, we have just one feature specification. We will often need more than one. For example, we need to say of *had* in one of its uses not just that it is a V but also that it is past tense and that it is an auxiliary, in other words that it is an item that can appear before the subject in a question. The following illustrates this last point:

(3) Had he been there?

Here, then, we need the following category:

(4) V[+PAST;+AUX]

(I use a semi-colon here and subsequently to separate distinct feature specifications.) Similarly, we need to say of *you* not just that it is an N but also that it is a pronoun and that it is second person. Thus, for *you*, we need the following category:

(5) N[+PRO;+2ND]

Finally, we need to say of *I* not just that it is an N but also that it is a pronoun, that it is first person, and that it is singular. Here, then, we need the following category:

(6) N[+PRO;+1ST;+SING]

(In fact, we also need to say that *I* has nominative Case, in contrast with *me*, which has objective case. We will be concerned with this matter in Chapter 9.)

It seems, then, that we need to associate most linguistic expressions not just with a basic category but also with various feature specifications that provide additional information about them. This provides some justification for the suggestion that syntactic categories are complex entities.

There is one further point that we should note here. In (1), (2), (4), (5) and (6), the various elements of the categories appear one after another on a single line. An alternative is to place each element on a separate line. This would give us the following instead (1), (2), (4), (5) and (6):

(7)   N
      [+SING]

(8)   V
      [+PAST]

(9)   V
      $\begin{bmatrix} +PAST \\ +AUX \end{bmatrix}$

(10)   N
      $\begin{bmatrix} +PRO \\ +2ND \end{bmatrix}$

(11)   N
      $\begin{bmatrix} +PRO \\ +1ST \\ +SING \end{bmatrix}$

We will use both modes of representation in subsequent discussion.

4.3 Phrasal and lexical categories

Some further evidence that categories are complex entities comes from the fact that phrasal categories go together with, or are 'projections' of, specific lexical categories. This was first highlighted in Harris (1951) and was taken up in Chomsky (1970), a paper which introduced what became known as X-bar theory, a body of ideas about constituent structure developed in the 70s and absorbed in one way or another into most current approaches.

NP and N′ go together with N in that they typically occur in structures of the following form:

(12)

Here, N is immediately dominated by N′, which in turn is immediately dominated by NP. In such structures, N is standardly referred to as the head of N′, and either N′ or N is referred to as the head of NP. If we want, we can say that N′ is the immediate head of NP and N the ultimate head. It seems, then, that NP and N′ are not just convenient labels. Rather they are categories that really are nominal, the full phrasal and intermediate phrasal counterparts of N.

AP and A′ go together with A in the same way. They typically appear in structures of to following form:

(13)

It seems, then, that AP and A′ too are not just convenient labels, but categories that really are adjectival.

We can argue in much the same way that PP and P′ go together with P and hence are really prepositional and that VP and V′ go together with V and hence are really verbal.

It should be stressed that we are not suggesting here that structures like (12) and (13) are the only structures that occur. For example, it is often assumed that pre-nominal adjectives such as *old* in (14) combine with an N′ to form a larger N′, i.e. that they appear in the structure in (15).

(14) an old photo of Mary
(15)

Here, the higher N′ does not immediately dominate N. However, the lower N′ probably will. Hence, the existence of such structures does not call into question the assumption that N' is a category that is really nominal. There are also coordinate structures like the following:

(16)

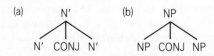

In (16)a., as in (15), the higher N' does not immediately dominate N, but again the lower N' probably will. Similarly, in (16)b., the higher NP does not immediately dominate N', but the lower NP will probably will.

It seems, then, that phrasal categories are associated with particular lexical categories. How is this important? Quite simply if NP and N' really are nominal, AP and A' are really adjectival, etc., they should be identified as such. In other words, we should analyze our original categories in terms of two elements: one indicating whether they are nominal, adjectival, etc., and one indicating whether they are lexical, intermediate phrasal or full phrasal. How can we do this? One possibility is to use feature specifications like [+NOMINAL] for the former, and the numbers 0, 1 and 2 for the latter, 0 meaning lexical, 1 meaning intermediate phrasal, and 2 meaning full phrasal. We would then have the following instead of N, N' and NP:

(17) $\begin{bmatrix} +\text{NOMINAL} \\ 0 \end{bmatrix}$ $\begin{bmatrix} +\text{NOMINAL} \\ 1 \end{bmatrix}$ $\begin{bmatrix} +\text{NOMINAL} \\ 2 \end{bmatrix}$

We would have similar complexes instead of A, A' and AP, P, P' and PP, and V, V' and VP. And instead of (1), we would have the following:

(18) $\begin{bmatrix} +\text{NOMINAL} \\ 0 \\ +\text{SING} \end{bmatrix}$

This revision gives us some further evidence that categories are complex entities. As we will see in the next chapter, it enables us to provide for a variety of different structures with a single ID rule.

There is one further point that we can note here. This is that full phrasal categories are often referred to as 'maximal projections'. One consequence of this is that it is quite common to use N^{max}, V^{max} etc. instead of NP, VP, etc.

4.4 Cross-categorial generalizations

Some further evidence for the position that categories are complex entities comes from what are known as cross-categorial generalizations: generalizations affecting different lexical categories or different phrasal categories. Such generalizations were an important focus of interest in the 70s. They suggest that the basic categorial status of a category is a complex matter.

We can look first at the following data:

(19) a. Stefan fears spiders.

  b. Stefan is in the kitchen.
  c. * Stefan is afraid spiders.
  d. * Stefan's fear spiders is surprising.

The c. and d. examples are, of course, grammatical if *of* is inserted before *spiders*. These examples show that verbs and prepositions but not adjectives and nouns can combine with an NP. We can capture this fact if verbal and prepositional categories have an element in common distinguishing them from adjectival and nominal categories.

We can look now at the following data:

(20) a. It was Stefan that Maja was arguing with.
  b. It was with Stefan that Maja was arguing.
  c. * It was very foolish that Maja was.
  d. * It was gone home that Maja had.

These examples show that NP's and PP's but not AP's and VP's can appear in focus position in a cleft sentence. This suggests that nominal and prepositional categories have an element in common distinguishing them from adjectival and verbal categories.

We can account for data like this if we analyze the basic categorial status of categories in terms of a pair of feature specifications as follows:

(21) nominal $= [+N; -V]$
     verbal $= [-N; +V]$
     adjectival $= [+N; +V]$
     prepositional $= [-N; -V]$

Given this analysis, we can say of the data in (19) that $[-N]$ categories but not $[+N]$ categories can combine with an NP, and we can say of the data in (20) that $[-V]$ categories but not $[+V]$ categories can appear in focus position in a cleft sentence.

With this revision, we will have the following instead of the complexes in (17):

(22) $\begin{bmatrix} +N \\ -V \\ 0 \end{bmatrix}$ $\begin{bmatrix} +N \\ -V \\ 1 \end{bmatrix}$ $\begin{bmatrix} +N \\ -V \\ 2 \end{bmatrix}$

We will have similar complexes for verbal, adjectival and prepositional categories. And we will have the following instead of (1):

(23) $\begin{bmatrix} +N \\ -V \\ 0 \\ +SING \end{bmatrix}$

Here, then, we have some further evidence that categories are complex entities.

4.5 Features

The foregoing discussion suggests that syntactic categories are sets of feature specifications together with a number indicating their phrasal status. But what exactly is a feature specification? We can say that a feature specification is a feature together with one of a number of possible values. There are a number of additional points that we should note about features.

Firstly, we should note that we might treat the number indicating the phrasal status of a category as the value of another feature. For example, we might introduce the feature BAR. We would then have the following instead of the complexes in (22).

$$(24) \quad \begin{bmatrix} +N \\ -N \\ 0BAR \end{bmatrix} \qquad \begin{bmatrix} +N \\ -V \\ 1BAR \end{bmatrix} \qquad \begin{bmatrix} +N \\ -V \\ 2BAR \end{bmatrix}$$

Secondly, we should note that we might reverse the order of feature and value. This would give us the following instead of the complexes in (24).

$$(25) \quad \begin{bmatrix} N,+ \\ V,- \\ BAR,0 \end{bmatrix} \qquad \begin{bmatrix} N,+ \\ V,- \\ BAR,1 \end{bmatrix} \qquad \begin{bmatrix} N,+ \\ V,- \\ BAR,2 \end{bmatrix}$$

Here and subsequently, I use a comma to separate a feature from a following value.

Finally, we should note that we might assume more complex feature values than '+' and '−' and numbers. Various kinds of complex feature values have been exploited within PSG. In particular, as we will see in Chapters 7 and 12, Generalized Phrase Structure Grammar has employed features with a category as their value, and as we will see in the next chapter, Head-driven Phrase Structure Grammar has made use of a feature with a list of categories as its value.

One further point that we should note here is that it is standard practice to use simplified categories in rules and trees. Thus, while the 'real' category might be (26), one might use something like (27) or even just (28) if there is no reason to give the full details.

$$(26) \quad \begin{bmatrix} N,+ \\ V,- \\ BAR,2 \\ PERS,3 \\ NUMB,SING \end{bmatrix} \qquad (27) \quad \begin{matrix} NP \\ \begin{bmatrix} PERS,3 \\ NUMB,SING \end{bmatrix} \end{matrix} \qquad (28)\ NP$$

This is similar to the standard practice of using simplified trees when not all the details of the structure of a sentence are important.

4.6 Categories in rules and the lexicon and categories in trees

There is one further matter that we must consider here: the relation between categories in rules and the lexicon and categories in trees. We will look first at the situation with categories in rules. Then, we will consider the situation with categories in the lexicon.

It is clear that categories in trees must match categories in rules. For example, if the rule contains an NP, the tree must contain an NP and not a VP or an AP. We must ask, however, what exactly we mean by 'match' here. One might suggest the following:

(29) A category in a tree matches a category in a rule iff they are identical.

This would be the right answer if our categories were simple and unanalyzable. It is clear, however, that it is not the right answer if our categories are complex entities.

We can show this by considering the following, rather similar examples:

(30) Stefan saw the girl.
(31) Stefan saw the girls.

These are identical except that the former has a singular object NP whereas the latter has a plural object NP. It is clear from the following examples that we need to distinguish singular and plural NP's in English:

(32) The girl $\left\{ \begin{array}{l} \text{likes} \\ \text{* like} \end{array} \right\}$ Stefan.

(33) The girls $\left\{ \begin{array}{l} \text{like} \\ \text{* likes} \end{array} \right\}$ Stefan.

Thus, for the VP's in (30) and (31), we will have something like the following structures.

(34)

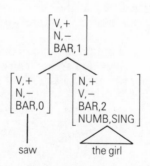

(35)

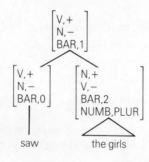

These trees are similar but not identical because the NP categories have different values for the feature NUMB. Hence, if we assume that tree categories must be identical to the corresponding rule categories, we will need two different phrase structure or immediate dominance rules. If we assume phrase structure rules, we might have the following:

$$(36) \quad \begin{bmatrix} V,+ \\ N,- \\ BAR,1 \end{bmatrix} \rightarrow \begin{bmatrix} V,+ \\ N,- \\ BAR,0 \end{bmatrix} \quad \begin{bmatrix} N,+ \\ V,- \\ BAR,2 \\ NUMB,SING \end{bmatrix}$$

$$(37) \quad \begin{bmatrix} V,+ \\ N,- \\ BAR,1 \end{bmatrix} \rightarrow \begin{bmatrix} V,+ \\ N,- \\ BAR,0 \end{bmatrix} \quad \begin{bmatrix} N,+ \\ V,- \\ BAR,2 \\ NUMB,PLUR \end{bmatrix}$$

Since the trees are almost identical it seems unsatisfactory to invoke two different rules. We can avoid this if we replace (29) by the following:

(38) A category in a tree matches a category in a rule iff the latter subsumes the former.

Of course, this only makes sense if we know what it means for one category to subsume another. We can define this as follows:

(39) A category X subsumes a category Y iff Y contains all the feature specifications in X together possibly with certain additional feature specifications.

Given this, we can replace the rules in (36) and (37) by the following rule:

$$(40) \quad \begin{bmatrix} V,+ \\ N,- \\ BAR,1 \end{bmatrix} \rightarrow \begin{bmatrix} V,+ \\ N,- \\ BAR,0 \end{bmatrix} \quad \begin{bmatrix} N,+ \\ V,- \\ BAR,2 \end{bmatrix}$$

The important point about this rule is that the second category on the right hand side does not contain the feature NUMB. Hence, it subsumes the NP categories in (34) and (35) since they contain all the feature specifications that it contains as well as one other.

This example illustrates a very important point, namely that rules containing complex categories allied to the principle in (38) can cover a number of different situations. Thus, an analysis employing complex categories requires fewer rules than one employing simple categories, possibly far fewer. Here, we see in very concrete terms the advantage of complex categories.

We can turn now to relation between categories in the lexicon and categories in trees. Once again we can say that the categories must match. If a lexical item is identified in the lexicon as an N, then it can only appear in an N position in a tree. Again, however, we must ask what we mean by match. Again, we might assume that the categories must be identical, but again it is clear that this is unsatisfactory.

This becomes clear if we consider the noun *sheep*. This can be singular or plural. Hence, it can be assigned to the following category:

(41)
$$\begin{bmatrix} N,+ \\ V,- \\ BAR,0 \end{bmatrix}$$

The important point about this category is that it contains no value for the feature NUMB. Consider now the following sentences:

(42) The sheep was in the garden.
(43) The sheep were in the garden.

(42) contains a verb which requires a singular subjct, while in (43) we have a verb which requires a plural subject. This suggests that the subjects will have something like the following structures. (For simplicity, we ignore intermediate categories.)

(44)   (45)

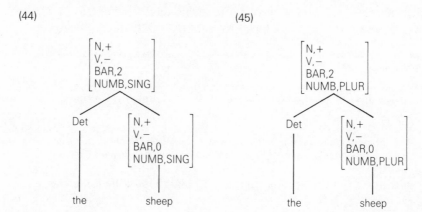

If this is right, however, we cannot say that a category in a tree and a category in the lexicon match only if they are identical. Rather, we must say the following:

(46) A category in a tree matches a category in the lexicon iff the latter subsumes the former.

Thus, we have just the same relation between categories in the lexicon and categories in trees as between categories in rules and categories in trees.

One might suppose that the noun *sheep* is something of a special case, and that categories in trees will generally be identical to the corresponding categories in the lexicon. In fact, however, it is very common, at least in PSG, for a lexical item to be associated with a more specific category in a tree than in the lexicon. We will see this in later chapters.

4.7 Summary

In this chapter we have looked more closely at syntactic categories and considered reasons for assuming that they are not simple, unanalyzable entities but complex entities made up from smaller elements. In 4.2, we saw how the need for a richer classification of expressions provides some motivation for this assumption. Then, in 4.3 we saw how the relation between lexical and phrasal categories provides further motivation, and in 4.4, we considered the relevance of cross-categorial generalizations. In 4.5, we looked at features, the basic building blocks of categories. Finally, in 4.6, we looked at the relation between categories in rules and the lexicon and categories in trees. We saw that a category in a tree matches a corresponding category in a rule or in the lexicon as long as the latter subsumes the former. This means that categories in trees can be more specific than the corresponding categories in rules or the lexicon.

Notes

The view that syntactic categories are complex entities is generally seen as originating in Harman (1963), but it only gained general acceptance after it was adopted in Chomsky (1965). Chomsky proposed not that all syntactic categories are complex but just that lexical categories are, but in Chomsky (1970) he proposed that all categories are sets of features.

For textbook discussion of prenominal adjectives, *see* Radford (1988, 4.7). For discussion of coordinate structures, *see* Sag *et al.* (1985) and Goodall (1987).

The fact that phrasal categories go together with lexical categories was also highlighted in Lyons (1968). The most important presentation of X-bar theory as it developed in the 70s is Jackendoff (1977). For technical discussion of X-bar theory, see Kornai and Pullum (1990).

A number of syntacticians, notably Abney (1987), have argued that what have traditionally been regarded as NP's are in fact projections of Det and hence really DP's. Examples like the following seem to provide some support for this view:

(1) all of the men

Here, the only N *men* is within a PP and hence cannot be head of the whole phrase. It seems plausible, then, to suggest that the Det *all* is a head. There are, however, examples of what are traditionally regarded as NP's which contain no overt Det. These cast some doubt on the idea that these phrases are DP's. This is an important unresolved issue.

Adverbs are commonly analyzed as a special kind of adjective and adverb phrases as a special kind of adjective phrase. See Radford (1988, 3.7.) for some discussion.

The analysis of the basic categorial status of categories in terms of the features N and V was introduced in Chomsky (1974). It is assumed in GB and GPSG, but not in HPSG, which simply assumes a feature MAJ with the values N, V, A, P, etc.

HPSG and a number of other approaches have made use of features which have a number of other features as their value. Such features permit a simple account of situations in which a number of features have the same value in categories that are related in some way. If these features are the value of some other feature, all one has to do is to ensure that the categories have the same value for this feature.

HPSG and other approaches also allow negative and disjunctive feature values. In other words, they allow one to say that an expression does not have a particular value for a certain feature or that it has one of two possible values. See Kartunnen (1984), for discussion.

For further discussion of complex categories and their descriptive potential, see Shieber (1987) and Gazdar and Mellish (1989, 7.).

The nature of syntactic categories has had much less attention in GB than in PSG. However, a collection of largely GB-based papers on features and related matters appears in Muysken and van Riemsdijk (1985).

For further discussion of subsumption, see Shieber (1987, 3.) and Gazdar and Mellish (1989, 7.).

Exercises

Exercise 1

Replace the informal classification of expressions in the following statements with precise categories using the features N, V, BAR and others:

(1) *Been* is the past participle of an auxiliary verb.
(2) *Them* is an objective third person plural pronoun.
(3) *Taller than Ben* is a comparative adjective phrase.
(4) *The girls* is a feminine plural noun phrase.
(5) *Picture of Debbie* is a neuter, singular N'.

Exercise 2

Identify the lexical categories in the following trees which do not have associated phrasal categories and the phrasal categories which do not have associated lexical categories. Assume that any category which is not a lexical category is a phrasal category.

(1)

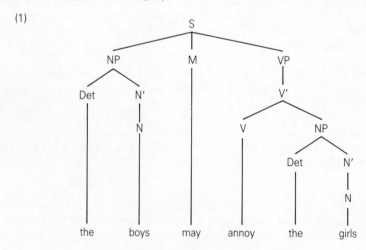

(2)

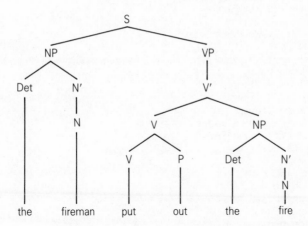

(3)

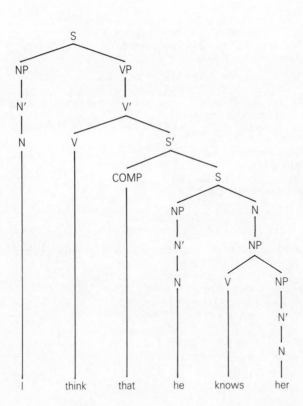

Exercise 3

Discuss which of the following facts can and which cannot be easily described using the features N and V introduced in 4.4.

(1) In English; NP's, AP's and PP's but not VP's can appear in clause-initial position in *wh*-questions. The phrases are bracketed.

(1) a. [Which house] did you buy?
   b. [How tall] is your son?
   c. [In which county] did he live?
   d. * [Read which book] may he?

(2) In Welsh, finite verbs and prepositions agree with a following pronoun. The following illustrate:
   (2) a. Gwelais i Emrys.
       saw-1SG I Emrys
       'I saw Emrys.'
     b. Gwelasant hwy Emrys.
        saw-3PL   they Emrys
        'They saw Emrys.'
     c. arnaf   i
        on-1SG I
        'on me'
     d. arnynt hwy
        on-3PL they
        'on them'

(3) In Polish, adjectives and nouns are marked for case. The following illustrates:
   (3) Jan   wygląda mi   na inteligentnego.
       Jan-NOM   looks   me-DAT on inelligent-ACC
       'Jan looks intelligent to me.'

   (NOM − nominative; DAT − dative; ACC − acc)

(4) In Welsh, a non-finite verb and a noun is a preceded by a clitic if it is followed by a pronoun. The following illustrate:
   (4) a. ei   mam   ef
        3SGM mother   he
        'his mother'
     b. Ceisiodd hi ei   weld ef
        tried   she 3SGF see he
        'She tried to see him.'

Exercise 4

Which categories in the following are subsumed by which other categories?

(1) [BAR,2;N,+;V,−]
(2) [BAR,2;N,+;V,−;CASE,ACC]
(3) [BAR,2;N,−;V,+;VFORM,FIN;PAST,+]
(4) [BAR,0;N,+;V,−;CASE,ACC]
(5) [BAR,2]
(6) [BAR,2;N,+;V,−;PERS,3;NUMB,SG]
(7) [BAR,2;N,−;V,+;VFORM,FIN]
(8) [BAR,0;N,−;V,+]

5

Heads and complements

5.1 Introduction

An important fact that we have ignored so far is that lexical items of the same broad class, V, N. A or P, can differ in their behaviour. Particularly important is the fact that lexical heads of the same class can differ in the categories that they combine with, or, more precisely, in the complements that they take. The following illustrate:

(1) a. Stefan put the book on the shelf.
    b. * Stefan put Ben that he should work harder.
(2) a. Stefan persuaded Ben that he should work harder
    b. * Stefan persuaded the book on the shelf.

The verb *put* takes an NP and a PP as its complements whereas the verb *persuade* takes an NP and an S. Thus, the a. examples are grammatical but the b. examples are quite impossible. It is clear, then, that we need a subclassification of lexical heads on the basis of what complements they take. This is standardly known as subcategorization and has been a major concern of syntactic theory since the 60's.

In this chapter, we will look first at what exactly we mean by a complement and in particular at how complements differ from adjuncts. Then, we will consider the approach to subcategorization developed by Chomsky in his book *Aspects*. Next, we will consider the GB approach and after that we will consider PSG ideas about subcategorization. Finally, we will look at the relation between complements and meaning.

5.2 Complements and adjuncts

In English, complements follow the lexical heads with which they are associated. However, not all constituents that follow a lexical head within the phrase that it heads are complements. Others are so-called adjuncts. In (3) *Maja* is a complement but *in the garden* is an adjunct, and in (4) *to London* is a complement but *on Thursday* is an adjunct.

(3) Stefan saw Maja in the garden.
(4) Stefan went to London on Thursday.

The complement-adjunct distinction is relevant to all categories but we will only consider it in connection with verbs.

An important difference between complements and adjuncts is that complements are associated with specific lexical heads in a way that adjuncts are not. More precisely, particular lexical heads co-occur with particular complements, whereas an adjunct of a particular type is generally possible in any phrase of a particular kind whatever its head is. Hence, we can add *in the garden* or *on Thursday* to (1)a. and (2)a. without any problems.

A second point to note is that complements tend to be obligatory whereas adjuncts are always optional. Thus, a constituent that is obligatory must be a complement, but a constituent that is optional may be either a complement or an adjunct. The following show that *Maja* is obligatory in (3), whereas *in the garden* is optional

(5) a. * Stefan saw in the garden.
    b. Stefan saw Maja.

Hence, *Maja* must be a complement, but *in the garden* could be a complement or an adjunct.

We say that complements 'tend' to be obligatory because there are complements that are optional. Consider the following:

(6) a. Stefan was eating the carrot.
    b. Stefan was eating.

In (6)a., *eating* is followed by an NP. As (6)b. shows, this is optional. There are reasons, however, for saying that this NP is a complement. One is that it is understood in (6)b. that Stefan was eating something. We just don't know what. Another is that the NP is obligatory with the related verb *devour*. Thus, while (7)a. is fine, (7)b. is unacceptable.

(7) a. Stefan was devouring the carrot.
    b. * Stefan was devouring.

We will introduce a further reason shortly.

It is commonly assumed that there is a structural contrast between complements and adjuncts. Specifically, it is assumed that complements combine with a lexical category to form a related intermediate phrasal category, whereas adjuncts combine with an intermediate category to form the same intermediate category. This means that we have structures of the following form:

(8)

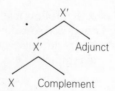

Assuming this structural contrast between complements and adjuncts, we can provide an explanation for the following data:

(9) a. Stefan will wash his socks in the bathroom and Ben will do so too.
   b. Stefan will wash his socks in the bathroom and Ben will do so in the kitchen.
(10) a. Stefan will put his socks in the bathroom and Ben will do so too.
   b. * Stefan will put his socks in the bathroom and Ben will do so in the kitchen.

If we assume that *wash* takes just an NP complement whereas *put* takes an NP and a PP complement, these will involve the following structures:

(11)

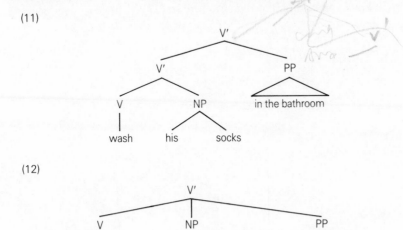

(12)

Given these structures, we just need to assume the following to account for the data in (9) and (10):

(13) *Do so* derives its interpretation from a preceding V'.

In (11), both *wash his socks in the bathroom* and *wash his socks* are V' constituents. Hence, *do so* derives its interpretation from a V' in both (9)a. and (9)b. In contrast, in (12), *put his socks in the bathroom* is a V', but *put his socks* is not. Hence, only in (10)a. does *do so* derive its interpretation from a V'. Here, then, we have a way of distinguishing verbal complements from verbal adjuncts.

We can use *do so* to provide some further evidence that we have an optional complement with *eat*. Consider the following data:

(14) a. Stefan ate a carrot and Maja did so too.
   b. * Stefan ate a carrot and Maja did so a radish.

In (14)a., *do so* derives its interpretation from *ate a carrot*. In (14)b, *do so* derives its interpretation from *ate*. Since the latter is unacceptable we can conclude that *ate* by itself is not a V' and hence that *a carrot* must be a complement.

What complements lexical heads take depends on how one analyzes sentences in which they appear. There is little disagreement in this area. Everyone agrees that there are many different possibilities with verbs, but far fewer possibilities with nouns, adjectives and prepositions, and everyone agrees that verbs and prepositions can take an NP complement while nouns and adjectives cannot, a point that we highlighted in 4.4. There is, however, disagreement about examples like the following:

(15) Stefan considers Ben to be a fool.

Within GB, this will have something like the structure in (16), whereas within PSG, it will have something like the structure in (17).

(16)

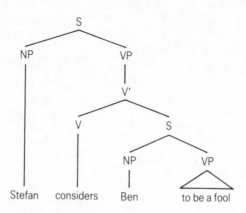

(17)

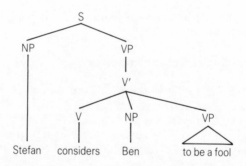

On the first analysis, *considers* takes an S complement, which, following Radford (1988), we can call an exceptional clause, whereas on the second, it takes an NP and a VP complement. There are similar disagreements about the following examples:

(18) Stefan considers Ben foolish.
(19) Stefan considers Ben a fool.
(20) Stefan wanted Ben out of the room.
(21) Stefan made Ben do it.

In GB, all these examples have a single clausal complement, standardly known as a small clause, whereas in PSG, they have two separate complements. For example, (18) will have something like the structure in (22) in GB and something the structure in (23) in PSG.

(22)

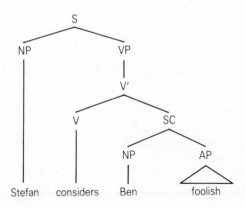

(23)

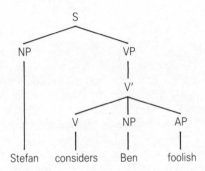

Apart from examples like these, there is general agreement about what complements lexical items take.

5.3 The *Aspects* approach to subcategorization

Until about ten years ago, most syntacticians accepted the approach to subcategorization developed by Chomsky in his *Aspects of the Theory of Syntax* (Chomsky, 1965). This approach has a serious weakness. It is important to understand this weakness, so that one understands why somewhat different approaches have been developed more recently.

The *Aspects* framework assumes phrase structure rules. If we assume phrase structure rules, we might have the following rules to provide for a variety of verb phrases:

(24) a. V′ → V
     b. V′ → V NP
     c. V′ → V PP
     d. V′ → V S
     e. V′ → V NP PP
     f. V′ → V NP S

These rules will provide for the underlined strings in the following:

(25) a. Stefan *paused*.
    b. Stefan *saw Maja*.
    c. Stefan *went to London*.
    d. Stefan *thinks that Maja likes him*.
    e. Stefan *put the book on the shelf*.
    f. Stefan *persuaded Maja that he liked her*.

To account for subcategorization facts, the *Aspects* framework associates lexical heads with subcategorization frames, which indicate what complements they take. For the verbs in the above examples, *pause, see, go, think, put* and *persuade*, we would have the following frames:

(26) a. [– Ø]
    b. [– NP]
    c. [– PP]
    d. [– S]
    e. [– NP PP]
    f. [– NP S]

Each of these frames contains ' – ' followed by one or more categories. This makes it clear that the complements follow the verb. The first frame contains the symbol 'Ø', which indicates that the verb *pause* takes no complements at all. All the other frames contain ordinary categories indicating that the verbs do take various complements. Given such frames, all we have to do to account for subcategorization facts is to stipulate that lexical heads can only appear in a context specified in a subcategorization frame with which they are associated.

This approach handles the facts quite well. It does, however, have one serious weakness first pointed out in Heny (1979). This is that it involves some redundancy. An inspection of the subcategorization frames in (26) reveals that they are identical to the right hand sides of the rules minus the V categories. This means that the subcategorization frames repeat the information in the rules or that the rules repeat the information in the subcategorization frames. Such redundancy is unsatisfactory. It should be noted that it has nothing to do with the fact that the rules are phrase structure rules. We would have just the same redundancy if we assumed immediate dominance rules.

There are two possible responses to this weakness. Either one finds some way of eliminating rules like those in (24), or one somehow eliminates subcategorization frames. Both options have been explored in recent work.

5.4 GB and subcategorization

GB takes the first of these options. Since Stowell (1981), it has abandoned rules like those in (24) and assumed a single, category-neutral immediate dominance rule.

We can call this rule the head-complement rule, and formulate it as follows:

(27) X' → X,YP*

This says that an intermediate phrasal category can immediately dominate the related lexical category together with any number of full phrasal categories.

(The '*' means 'any number'.) It is category-neutral in the sense that it does not refer to any specific categories. One point to note is that the rule presupposes a feature system of the kind that we introduced in the last chapter, in which related lexical and intermediate categories are identified as such. Another point to note is that it shows very clearly that we cannot require categories in trees to be identical to the corresponding categories in rules. Given such a general rule, the corresponding categories in trees will always be much more specific. A final point to note is that the rule embodies the assumption, advocated, for example, in Jackendoff (1977) and Stowell (1981), that complements are always maximal projections.

The rule will allow all sorts of ill-formed local trees. For example, it will allow the following:

(28)

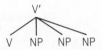

There is, however, nothing new in an immediate dominance rule that allows local trees that are not well-formed. The rule in (29) allows both the trees in (30)

(29) V' → V,NP
(30)

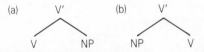

This is no problem, however, since (30)b. is ruled out by the requirement that a lexical category precedes any phrasal category that is its sister. Structures like (28) will be ruled out if syntactic structures are required to satisfy the sub-categorization requirements of the lexical items they contain. This requirement is embodied in what is known as the Projection Principle, which we can formulate as follows:

(31) Syntactic representations are projections of the lexicon in that they observe the subcategorization properties of lexical items.

Given this principle, (28) will be ruled out because there is no verb that requires three NP complements and hence no verb that can appear in such a structure.

One point to note about this approach is that whether or not a local tree is well-formed is a complex matter. A lexically headed local tree must match the head-complement rule and conform to the Projection Principle and linear precedence requirements. We can illustrate this point with the following examples:

(32)

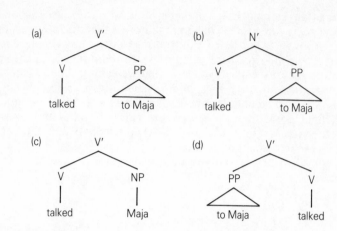

(32)a. is well-formed. It matches the head-complement rule, and conforms to the Projection Principle and linear precedence requirements. All the other trees are ill-formed. (32)b. is ill-formed because it does not match the head-complement rule. (32)c. is ill-formed because it does not conform to the Projection Principle. Finally, (32)d. is ill-formed because it violates a linear precedence requirement.

Here, then, we have an approach to subcategorization that successfully avoids the redundancy that is a feature of the *Aspects* approach.

5.5 PSG and subcategorization

We can turn now to PSG. Here, two different approaches to subcategorization have been developed. Generalized Phrase Structur Grammar (GPSG) takes the second of the options that we highlighted at the end of 5.3., abandoning subcategorization frames. Head-driven Phrase Structure Grammar (HPSG) follows GB in taking the first of the two options, abandoning category-specific rules.

GPSG assumes a feature SUBCAT, which takes as its value an arbitrary number. Within GPSG, then, we might have the following immediate dominance rules to provide for the VP's in (25).

(33) a. V′ → V[SUBCAT, 1]
      b. V′ → V[SUBCAT, 2], NP
      c. V′ → V[SUBCAT, 3], PP
      d. V′ → V[SUBCAT, 4], S
      e. V′ → V[SUBCAT, 5], NP,PP
      f. V′ → V[SUBCAT, 6], NP,S

To ensure that *pause* appears in the right context, we must say that it is not just a V but a V[SUBCAT, 1]. Similarly, to ensure that *see* appears in the right context, we must say that it is not just a V but a V[SUBCAT, 2]. Similar remarks apply to the other verbs. Here, then, there is no need for subcategorization frames.

HPSG also assumes a feature SUBCAT but one which takes as its value not an arbitrary number but a list of categories, which we can refer to as a

SUBCAT list. I will assume here that this list includes just the complements that the head requires. (I will consider a different position in the next chapter.) I will also assume with Pollard and Sag (1988) that the categories are listed in the opposite order from that in which they appear in the tree. Given these assumptions, if a head takes an NP followed by a PP, it will be [SUBCAT, $\langle$PP, NP$\rangle$]. The list is surrounded by angle brackets and its members are separated by commas. Within this version of the framework, we will have the following categories for the verbs in (25).

(34) a. V[SUBCAT, $\langle\rangle$]
      b. V[SUBCAT, $\langle$NP$\rangle$]
      c. V[SUBCAT, $\langle$PP$\rangle$]
      d. V[SUBCAT, $\langle$S$\rangle$]
      e. V[SUBCAT, $\langle$PP, NP$\rangle$]
      f. V[SUBCAT, $\langle$S, NP$\rangle$]

In (34)a. the value of SUBCAT is an empty list, which means that no complements are required. Phrasal categories will also be [SUBCAT, $\langle\rangle$] since they require no complements. NP and PP are abbreviations for N[SUBCAT, $\langle\rangle$] and P[SUBCAT, $\langle\rangle$], respectively. We will consider the meaning of S in the next chapter. Categories like those in (34) interact with a single category-neutral head-complement rule, and a general principle known as the Sub-categorization Principle. Simplifying somewhat, we can formulate the rule as follows:

(35) X[SUBCAT,$\langle\rangle$] → X[SUBCAT,$\langle$ . . . $\rangle$], C∗

'$\langle$ . . . $\rangle$' here stands for any list (including the empty list) and C stands for a complement. We can paraphrase the rule as follows:

(36) A category that requires no complements can immediately dominate a related category that may require complements together with any number of complements.

Nothing in this rule ensures that we have the correct number and kind of complements. The Subcategorization Principle does this. It is rather like the Projection Principle. We can formulate it as follows:

(37) When a head and its mother have different values for SUBCAT, the categories that are on the SUBCAT list of the head and not on the SUBCAT list of the mother must be identical to the sisters of the head.

This ensures that a lexical head has just the complements that it requires and no others. The category in (34)b. will interact with the rule and the Principle to allow the tree in (38).

(38)

Similarly, the category in (34)e. will interact with the rule and the Principle to allow the tree in (39).

(39)

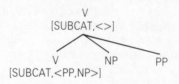

In this analysis, as in the GB analysis, whether or not a local tree is well-formed is a complex matter. A lexically headed local tree must match the head-complement rule and conform to the Subcategorization Principle and linear precedence requirements. The following illustrate:

(40)

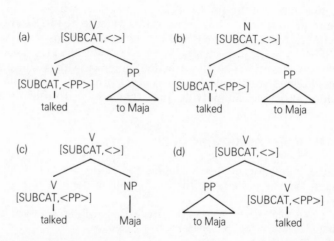

Only (40)a. is well-formed. It matches the head-complement rule, and conforms to the Subcategorization Principle and linear precedence requirements. All the other trees are ill-formed. (40)b. does not match the HPSG head-complement rule, (40)c. does not conform to the Subcategorization Principle, and (40)d. violates a linear precedence requirement.

A technical point that we should note here is that the Subcategorization Principle can lead to a lexical item being associated with a more specific category in a tree than in the lexicon. As we saw in the last chapter, this is something which we must allow. We have suggested the following lexical category for the verb *saw*:

(41) V[SUBCAT,⟨NP⟩]

The SUBCAT list contains just an NP with no indication of number. Notice now that *saw* can have either a singular or a plural NP complement.

(42) Maja saw the spider.
(43) Maja saw the spiders.

Given the Subcategorization Principle, *saw* will have the category in (44) in (42) and the category in (45) in (43).

(44) V[SUBCAT,⟨   NP   ⟩]
         [NUMB,SING]
(45) V[SUBCAT,⟨   NP   ⟩]
         [NUMB,PLUR]

Both are subsumed by (41). Hence, there is no problem here. As we will see in later chapters, this 'fleshing out' of categories by the Subcategorization Principle is of some importance within HPSG.

One point to note about this analysis is that we have not identified the verbs as lexical or their mothers as phrasal. In (35) and (36), the verbs and their mothers are distinguished by the SUBCAT feature. This will often be the case since a verb will often require a complement or complements, whereas its mother never will. But, of course, there are verbs which do not require a complement, simple intransitive verbs like *run*. There are also many nouns and adjectives that do not require a complement. To distinguish such items from their mothers, HPSG employs a feature LEX with the values '+' for lexical categories and '−' for phrasal categories. Assuming this feature, we will have +LEX in the categories in (34) and in the verbs in (38) and (39) and −LEX in the mothers (and NP and PP will be abbreviations for N[−LEX;SUBCAT,⟨⟩] and P[−LEX;SUBCAT,⟨⟩], respectively). In addition, the head-complement rule will be reformulated as follows:

(46) X[−LEX; SUBCAT,⟨⟩] → X[+LEX; SUBCAT,⟨ . . . ⟩], C∗

We can paraphrase as follows:

(47) A phrasal category that requires no complements can immediately dominate a
     related lexical category that may require complements together with any number
     of complements.

Thus, the LEX feature ensures that lexical heads and their mothers are always distinguished even when the head requires no complements. We will, however, ignore it in subsequent discussion.

A natural question to ask here is: how are full and intermediate phrasal categories distinguished within this framework? They are in fact distinguished by the presence in the latter and the absence in the former of feature specifications indicating that they require a specifier of some kind. We will not go into this, however.

Here, then, as in GB, we have an approach to subcategorization that avoids the redundancy of the *Aspects* approach. Superficially, it is rather different from the GB approach. It should be clear, however, that it is in reality rather similar.

5.6 Complements and meaning

One thing that is clear in this area is that what complements a lexical head takes has something to do with its meaning. For example, the fact that *die* is an intransitive verb taking no complement is clearly related to the fact that it denotes a process which involves a single person identified by its subject. Similarly, the fact that *kill* is a transitive verb taking an NP complement obviously has something to do with the fact that it denotes an action which involves two people, the killer, identified by the subject, and the victim, identified by the complement.

It is natural to ask whether we can say anything more precise than this about the relation between complements and meaning. GB in particular has given a positive answer to this question. One claim that is made within GB is that the number of complements a lexical head takes is predictable from its semantic properties.

This claim involves the notion of a semantic role or a θ-role. We can illustrate this notion with the following examples:

(48) Stefan went from London to Brighton.
(49) Stefan put the book on the shelf.

We can say that *Stefan* in both these examples is the agent, since it identifies the entity responsible for the action. In (48), we can say that *from London* is the source and that *to Brighton* is the goal. The former identities the position from which movement occurs and the latter identifies the position at which move-ment terminates. Finally, in (49), we can say that *the book* is the theme and *on the shelf* the location. The former identifies the person or thing to which something happens, and the latter identifies a place.

It is proposed in GB that lexical heads are associated with a specific number of θ-roles and that every complement must be assigned a θ-role. One conse-quence of this is that the number of complements a lexical head takes will typically be the number of θ-roles associated with it minus one, which is assigned to its subject. We say 'typically' because, as discussed in the next chapter, there are cases where no θ-role is associated with the subject position. In these cases, the number of complements is identical to the number of θ-roles associated with the lexical head. Another consequence of the proposal that a lexical head assigns a θ-role to all its complements is that the post-verbal NP in examples like the following cannot be a complement:

(50) a. I believe it to be easy to fool Maja.
      b. I consider it easy to fool Maja.

As we will see in the next chapter, the *it* that appears in these examples is analyzed in GB as an element that has no θ-role. Here, then, we have one reason for assuming that these verbs take a single clausal complement and not two separate complements.

It has also been suggested within GB that the nature of the complements a lexical head takes is largely determined by semantic considerations. It may well be that a complement with certain semantic properties normally appears as an NP, that a complement with certain other semantic properties normally appears as a PP, and so on. It is clear, however, that what complements appear is not completely predictable from semantic considerations. Various kinds of data show this. Consider the following:

(51) a. It is likely that Stefan will be late.
      b. It is probable that Stefan will be late.

(52) a. Stefan is likely to be late.
    b. * Stefan is probable to be late.

The examples in (51) seem to have essentially the same meaning, so it seems that *likely* and *probable* mean the same. The examples in (52) show, however, that they do not take exactly the same complements. Consider also the following:

(53) a. I asked what time it was.
    b. I inquired what time it was.
(54) a. I asked the time.
    b. * I inquired the time.

The examples in (53) seem to have the same meaning, which suggests that *ask* and *inquire* mean the same. Both take a complement that identifies a question, and with both, the complement can be a clause. The examples in (54) show, however, that *ask* but not *inquire* also allows the complement to be an NP.

It is clear, then, that what complements a lexical head takes is related to its meaning. It is also clear, however, that what complements appear is not completely predictable from semantic considerations.

5.7 Summary

We have been concerned in this chapter with the way that lexical heads of the same class differ in the complements that they take, a phenomenon traditionally discussed under the heading of subcategorization. We looked first in 5.2 at the distinction between complements and the superficially similar adjuncts. Then, in 5.3, we looked at what we called the *Aspects* approach to subcategorization, essentially the approach developed in Chomsky (1965). This employs both a variety of category-specific rules for head-complement combinations and subcategorization frames in the lexicon, and consequently involves a degree of redundancy. To avoid this redundancy, one must eliminate one or other of the devices. In 5.4, we looked at how GB eliminates category specific head-complement rules, highlighting in particular the role of the Projection Principle. Then in 5.5 we looked first at the GPSG approach, which eliminates subcategorization frames, and then at the HPSG approach, which like the GB approach eliminates category-specific head-complement rules. In connection with the latter, we highlighted the Subcategorization Principle. Finally, in 5.6, we looked at the relation between complements and meaning, suggesting that what complements a lexical head takes is partly but not completely predictable from its semantic properties.

Notes

The fact that *do so* can be used to distinguish between verbal complements and verbal adjuncts was first highlighted in Lakoff and Ross (1976). In much the same way as *do so* derives its interpretation from a preceding V', *one* derives its interpretation from a preceding N'. Hence, it provides a way of distinguishing between nominal complements and adjuncts. Consider the following contrast.

(1) This student from Korea is more dedicated than that one from Japan.
(2) * This student of linguistics is more dedicated than that one of psychology.

In both, *one* derives its interpretation from *student*. The fact that (1) is grammatical suggests that *from Korea* is an adjunct. The fact that (2) is ungrammatical, on the other hand suggests that *of linguistics* is a complement. See Radford (1988, 5.2.), for further discussion.

An important fact about subcategorization is that lexical heads often require not just a certain type of PP, but a PP headed by a particular preposition. The following illustrate:

(3) He relies $\left\{ \begin{array}{l} \text{on} \\ \text{* in} \\ \text{* by} \\ \text{* with} \\ \text{* from} \end{array} \right\}$ her.   (4) He is fond $\left\{ \begin{array}{l} \text{of} \\ \text{* to} \\ \text{* for} \\ \text{* by} \\ \text{* with} \end{array} \right\}$ her.

PSG uses a feature PFORM, whose value is the name of a preposition to identify a PP as headed by a specific preposition. Thus, for PSG, *relies* takes a PP[PFORM,ON] and *fond* a PP[PFORM,OF].

The constituent structure of sentences like (15) and (18) – (21) in the text has been discussed extensively but it remains unresolved. As McCloskey (1988) notes, 'It is one of the enduring embarrassments of the field that this apparently routine question of constituency has proven so difficult to resolve one way or the other.' The main early discussions are Postal (1974) and Bresnan (1976). Williams (1983) is an important GB critique of the small clause analysis. Postal and Pullum (1988) contains some important recent criticisms of exceptional clause and small clause analyses. Proponents of small clauses have argued that strings like the bracketed string in the following provide a further example:

(5) With [Ben in charge], anything is possible.

See Hoekstra (1984) and Beukema and Hoekstra (1984).
    Proponents of small clauses disagree about the categorial status of the small clause node. Throughout the book, I use the label SC, assuming that the small clause category is unrelated to the category of the predicate. A number of syntacticians have suggested, however, that it is a projection of the head of the predicate. Stowell (1981) proposes that small clauses have the form in (6), and Chomsky (1986) proposes that they have the form in (7).

(6)   (7)

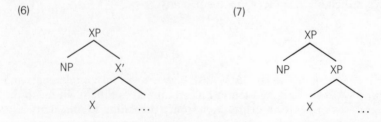

See Radford (1988, 9.12) for some discussion.

Under certain circumstances what we might regard as an extra complement is possible. Consider, for example, the following:

(8) The problem is harder [than we thought]
(9) They are more confident [than they used to be]
(10) He is as angry [as they said]
(11) Stefan is so tired [that he can't keep his eyes open]
(12) Maja is too intelligent [to be deceived]

In (8), the bracketed string is only possible because we have the comparative form *harder* and not the basic form *hard*. In (9), the bracketed string is only possible because the adjective is preceded by the specifier *more*. In much the same way, the bracketed strings in (10)–(12) are only possible because we have the specifiers *as*, *so* and *too*. For some discussion of these extra complements, see Jackendoff (1977, 8.).

The GPSG approach to subcategorization is discussed in Gazdar et al. (1985, 2.5.).

The version of HPSG that is presented in the text is essentially that proposed in Borsley (1987, forthcoming). As noted in the next chapter, the version of HPSG that is presented in Pollard and Sag (1988) involves a SUBCAT feature which indicates both what complements a lexical head takes and what sort of subject it requires.

The value of SUBCAT is in fact a list of signs, combinations of syntactic, semantic and phonological information, in Pollard and Sag (1988) and a list of SYNSEM objects, combinations of syntactic and semantic information in Pollard and Sag (forthcoming). Thus, we are simplifying somewhat in treating its value as a list of categories.

The HPSG idea that categories should incorporate information about what other categories they combine with has its origins in so-called Categorial Grammar, an approach to grammar originally developed between the wars by the Polish logician Ajdukiewicz. In one version of Categorial Grammar all categories apart from a small number of basic categories are of the form α/β or $\alpha\backslash\beta$, where α and β are categories. An α/β is an expression which combines with a following β to form an α, and an $\alpha\backslash\beta$ is an expression which combines with a preceding β to form an α. Within this approach, an English VP might be analyzed as a S\NP, an expression which combines with a preceding NP to form an S, and an English transitive verb might be analyzed as an (S\NP)/NP, an expression that combines with a following NP to form an expression which combines with a preceding NP to form an S. Categorial Grammar is an important focus of current research. For introductions to the basic ideas, see Lyons (1968, 6.3.) and Flynn (1983). For recent work in Categorial Grammar, see the papers in Oehrle, Bach and Wheeler (1988).

Thematic roles were introduced into syntactic theory as thematic relations in Gruber (1965), and their position in transformational grammar was consolidated in Jackendoff (1972). In the 60's and 70's, they were at the heart of a framework known as Case Grammar, in which they were referred to as (semantic) cases. See Fillmore (1968, 1977) and Anderson (1971, 1977).

Jackendoff (1983, 1987) argues that θ-roles can be defined in terms of the semantic representations that are associated with lexical items. For recent discussion of θ-roles, see Wilkins (1988).

The assumption that dummies do not appear in complement position is contested by Postal and Pullum (1988) on the basis of examples like the following:

(13) I take it that you will pay.
(14) I have it on good authority that the CIA was never informed.
(15) Don't spread it around that I am giving you this assignment.
(16) John will see to it that you have a reservation.

Current GB ideas about the relations between complements and meaning owe much to Pesetsky (1982). Jackendoff (1985) provides some interesting discussion of this relation. Pollard and Sag (1988, 5.3.) argue that subcategorization cannot be reduced to semantic considerations. The *likely/probable* contrast is highlighted in Hudson (1972). The *ask/inquire* contrast is highlighted in Grimshaw (1979).

Exercises

Exercise 1

Decide which of the post-verbal constituents in the following examples are complements of the verb and which are adjuncts and provide appropriate subcategorization frames for the verbs.

(1) He keeps a picture of his wife on his desk.
(2) He met the man from the Embassy in the park.
(3) We moved the stereo from the lounge to the bedroom before the party.
(4) I gave the students an assignment about prepositional phrases this week.
(5) They seemed intelligent to me when I interviewed them.
(6) We appealed to him to work harder last week.

Exercise 2

Explain how the ungrammaticality of (2) and (3) appears to provide an argument against the assumption that *him to be a genius* in (1) is an exceptional clause. Then explain how the ungrammaticality of (5) and (6) undermines this argument. Next show how the grammaticality of (7) seems to provide an argument in favour of the assumption that *him to be a genius* is an exceptional clause. Finally, show how the grammaticality of (8) undermines this argument.

(1) Everyone considered him to be a genius.
(2) * Him to be a genius was considered by everyone.
(3) * What everyone considered was him to be a genius.
(4) Everyone thought he was a genius.
(5) * He was a genius was thought by everyone.
(6) * What he thought was he was a genius.
(7) We consider him to be a genius and her to be a fool.
(8) We gave him a hamster and her a snake.

Exercise 3

Provde HPSG trees with appropriate categories for the bracketed strings in the following sentences. Ignore the internal structure of complements.

(1) They [said to him that he was mistaken]
(2) We [talked to her about the situation]
(3) He appeared [from under the bed]
(4) He likes [stories about dragons]
(5) It was [apparent to everyone that he was lying]
(6) They stayed [until the beer ran out]

Exercise 4

Many Welsh prepositions have a variety of different forms, each used in just some of the situations in which a typical English preposition appears. The following illustrate the full range of forms of the preposition *gan* 'with'.

(1) gan   y   bachgen/y bechgyn/* i/* ti   /* ef/* hi/* ni/* chwi/
    with   the   boy   the boys   I you-SG   he she we you-PL
    * hwy
      they
(2) gennyf i/* ti/   * ef/* hi/* ni/* chwi/   * hwy/* y   bachgen/
    with   I you-SG he ·she we you-PL.   they   the   boy
    *-y bechgyn .
      the boys
(3) gennyt ti/   * i/* ef/* hi/* ni/* chwi/   * hwy/* y   bachgen/
    with   you-SG I he she we you-PL   they   the   boy
    * y bechgyn
      the boys
(4) ganddo ef/* i/* ti/   * hi/* ni/* chwi/   * hwy/* y   bachgen/
    with   he I you-SG she we you-PL   they   the   boy
    * y bechgyn
      the boys
(5) ganddi hi/* i/* ti/   * ef/* ni/* chwi/   * hwy/* y   bachgen/
    with   she I you-SG he we you-PL   they   the   boy
    * y bechgyn
      the boys
(6) gennym ni/* i/* ti/   * ef/* hi/* chwi/   * hwy/* y   bachgen/
    with   we I you-SG he she you-PL   they   the   boy
    * y bechgyn
      the boys
(7) gennych chwi/   * i/* ti/   * ef/* hi/* ni/* hwy/* y   bachgen/
    with   you-PL   i you-SG he she we they   the   boy
    * y bechgyn
      the boys
(8) ganddynt hwy/* i/* ti/   * ef/* hi/* ni/* chwi/ * y   bachgen/
    with   they I you-SG he she we you-PL the   boy
    * y bechgyn
      the boys

Provide HPSG type categories with appropriate SUBCAT feature specifications for each of these forms.

6

Subjects and predicates

6.1 Introduction

A typical sentence in English and many other languages consists of a subject (often but not always referring to the topic of the sentence, i.e. what it is about) and a predicate saying something about whoever or whatever the subject refers to. In much the same way as lexical heads take particular complements, so predicates combine with particular subjects. The following illustrate this point:

(1) * Stefan talked Maja.
(2) * They likes her.

Just as (1) is ungrammatical because the lexical head *talked* does not have the right kind of complement, so (2) is ungrammatical because the predicate *likes her* does not have the right kind of subject. Clearly, this is a matter which any approach to syntax must take account of. In this chapter, we will look first at the various ways in which subjects and predicates can agree. Then, we will consider GB ideas about subjects and predicates. Finally, we will look at the position of subjects and predicates in PSG.

6.2 Subject-predicate relations

There are various ways in which subjects and predicates may agree. Firstly, finite verbs, verbs which are marked for tense, vary in form according to the person and number of the subject. The following illustrate:

(3) a. He knows her.
    b. * He know her.

The form *knows* appears with a third person singular subject. The form *know* appears with other person and number combinations.

Secondly, some predicates require or allow what is known as a dummy (or expletive, or pleonastic) subject, a subject with no semantic function. The following illustrate:

(4) a. It rained all day.
    b. * Stefan rained all day.
(5) a. It was easy to fool Maja.
    b. * Stefan was easy to fool Maja.

Here, we have two predicates which require a dummy *it*. *It* is shown to be a dummy by the fact that there is no possibility of enquiring about its reference, as there is with a normal pronoun.

(6) * What rained all day?
(7) * What was easy to fool Maja?

Also relevant here are the following examples:

(8) a. There is a man in the field.
     b. * There is reading a book.

These show that some predicates but not others take a dummy *there*. *There* is shown to be a dummy here by the fact that it cannot be accompanied by a gesture indicating an intended location in the way that it can in the following example:

(9) Stefan is there.

Thirdly, some predicates but not others allow a clause in subject position. The following illustrate:

(10) a. That Stefan was late annoyed Maja.
     b. * That Stefan was late kicked Maja.

Finally, some idioms require specific NP's as subjects. The following illustrates:

(11) The cat is out of the bag.

This contrasts with the following, where we can have any non-dummy NP in subject position:

(12) $\left\{ \begin{array}{l} \text{Maja} \\ \text{She} \\ \text{The girl next door} \end{array} \right\}$ kicked the bucket.

All the above examples involve finite clauses, clauses containing a verb which is marked for tense, but we have some of the same phenomena in non-finite clauses, clauses which have no tense-marking. Non-finite verbs do not vary in form according to what subject they combine with, but some non-finite VP's require or allow a dummy subject. The following illustrate:

(13) a. It is possible for it to rain all day.
     b. * It is possible for Stefan to rain all day.
(14) a. It is possible for it to be easy to fool Maja.
     b. * It is possible for Stefan to be easy to fool Maja.
(15) a. It is possible for there to be a man in the field.
     b. * It is possible for there to be reading a book.

It does not seem to be possible for a non-finite clause to have a clausal subject.

(16) * It is possible for that Stefan was late to annoy Maja.

We do, however, have idiomatic examples where a specific NP is required as subject.

(17) It is possible for the cat to be out of the bag.

We have a similar situation in examples which may or may not involve non-finite clauses. We can look first at the following:

(18) a. I expect it to rain all day.
     b. * I expect Stefan to rain all day.
(19) a. I expect it to be easy to fool Maja.
     b. * I expect Stefan to be easy to fool Maja.
(20) a. I expect there to be a man in the field.
     b. * I expect there to be reading a book.
(21) I expect the cat to be out of the bag.

These examples involve exceptional clauses for GB, but two separate complements for PSG. It is clear, however, that they involve a subject and a predicate. If we assume that they do not combine to form a clause, we might call the subject a functional subject to distinguish it from ordinary subjects.

Another type of example which may or may not involve a clause is exemplified by the following:

(22) a. I consider it easy to fool Maja.
     b. * I consider Stefan easy to fool Maja.

Like (18)–(21), these examples involve small clauses for GB, but two separate complements for PSG. Again, however, it is clear that they involve a subject and predicate, and again we might call the subject a functional subject if we assume that there is no clause.

6.3 Subjects and predicates in GB

We can look now at GB ideas about subjects and predicates. There are two points that we can highlight here.

The first is that it is assumed in GB following Rothstein (1983) that predicates require subjects. We can formulate this as follows:

(23) A predicate must have a subject.

This is often combined with the Projection Principle, discussed in the last chapter, to form the Extended Projection Principle. One consequence can be illustrated with the following Polish examples:

(24) a. Ja widziałem Stefana.
        I saw-1SGM Stefan-ACC
        'I saw Stefan.'
     b. Widziałem Stefana.

These have the same meaning in the sense that if one is true so is the other and if one is false the other is too (as long as they are said by the same person about the same Stefan). The only difference is one of emphasis. A speaker would use the a. example if she wanted to stress that it was she and not somebody else that saw Stefan. Given (23), the b. example must have a subject just as the a. example does. For GB, it will have exactly the same kind of subject as the a. example except that it lacks phonetic content. In other words, it will have a phonetically empty pronoun as its subject. Such a pronoun is often referred to as a *pro*. We might represent the sentence as follows:

(25)

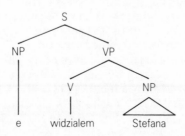

Here, following standard practice, we use *e* to indicate that the subject is phonetically empty. Alternatively, we might use *pro* instead of *e*. Languages which allow sentences like (24)b. are commonly known as null-subject or pro-drop languages.

A second important point relates to the possibility of dummy subjects and involves the notion of a θ-role, which we introduced in the last chapter. As we noted, it is assumed within GB that lexical heads assign a θ-role to all their complements but that they do not always assign a θ-role to their subject. When a lexical head assigns a θ-role to its subject, it is said to have an external θ-role. When it does not assign a θ-role to its subject, it is said to have no external θ-role. A dummy subject appears when a lexical head does not assign a θ-role to its subject, i.e. when it has no external θ-role. Thus, we can account for the occurrence of dummy subjects with the verbs *rain* and the adjective *easy* and the verb *be* in certain uses if we say that they have no external θ-role. Of course, there is nothing here to tell us which of the two dummies appears. Thus, this is only a partial account of the occurrence of dummy subjects.

One further point that we should note here is that it is assumed in GB that there are sentences which have a non-dummy subject even though there is no θ-role associated with their subject position. We will discuss this in Chapters 9 and 10.

6.4 Subjects and predicates in PSG

We can now consider how subjects and predicates can be handled within PSG. In fact, we can consider two different approaches.

The first, developed in Pollard and Sag (1988), treats subjects as the realization of a further category in the SUBCAT list. In this approach, a verb like *likes*, which takes an NP complement and a third person singular subject, will have the category in (26).

(26) V[SUBCAT,⟨NP, NP ⟩]
　　　　　　 [+3SG]

Similarly, a verb like *gives*, which takes an NP and a PP complement, and a third person singular subject will have the category in (27).

(27) V[SUBCAT,⟨PP,NP,   NP   ⟩]
                          [+3SG]

Given such categories, we will need a different head-complement rule combining a head not with all the categories on its SUBCAT list but with all except the last one, which will appear as the SUBCAT list of the mother. Then, for subject-predicate combinations, we will need a rule combining a category with a single item on its SUBCAT list with that item.

A rather different approach to subjects has been developed in GPSG, which does not necessitate a revision of the analysis of complements introduced in the last chapter. This uses a category-valued feature to indicate what kind of subject an item requires. In Gazdar *et al.* (1985), this feature is called AGR. In Hukari (1989), it is called SUBJ. I will follow Hukari here. Given this feature, we will have (28) and (29) instead of (26) and (27).

(28)
$$\begin{bmatrix} V \\ \text{SUBCAT,⟨NP⟩} \\ \text{SUBJ,\quad NP} \\ \text{[+3SG]} \end{bmatrix}$$

(29)
$$\begin{bmatrix} V \\ \text{SUBCAT,⟨PP,NP⟩} \\ \text{SUBJ,\quad NP} \\ \text{[+3SG]} \end{bmatrix}$$

To utilize the SUBJ feature, we first need to ensure that a predicate has the same value for the feature as its head. We can do this be revising the head-complement rule as follows:

(30) X[SUBCAT,⟨⟩;SUBJ,Y] → X[SUBCAT,⟨ . . .⟩,SUBJ,Y], C∗

'Y' here stands for any category. We can paraphrase this as follows:

(31) A category that requires no complements but requires a subject of some kind can immediately dominate a related category that may require complements and requires the same kind of subject together with any number of complements.

Then we need a rule combining a subject and a predicate. We can propose the following, which we can call the subject-predicate rule:

(32) X[SUBCAT⟨⟩] → Y, X[SUBCAT⟨⟩;SUBJ,Y]

We can paraphrase this as follows:

(33) A category that requires no complements and no subject can immediately dominate a related category that requires no complements but requires a subject together with the subject that it requires.

Given these rules, we will have trees like the following:

(34)

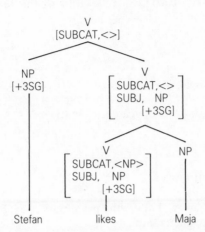

The lower part of this tree is licensed by the revised head-complement rule, interacting with the Subcategorization Principle, and the upper part of the tree is licensed by the subject-predicate rule. One point to note about this analysis is that it treats VP and S as very similar categories. S is just like VP except that it lacks the SUBJ feature.

We can return now to the data that we introduced in section 1. Essentially, all we need to account for this data is the right categories. I will repeat the examples as appropriate. Consider firstly the examples in (3).

(3) a. He knows her.
    b. * He know her.

(29) is the category that we need for *knows* in (3)a., which will have a structure just like (34). We can rule out (3)b. by assigning *know* to the following category:

(35)
$$\begin{bmatrix} V \\ \text{SUBCAT,}\langle NP \rangle \\ \text{SUBJ,}\quad NP \\ [-3SG] \end{bmatrix}$$

Given this category, a predicate headed by *know* will combine with a non-third person singular subject. Here, then, we have an account of the data in (3).

We can turn now to the examples in (4) and (8).

(4) a. It rained all day.
    b. * Stefan rained all day.
(8) a. There is a man in the field.
    b. * There is reading the book.

Within PSG, dummies are distinguished from normal NP's by a feature NFORM which takes as its values NORM, THERE and IT. Ordinary NP's are [NFORM,NORM], which means, of course, that the NP's that we have just been considering should be [NFORM,NORM]. Dummy *it* is [NFORM,IT], and dummy *there* is [NFORM,THERE]. Utilizing this feature, we can assign *rained* to the category in (36).

(36)
$$\begin{array}{c} V \\ \left[\begin{array}{ll} SUBCAT,\langle\rangle \\ SUBJ, & NP \\ & [NFORM,IT] \end{array} \right] \end{array}$$

Similarly, we can assign *be* to the category in (37).

(37)
$$\begin{array}{c} V \\ \left[\begin{array}{ll} SUBCAT,\langle PP,NP\rangle \\ SUBJ, & NP \\ & [NFORM,THERE] \end{array} \right] \end{array}$$

With these categories, we will allow the grammatical examples in (4) and (8), but not the ungrammatical examples.

Next we can consider the examples in (10).

(10) a. That Stefan was late annoyed Maja.
　　 b. * That Stefan was late kicked Maja.

Here, we simply need to assign *annoyed* but not *kicked* to the following category:

(38)
$$\begin{array}{c} V \\ \left[\begin{array}{l} SUBCAT,\langle NP\rangle \\ SUBJ,S \end{array} \right] \end{array}$$

This will ensure that *annoyed* but not *kicked* allows a clausal subject.

Given an appropriate analysis of infinitival *to* (something which we consider in chapter 10), this approach should extend to the data in (13)–(15).

(13) a. It is possible for it to rain all day.
　　 b. * It is possible for Stefan to rain all day.
(14) a. It is possible for it to be easy to fool Maja.
　　 b. * It is possible for Stefan to be easy to fool Maja.
(15) a. It is possible for there to be a man in the field.
　　 b. * It is possible for there to be reading a book.

We need a somewhat different approach, however, to the examples in (18)–(20) and (22).

(18) a. I expect it to rain all day.
　　 b. * I expect Stefan to rain all day.
(19) a. I expect it to be easy to fool Maja.
　　 b. * I expect Stefan to be easy to fool Maja.
(20) a. I expect there to be a man in the field.
　　 b. * I expect there to be reading a book.
(22) a. I consider it easy to fool Maja.
　　 b. * I consider Stefan easy to fool Maja.

These examples do not involve clauses within PSG. All we need, however, to handle these examples is appropriate categories for the main verbs.

For *expect*, we can propose the following category:

(39)
$$
\left[
\begin{array}{l}
\text{SUBCAT,}\Big\langle
\begin{array}{c}
\text{V} \\
\left[
\begin{array}{l}
\text{VP} \\
+\text{INF} \\
\text{SUBJ,} \quad \text{NP} \\
\qquad\quad [\text{NFORM,}\alpha]
\end{array}
\right]
\end{array}
\;,\;
\begin{array}{c}
\text{NP} \\
[\text{NFORM,}\alpha]
\end{array}
\Big\rangle \\
\text{SUBJ,NP}
\end{array}
\right]
$$

'VP' here is an abbreviation for V[SUBCAT,⟨⟩] (or, to be more precise V[−LEX; SUBCAT,⟨⟩]). The crucial feature of this category is that the NFORM feature within the value of the SUBJ feature in the first SUBCAT list category and the NFORM feature within the second SUBCAT list category have the same variable as their value. The Subcategorization Principle will ensure that these categories are identical to the sisters of *expect*. This will mean that the variables will be replaced by ordinary values or constants, or, to use a technical locution, that they will be instantiated. To handle the data, we just need to ensure that the variables are instantiated in the same way. We can do this with the following stipulation:

(40) For a category X to subsume a category Y, all instances of a single variable in X must be instantiated in the same way in Y.

Remember that a category in the lexicon must subsume the corresponding category in a tree. Given (40), (39) will only subsume the corresponding category in the tree if the two NFORM features have the same value. This will ensure that *expect* takes an NP complement of the kind that is required as a subject by its VP complement.

Turning now to *consider*, we can propose the following:

(41)
$$
\left[
\begin{array}{l}
\text{SUBCAT,}\Big\langle
\begin{array}{c}
\text{V} \\
\left[
\begin{array}{l}
\text{AP} \\
\text{SUBJ,} \quad \text{NP} \\
\qquad\quad [\text{NFORM,}\alpha]
\end{array}
\right]
\end{array}
\;,\;
\begin{array}{c}
\text{NP} \\
[\text{NFORM,}\alpha]
\end{array}
\Big\rangle \\
\text{SUBJ,NP}
\end{array}
\right]
$$

This is very similar to (39). Again, the two NFORM features have the same variable as their value. Interacting with the Subcategorization Principle and (40), this will ensure that *consider* takes an NP complement of the kind that is required as subject by its AP complement. Thus, it is not difficult to account for the subject-predicate relations in (18)–(22) without assuming that they involve subordinate clauses.

6.5 Summary

In this chapter, we have been concerned with the relation between subjects and predicates. In 6.2, we considered the variety of ways in which subjects and predicates may agree. In 6.3, we looked at certain GB ideas about subjects. Finally, in 6.4, we looked at how subject-predicate structures can be handled within PSG.

Notes

For further discussion of the properties of dummy *it*, see Postal and Pullum (1988) and Bennis (1986).

An important point to note about sentences with a dummy *there* subject is that the verb agrees with the following NP which is understood as its subject. The following illustrate:

(1)   There $\left\{ \begin{array}{l} \text{is} \\ * \text{ are} \end{array} \right\}$ a fly in the soup

(2)   There $\left\{ \begin{array}{l} \text{are} \\ * \text{ is} \end{array} \right\}$ two flies in the soup.

A number of syntacticians, notably Koster (1978b) and Stowell (1981, Ch. 3.), have argued that what look like clauses in subject position are in fact clauses in topic position. In other words, they occupy the same position as the clause in the following, and the subject position is empty:

(3)   That Stefan was late nobody would believe.

Evidence that these clauses do not occupy subject position comes from the ungrammaticality of the following examples:

(4)   * Did that Stefan was late annoy Maja.
(5)   * I think that that Stefan was late annoyed Maja.

Here, we have clauses which can only be subjects. Notice, however, that similar examples with a *whether* clause are much better.

(6)   Is whether (or not) Ben did it of any importance.
(7)   I think that whether (or not) Ben did it is of no importance.

It looks, then, as if at least some types of clause can appear in subject position.

Since they precede their sisters, both clausal topics and clausal subjects necessitate a revision of the rule introduced in 3.4 that an S follows all its sisters.

In earlier GB work, e.g. Chomsky (1981, 1982), it is assumed that it is not predicates but clauses that require a subject. As noted in the text, Rothstein (1983) argues that it is predicates that require subjects and this position is accepted in Chomsky (1985).

As we note in chapter 11, subjects of ordinary clauses are analyzed as specifiers of an I (or INFL or INFLECTION) category within GB.

Null subject languages commonly have elaborate verb morphology which can be seen as making the subject redundant. For discussion of such languages, see Jaeggli and Safir (1989).

Exercises

Exercise 1

Identify the subjects in the following sentences referring where appropriate to related sentences. Bear in mind that a complex sentence can have more than one subject.

(1) In all probability nothing will come of it.
(2) Why did you say that there was a problem?
(3) Whether it is necessary to do something is not yet clear.
(4) Under no circumstances should it be admitted that you were there.
(5) That tabs are being kept on him is obvious.

Exercise 2

Consider each *it* in the following examples and try to decide whether or not it is a dummy.

(1) It is likely that it will upset Maja.
(2) It is likely to upset Maja.
(3) I found it easy to solve the problem.
(4) I found it easy to solve.
(5) It is said that it is dangerous.
(6) It seems that it is easy to eat.

Exercise 3

In the text, we note that Polish is a null subject language. Given this, it is plausible to assume that (1) below has two different structures. Give these structures.

(1) Stefan jest inteligentny, i   ciężko pracuje.
 Stefan is   intelligent   and hard   works
 'Stefan is intelligent and works hard.'

Exercise 4

Provide PSG categories of the kind given in the text for the italicized verbs in the following examples:

(1) He *complained* to her about her attitude.
(2) That he was late *suggests* that he isn't very keen.
(3) It *seems* to me that he is extravagant.
(4) He *told* her that he would come.
(5) That he was there *convinced* everyone that he could be trusted.

7

Noncanonical complements and subjects

7.1 Introduction

In the last two chapters, we looked at head-complement structures and subject-predicate structures. These structures play a major role in languages. Obviously, however, there are other important kinds of structure. Particularly important are sentences involving what we can call a 'noncanonical complement' or a 'noncanonical subject'. The remainder of the book will be largely devoted to sentences of this kind. Thus, this chapter is essentially an introduction to the rest of the book. In this chapter, we will introduce the range of sentence-types that fall into these two broad categories and consider in general terms how they might be analyzed. At one time, such sentences were almost universally seen as providing evidence for a transformational approach to grammar. Nowadays, however, this position is a controversial one. We will begin by looking at a range of sentences involving noncanonical complements, and then we will look at a variety of sentences involving noncanonical subjects. Next, we will illustrate the important point that many sentences involving a noncanonical complement or a noncanonical subject have related sentences with a canonical complement or subject. Then, we will look at what we can call the monostratal approach to these sentences, which is exemplified by PSG. Finally, we will consider what we can call the multistratal approach, which is exemplified by transformational grammar.

7.2 Noncanonical complements

First, then, we can look at sentences involving noncanonical complements. By a noncanonical complement, I mean a constituent which functions as the complement of a lexical head, i.e. satisfies its subcategorization requirements, but is not a sister of the head as complements normally are. Various kinds of sentence can involve noncanonical complements. We can look first at *wh*-questions.

By a *wh*-question, I mean a question involving a question word (or a *wh*-word) of some kind like *who*, *what*, or *how*, and requiring a more-specific answer than just *yes* or *no*. The following is a typical example:

(1) Who did Stefan annoy?

Very similar is the bracketed subordinate clause in the following example:

(2) I wonder [who Stefan annoyed]

In both these examples, there is no NP complement following *annoy*. This is normally necessary, as (3) illustrates.

(3) * Stefan annoyed.

The obvious explanation for the absence of the NP complement in (1) and (2) is that the *wh*-word functions as a complement. Some support for this view comes from the fact we cannot add an NP complement to examples like (1) and (2), as the following illustrate:

(4) * Who did Stefan annoy her?
(5) * I wonder who Stefan annoyed her.

If the *wh*-word functions as the complement of *annoy* in (1) and (2), then these will be ungrammatical for the same reason as the following:

(6) * Stefan annoyed her him.

In all three cases, the problem is that a particular subcategorization requirement is satisfied twice.

Another type of sentence that can involve noncanonical complements is the passive. We can look here at the following:

(7) Maja was annoyed.

Again, we have the verb *annoy* without a following NP complement. The obvious explanation for the absence of the complement is that the subject *Maja* functions as a complement. The fact that we cannot add a complement provides some support for this view.

(8) * Maja was annoyed Stefan.

If *Maja* functions as a complement in (7), this will be ungrammatical just like (4), (5) and (6) because a subcategorization requirement is doubly satisfied.

7.3 Noncanonical subjects

We can turn now to noncanonical subjects. By a noncanonical subject, I mean a constituent which functions as the subject of a predicate although it is not a sister of the predicate. Again, various kinds of sentence are relevant, and again we can begin by looking at *wh*-questions.

Relevant examples are (9) and the bracketed subordinate clause in (10).

(9) Who do you think annoyed Maja.
(10) I wonder [who you think annoyed Maja]

In both these examples, the predicate *annoyed Maja* is not immediately preceded by a subject. This is normally necessary, as (11) illustrates:

(11) * You think annoyed Maja.

The obvious explanation for the absence of the subject in (9) and (10) is that the *wh*-word functions as the subject. The ungrammaticality of the following provides some support for this view:

(12) * Who do you think he annoyed Maja?
(13) * I wonder who you think he annoyed Maja?

If the *wh*-word functions as the subject of *annoyed Maja* in (9) and (10), these examples will be ungrammatical for the same reason as the following:

(14) * He she annoyed Maja.

In all three cases, we have a predicate with two subjects.

Another type of sentence that is relevant here is what is known as a raising sentence. We can illustrate with the following:

(15) Stefan seemed to be a fool.

Here, the predicate *to be a fool* is not immediately preceded by a subject. This is normally necessary, as the following contrast illustrates:

(16) a. They consider Maja to be a fool.
     b. * They consider to be a fool.

The obvious explanation for the absence of the subject in (15) is that *Stefan*, the subject of *seemed to be a fool*, also functions as subject of *to be a fool*. This view receives some support from the ungrammaticality of the following:

(17) * Stefan seemed Maja to be a fool.

If *Stefan* functions as the subject of *to be a fool*, this will be another case of a predicate with two subjects.

Passives are also relevant here. Consider, for example, the following:

(18) Maja is considered to be a fool

This is a lot like (15). The obvious explanation for the absence of a subject with *to be a fool* is that *Maja* the subject of the larger predicate, *is considered to be a fool*, also functions as subject of this predicate. The ungrammaticality of the following supports this view:

(19) * Maja is considered Stafan to be a fool

This can be seen as another example of a predicate with two subjects.

There is one further point to note about examples like (18). For PSG, *Maja* in (16)a. is not just a subject of the following predicate but also a complement of the preceding verb. Hence, for PSG, *Maja* in (18) is both a noncanonical subject and a noncanonical complement.

7.4 Related sentences

One important point to note about sentences of the kind that we are concerned with here is that in many cases there are related sentences involving canonical complements or canonical subjects.

Related to (1) and the subordinate clause in (2), we have the following:

(20) Stefan annoyed who?
(21) Stefan annoyed someone.

(20) is what is known as an echo-question, a question which echoes someone's statement. (21) might be called an indefinite statement. Related to (7) is the following indefinite statement:

(22) Someone annoyed Maja.

Related to (9) and the subordinate clause in (10), we have the following:

(23) You think who annoyed Maja?
(24) You think someone annoyed Maja.

Related to (15), we have the following:

(25) It seemed that Stefan was a fool.

Finally, related to (18), we have the following:

(26) Someone considered Maja to be a fool.

Thus, all the examples we have considered so far have a related sentence with a canonical complement or a canonical subject. It is important to note, however, that this is not always the case.

We can look first at (27) and the bracketed subordinate clause in (28).

(27) Who the hell did Stefan annoy?
(28) I wonder [who the hell Stefan annoyed]

Neither of the following is possible:

(29) * Stefan annoyed who the hell?
(30) * Stefan annoyed someone the hell.

Here, then, there seems to be no related sentence with a canonical complement. The situation is similar with the following:

(31) Stefan is rumoured to be a spy.

Here, the following is ungrammatical:

(32) * They rumour Stefan to be a spy.

Here, then, there seems to be no related sentence with a canonical subject. Finally, we can consider the following:

(33) Stefan tends to annoy Maja.

Here, the following is ungrammatical:

(34) * It tends that Stefan annoys Maja.

Here, then, there seems to be no related sentence with a canonical subject.

7.5 The monostratal approach

How can we handle noncanonical complements and subjects? We can distinguish two approaches, which we can call the monostratal approach and the multistratal approach. For the former the syntactic structure of a sentence is always a single tree, whereas for the latter it can be a number of trees. We can look first at the former.

If the structure of a sentence is a single tree, the only way to handle sentences involving noncanonical complements and subjects is to somehow make lexical heads and predicates sensitive to the presence of certain categories higher in the tree. We can illustrate this with the various examples we have considered.

We can look first at the subordinate clause in (2). This will have something like the following structure:

(35)

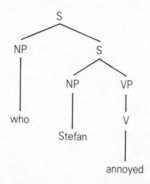

If this is the only structure that this clause has, the verb *annoyed* will somehow have to be sensitive to the presence of *who* higher up the tree.

The situation is similar with (7). Here, we will have something like the following structure:

(36)

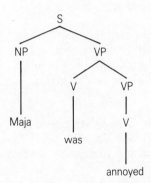

If this is the only structure that this example has, the verb *annoyed* must somehow be sensitive to the presence of *Maja* higher up the tree.

We can turn now to the subordinate clause in (10). Here, we will have something like the following structure:

(37)

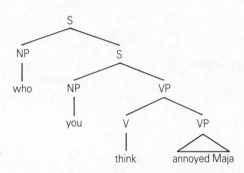

If this is the only structure that this clause has, the predicate *annoyed Maja* must somehow be sensitive to the presence of *who* higher up the tree.

Finally, we can consider (15). This will have something like the following structure:

(38)

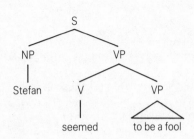

If this is the only structure it has, the predicate *to be a fool* must somehow be sensitive to the presence of *Stefan* higher up the tree.

Thus, if we adopt a monostratal approach, either a lexical head or a predicate must somehow be sensitive to a constituent higher in the tree. As we will see, this is essentially the approach that is taken within PSG.

7.6 The multistratal approach

We can turn now to the multistratal approach. If the syntactic structure of a sentence can involve more than one tree, there is no need to make lexical heads and predicates sensitive to a constituent higher up the tree. Instead, we can associate the sentence with an additional abstract structure in which the noncanonical complement or subject is in the canonical position for a complement or a subject.

We can look first at the subordinate clause in (2). Here, in addition to the ordinary structure in (35), we can have the following abstract structure, in which *who* is in the canonical complement position.

(39)

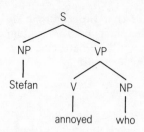

We can treat (7) in much the same way. Here, in addition to the ordinary structure in (36), we can have the following abstract structure with *Maja* in the canonical complement position.

(40)

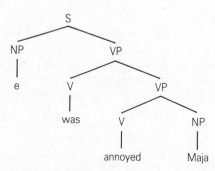

Notice that this structure involves an empty subject position, symbolized as in chapter 6 by *e*.

Next, we can consider the subordinate clause in (10). Here, in addition to the ordinary structure in (37), we can have the following abstract structure, in which *who* is in the canonical subject position.

(41)

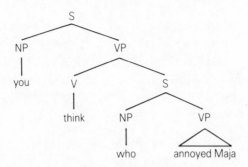

Finally, we can look at (15). Here, in addition to the ordinary structure in (38), we can have the following abstract structure, in which *Stefan* is in the canonical subject position.

(42)

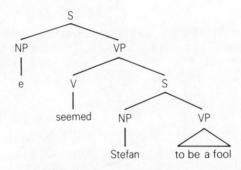

Again, we have an empty subject position here.

This is essentially the approach that is taken within transformational grammar. In transformational grammar, the additional abstract structures are regarded as more basic and the ordinary structures are seen as derived from them by various movement processes. Thus, (35) is derived from (39), (36) from (40), (37) from (41) and (38) from (42). We can distinguish two types of movement process. In the derivation of (35) from (39) and (37) from (41), we have an adjunction process. This makes the moved category the sister of some existing category and the daughter of another instance of that category. In the derivation of (36) from (40) and (38) from (42), we have a substitution process. This substitutes the moved category for an existing empty category. The empty category is standardly referred to as a 'landing site' for movement. Substitution processes are commonly known as structure-preserving, a term introduced in Emonds (1970), since unlike adjunction processes they do not change the structure of the sentence in any way but just rearrange the lexical material.

The examples we have considered so far are relatively simple. There are more complex cases where the abstract structure with which a sentence is associated must itself be associated with another more abstract structure. We can illustrate with the bracketed subordinate clause in (43).

(43) I wonder [who you think was annoyed]

The ordinary obvious structure of this clause is the following:

(44)

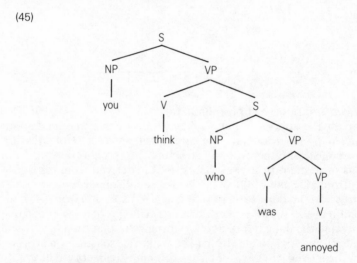

It is clear that *who* in this example is a noncanonical subject since it functions as the subject of *was annoyed* but is not its sister. This suggests that we need the following abstract structure:

(45)

Here, however, *who* is a noncanonical complement since it functions as the complement of *annoyed* but is not its sister. This suggests that we need another more abstract structure of the following form:

(46)

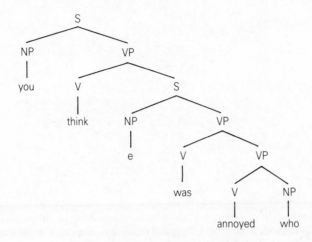

The situation is much the same with bracketed subordinate clause in (47).

(47) I wonder [who you think seemed to annoy Maja]

Here, the ordinary, obvious structure is the following:

(48)

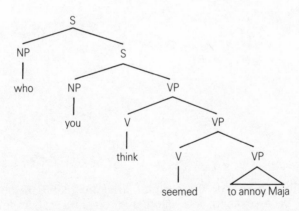

Here, *who* is a noncanonical subject because it functions as the subject of *seemed to annoy Maja* but is not its sister. It seems, then, that we need another more abstract structure of the following form:

(49)

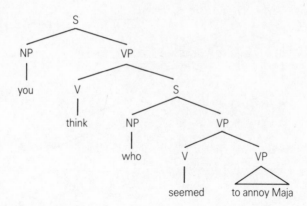

Here, however, *who* is still a noncanonical subject functioning as the subject of *to annoy Maja*. Hence, it seems that we need a further additional structure of the following form:

(50)

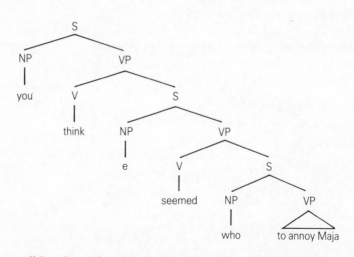

It is possible, then, for the abstract structure that is associated with a sentence to be associated with another more abstract structure. Thus, a sentence can have two structures apart from the ordinary obvious structure. It is possible to find examples where there will be three abstract structures. The subordinate clauses in the following is a relevant example:

(51) I wonder [who they said was believed to have been injured]

It shouldn't be too hard to work out what the abstract structures are.

Thus, for TG, the full structure of a sentence is a sequence of ordinary structures, a sequence, that is, of trees. The most basic structure is known as the deep or D- structure and the ordinary structure of a sentence is known as the surface or S- structure. Any intervening structures are known as intermediate structures.

7.7 Summary

In this chapter, we have looked at a number of sentence types which involve either a noncanonical subject or a noncanonical complement, a constituent which functions as the subject of a predicate or as the complement of some lexical head although it is not in the canonical position for a subject or a complement. In 7.2, we introduced a variety of examples involving a non-canonical complement, and in 7.3, we introduced a range of examples with a noncanonical subject. In 7.4, we highlighted the fact that many sentences involving a noncanonical complement or subject have related sentences with a canonical complement or subject. Then in 7.5, we introduced the monostratal approach to these sentences, an approach which is exemplified by PSG. Finally, in 7.6, we introduced the multistratal approach, which is exemplified by transformational grammar.

Notes

As well as noncanonical complements and subjects, we find what we might call noncanonical adjuncts. The following illustrate:

(1) When do you think she did it?
(2) Why do you think they left?
(3) Where do you think he is going.

In these examples the *wh*-words, *when*, *why* and *where* can be seen as noncanonical adjuncts. The following are related sentences with canonical adjuncts:

(4) I think she did it on Friday.
(5) I think she left because she was tired.
(6) I think he is going to Bangor.

The fact that examples like (27) and the subordinate clause in (28) do not have related sentences with a normal complement was pointed out by Brame (1978). The fact that examples like (31) do not have related sentences with a normal subject was pointed out in Postal (1974).

Exercises

Exercise 1

Identify the noncanonical complements and subjects in the following examples and the associated lexical heads and predicates:

(1) Who do you think he talked to about her?
(2) He is expected to create a good impression.
(3) Who did he seem to annoy?
(4) She proved to be a disaster.
(5) Who did he say wanted him?
(6) They are considered to be too old.

Exercise 2

All the following sentences involve either a noncanonical complement or a noncanonical subject. In each case, provide a related sentence with a canonical complement or subject.

(1) He has been given a week to complete his assignment.
(2) Which book did she say she was going to buy?
(3) He is absolutely certain to apply for the job.
(4) Who do you think she was talking about?
(5) Which man did you think would win the prize?
(6) It has often seemed to be likely that he will resign.

Exercise 3

Provide full TG analyses with D-structures, S-structures, and, where necessary, intermediate structures for the following sentences:

(1) Which books did she put in the attic?
(2) This book was written in 1843.
(3) He turned out to be a great success.
(4) Who did he say he had given the book to?
(5) He seems to have been fooled.
(6) They are believed to have been arrested.

8

Grammatical functions

8.1 Introduction

Before we look more closely at the constructions that we highlighted in the last chapter, I want to look at what are known as grammatical functions or grammatical relations. By this, I mean notions like subject, which we have used extensively in earlier discussion, and object, a notion often invoked in traditional grammatical descriptions. Can these notions be defined in some way? Or are they among the basic undefined terms or 'primitives' of syntactic theory? This is an important matter. Other things being equal, we prefer a simpler theory to a more complex one. Hence, it is desirable to keep the number of primitives to a minimum. We have already seen that it is generally assumed that notions like noun, verb, etc., are not primitives, but are defined in terms of certain features. The two approaches that we are paying most attention to in this book, GB and PSG, have generally assumed that it is possible to define the terms subject and object. There are, however, approaches which assume that they cannot be defined and hence that they are primitives. Here, then, we have an important issue in syntactic theory. In this chapter, we look at some aspects of this issue. We will begin by highlighting some problems that arise for the obvious definitions of subject and object. Then, we will look at two frameworks in which they are primitives. Next, we will consider the position of subject and object in GB. Finally, we will look at the situation in PSG.

8.2 Problems with the definition of subject and object

How might we define the notions subject and object? In both cases, problems arise. We can look first at subject.

We assumed in earlier discussion that subjects combines with predicates. Hence, we might propose the following definition:

(1) A subject is an expression that combines with a predicate.

Of course, we would have to say what exactly we mean by 'combines with' here. One might take it to mean 'is a sister of'. Given GB assumptions, this would work with all the examples we have considered so far. It would not work, however, given PSG assumptions. Recall that on these assumptions the italicized strings in examples like the following are not clauses, as they are on GB assumptions, but two separate complements of the preceding verbs

(2) Stefan considers *Ben to be a genius.*
(3) Stefan considers *Ben a genius.*

It follows that it is not just the subject *Ben* in these examples that is a sister of the following predicate but also the preceding verb. Thus, given PSG assumptions, sentences like (2) and (3) pose a problem for (1). There are, however, more serious problems. Particularly important are verb-initial sentences. A relevant example is the following English interrogative.

(4) Is Stefan in town?

In English, only auxiliaries can appear before the subject. Other languages, however, are less restrictive. In German, any verb can appear before the subject in an interrogative. (5) illustrates.

(5) Weiß er die Antwort?
    knows he the answer
    'Does he know the answer?'

Similarly, in Welsh the verb appears before the subject in declaratives, the basic type of sentence typically used to make statements, as (6) illustrates.

(6) Gwelodd Emrys ddraig.
    saw   Emrys dragon
    'Emrys saw a dragon.'

Why are such examples problematic? Simply because they do not contain a predicate in the way that the examples we considered earlier do. In each example, the elements that we might expect to form a predicate are separated by the subject. They suggest, then, that (1) is not a satisfactory definition after all.

Problems also arise when we attempt to define the notion object. Here, we might suggest the following definition:

(7) An object is an NP that combines with a verb to form a V' or a VP.

There are, of course, sentences where the object is not the only constituent that combines with the verb to form a V' or a VP. The following are relevant examples:

(8) Stefan gave the book to Maja.
(9) Stefan persuaded Maja that she should go home.

In (8), in addition to the object *the book*, we have the PP *to Maja*, and in (9), in addition to the object *Maja*, we have the clause *that she should go home*. These examples are no problem because the additional constituents are not NP's. A problem does arise, however, with examples like the following, which are commonly known as double-object sentences:

(10) Stefan gave Maja the book.
(11) Maja handed Stefan a spanner.

In these examples, we have two NP's that combine with a verb to form a V' or VP. Our definition will identify both as objects. The term double-object sentence might suggest that this is the right conclusion. There is evidence, however, that it is not. In general, it is only the first of these NP's that behaves like an object. For example, at least for most speakers, it is only the first NP that is missing in passive sentences, as the following illustrate:

(12) a. Maja was given the book.
     b. * The book was given Maja.
(13) a. Stefan was handed a spanner.
     b. * A spanner was handed Stefan.

It seems, then, that double-object sentences pose a serious problem for our definition of object.

Verb-initial sentences pose a further problem for our definition. Consider, for example, (5). Here, we seem to have something like the following structure:

(14)

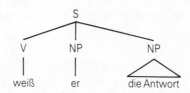

It seems natural to regard the second NP here as an object, but clearly it does not combine with a V' or a VP. Again, then, our definition seems unsatisfactory.

8.3 Subject and object as primitives

Problems like those we have just considered have led a number of syntacticians to assume that subject and object must be primitives. Two approaches are important here: Lexical Functional Grammar (LFG), in which they are known as grammatical functions, and Relational Grammar (RG), in which they are known as grammatical relations. The former is an approach which has developed since the late 70's. The latter is a framework whose origins go back to the early 70's.

For LFG, the syntactic structure of a sentence has two components, a constituent structure (or c-structure) and a functional structure or (f-structure). We can illustrate with the following simple example:

(15) Stefan likes Maja.

This will have (16) as its c-structure and (17) as its f-structure:

(16)

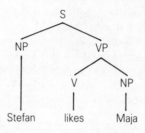

(17) $\begin{bmatrix} \text{SUBJ} & \text{[PRED 'STEFAN']} \\ \text{PRED} & \text{'LIKE} \langle (\text{SUBJ}) (\text{OBJ}) \rangle\text{'} \\ \text{OBJ} & \text{[PRED 'MAJA']} \end{bmatrix}$

PRED here is an abbreviation for predicate. Here, however, predicate has a rather different sense from that generally assumed in this book. It derives from work in logic. Essentially, it means the semantically most important element in a clause or phrase. The important point about (17) is that it makes it clear that *Stefan* is the subject and *Maja* the object. (17) looks very different from a constituent structure, but we could present essentially the same information as follows:

(18)

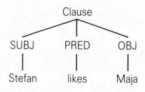

Obviously, this looks much more like a constituent structure. F-structure plays a central role in LFG. It is crucially involved in the description of a variety of phenomena: head-complement relations, subject-predicate relations and various phenomena that we will be concerned with in subsequent chapters.

For early RG, the syntactic structure of a sentence is a sequence of so-called relational networks in much the same way as the syntactic structure of a sentence is a sequence of constituent structures for transformational grammar. The following is a simple example of a relational network.

(19)

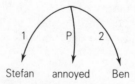

Here, labelled arrows or arcs identify the grammatical function of the constituents. The arc labelled '1' identifies *Stefan* as the subject of the sentence, the arc labelled 'P' identifies *annoyed* as the predicate (in the sense of predicate just introduced), and the arc labelled '2' identifies *Ben* as the object of the sentence. For RG, there is no separate constituent structure. Rather, what constituent structure is necessary is incorporated within the relational networks. Thus, if (19) is the only relational network assigned to the sentence *Stefan annoyed Ben*, *annoyed Ben* will not be treated as a constituent.

With a simple sentence like *Stefan annoyed Ben*, we might have just a single relational network. For many sentences, however, we will have more than one. For example, for the passive *Ben was annoyed*, we might have the underlying relational network in (20)a. and the superficial relational network in (20)b.

(20)

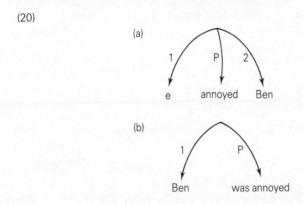

The derivation of (20)b. from (20)a. will involve a relation-changing process in much the same way as the parallel derivation in transformational grammar involves a movement process.

In more recent RG, we have not a sequence of relational networks but a single complex relational network. For example, instead of the two networks in (20), we might have the following:

(21)

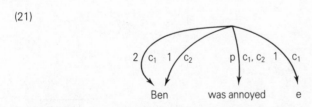

Here, arcs are labelled not just with grammatical function labels but also with what are known as coordinates, which indicate at what level or stratum the expression has the function in question. Thus, (21) indicates that *Ben* is object in the first stratum and subject in the second stratum, etc. Alternatively, we might represent this information as follows:

(22)

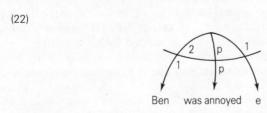

This is known as a stratal diagram.

8.4 Subjects and Objects in TG

As we noted at the outset, the two approaches that are the main concern of this book have generally assumed that subject and object can be defined. We can look first at how this position might be maintained within TG.

It is in fact quite easy to maintain the earlier definitions (1) and (7) within a transformational framework. One can simply say that the problematic S-structures derive from unproblematic D-structures. For example, we can assume that (4) is derived by a process of verb-fronting as follows:

(23)

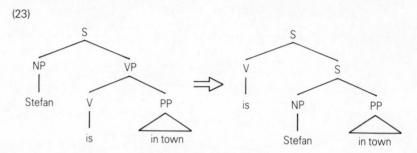

Assuming this analysis, *Stefan* combines with a predicate just like an ordinary subject. Similarly, we can assume that the German example in (5) has the following derivation:

(24)

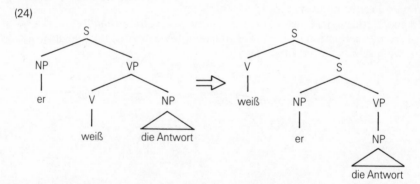

Given this analysis, *er* combines with a predicate in the same way as an ordinary subject. Thus, verb-initial sentences pose no problems for our definition of subject within a transformational framework. One point to note about these analyses is that verb-fronting is treated as an adjunction process. We will introduce a different view of verb-fronting in Chapter 12.

Verb-initial clauses are also no problem for our definition of object if they are derived in this way. In D-structure the object is an NP that combines with a verb to form a V' or a VP just as it is in typical subject-initial sentences.

What, then, of the problem that double object sentences pose for our definition? One way of maintaining something like our original definition is to assume, following in essence Larson (1988a), that VP's are derived from an abstract structure by a movement process. Specifically, we can assume D-structures in which a verb that takes an object and some other complement combines with the other complement to form what we might call a transitive verb phrase (TVP), which then combines with the object to form a VP. This will give us a structure like the following for (10):

(25)

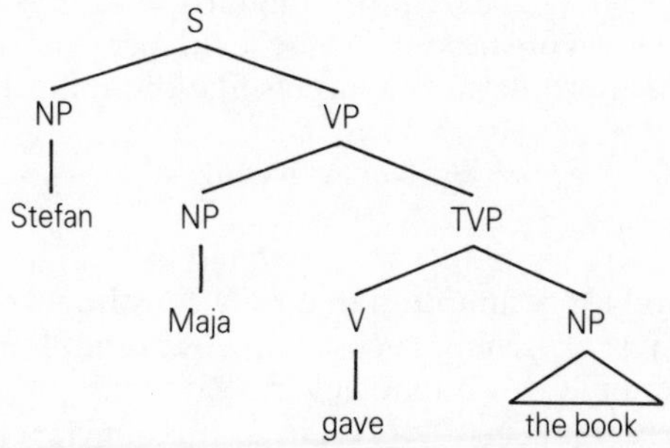

We can derive the S-structure from this by moving the verb *gave* to give the following structure:

(26)

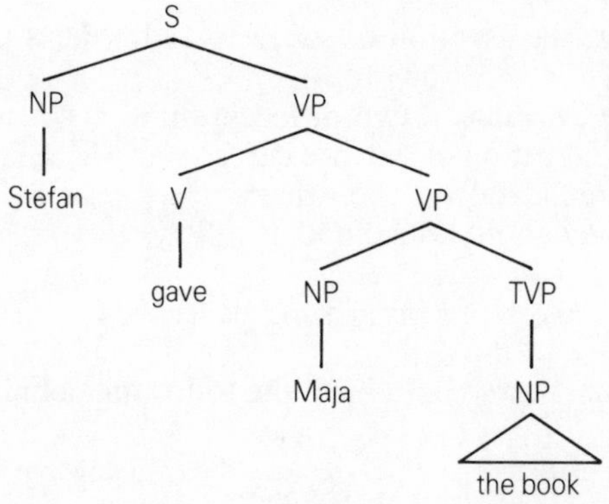

If we assume a TVP in all sentences, we will have the following derivation for a simple sentence where the verb has just one complement.

(27)

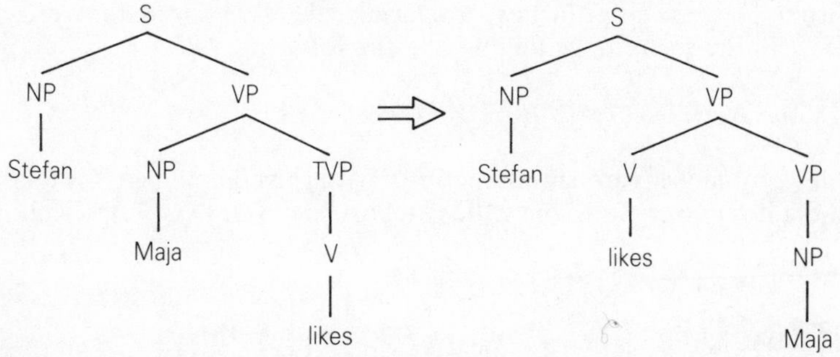

Given this approach to VP's, we can apparently define an object as follows:

(28) An object is an NP that combines with a TVP.

This is clearly very similar to our original definition.

There is one further point that we can note here. An important difference between the structure in (25) and more standard structures is that it treats the two complements as a constituent. Some evidence for this feature of the analysis comes from coordination examples like the following:

(29) Stefan gave Maja the book and Sue the record.

This is very similar to the example that we cited in Chapter 2 (77) as posing a problem for the standard assumption that only constituents can be conjoined. Given the analysis just sketched, such examples are no longer a problem for this assumption. It should be said, however, that strings like *Maja the book* do not behave like constituents in other respects. It is not clear, then, whether the fact that the analysis identifies them as constituents is really an advantage.

8.5 Subjects and objects in PSG

We can now look at the position of subjects and objects in PSG, and more specifically in HPSG.

In Chapter 6, we introduced two different approaches to subjects, one in which they are the realization of an extra category in a SUBCAT list, and one in which they are the realization of the value of a separate SUBJ feature. In the first approach, subject could be defined as follows:

(30 A subject is an expression which realizes the final item in a SUBCAT list.

In the second approach, we could have the following definition:

(31) A subject is an expressions which realizes the category that is the value of a SUBJ feature.

In the first approach, subject is clearly not a primitive. In the second approach, however, one might regard it as a primitive. Thus, this approach can be seen as accepting that relational grammar and lexical functional grammar are partially correct.

In either of these approaches, a special rule is required for verb-initial sentences. In the second, we might have the following rule:

(32) X[SUBCAT,⟨⟩] → X[SUBCAT,⟨ . . . ⟩; SUBJ,Y], Y, C*

This rule combines a verb simultaneously with the complements it takes and the subject it requires. If we have the category in (33) for *is*, (32) will allow the tree in (34).

(33)
$$
\begin{bmatrix}
\text{V} \\
\text{SUBCAT,⟨PP⟩} \\
\text{SUBJ,\quad NP} \\
\qquad \text{[+3SG]}
\end{bmatrix}
$$

(34)

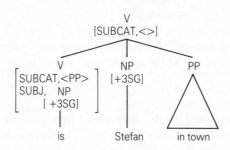

We can turn now to objects. If subjects are the realization of an extra category in the SUBCAT list, we might define object as follows:

(35) An object is an NP that realizes the penultimate category in the SUBCAT list of a verb.

If, on the other hand, subjects are the realization of an extra category in the SUBCAT list, object might be defined as follows:

(36) An object is an NP that realizes the final category in the SUBCAT list of a verb.

Clearly, if we adopt either of these positions, object is not a primitive.

8.6 Summary

In this chapter, we have been concerned with the status of the notions subject and object. In particular, we have considered whether they can be defined or whether they must be included among the basic terms or primitives of syntactic theory. In 8.2, we highlighted certain problems that arise for the obvious definitions of these notions. Then, in 8.3, we looked at two grammatical frameworks which treat them as primitives: lexical functional grammar (LFG) and relational grammar (RG). Next, in 8.4, we considered how the two notions could be defined within a transformational framework. Finally, in 8.5, we considered the situation in PSG. We considered two different approaches. Within one, subject is not a primitive, but within the other, it is. Within both, however, object is not a primitive.

Notes

The question of whether subject and object can be defined was originally raised in Chomsky (1965). Chomsky suggested there that subject could be defined as an NP immediately dominated by S and object as an NP immediately dominated by VP.

The main references for RG are Perlmutter (1983) and Perlmutter and Rosen (1984). Blake (1990) provides a textbook introduction. Closely related to RG is Arc Pair Grammar, first presented in Johnson and Postal (1980). LFG has its origins in the realistic transformational grammar framework of Bresnan

(1978). The main reference is Bresnan (1982a). For textbook introductions, see Horrocks (1987, 4.) and Sells (1985, 4.).

For an extensive GB-based discussion of grammatical functions, drawing on a variety of languages, see Marantz (1984). For a critique of the idea that grammatical functions are primitives, especially as it has been developed within LFG, see Williams (1984b).

Larson's transformational analysis of VP's, which we introduced in 8.4, draws on the PSG analysis of Jacobson (1987), which draws in turn on the analysis developed by Dowty (1982) within the framework known as Montague grammar. Larson's analysis is criticized by Jackendoff (1990). A variety of GB analyses to double-object sentences, have been advanced in Stowell (1981b, 5.), Kayne (1981), and Baker (1988, 5.).

Exercises

Exercise 1

Provide analyses for the following sentences which are compatible with the assumption that a subject is an expression that combines with a predicate. Where necessary, assume a verb-movement process. Remember that the constituents of a VP need not appear in the same order as in English.

(1) Naomi-ga   kare-wo   mituketa.
    Naomi NOM   he   ACC   found
    'Naomi found him.'
    Japanese (Gunji, 1987)
(2) Nividy kisoa ho'an ny   ankizy   Rakoto.
    bought pig for   the children Rakoto
    'Rakoto bought some pork for the children.'
    Malagasy (Pullum, 1977)
(3) Toto-komo   yonoye kamara
    man-COLLECTIVE   ate   jaguar
    'The jaguar ate people.'
    Hixkaryana (Pullum, 1980)
(4) Anana   nota apa
    pineapple I   fetch.
    'I fetch pineapple.'
    Apurina (Pullum, 1980)

Exercise 2

Provide analyses employing a TVP category for the following examples. Ignore the internal structure of the complements.

(1) He gave the book to her.
(2) She told him that she would be early.
(3) I bought some flowers for her.
(4) He worded the letter carefully.

Exercise 3

Provide HPSG analyses of the kind introduced in 8.5 for the following Welsh sentences. Ignore the internal structure of complements, and assume that *yn hywr* in (2) is an AP and *ddarllen y llyfr* in (3) a VP.

(1) Prynodd Emrys geffyl.
    bought   Emrys horse
    'Emrys bought a horse.'
(2) Mae Megan yn hwyr.
    is   Megan in late
    'Megan was late.'
(3) Ceisiodd Megan ddarllen y   llyfr.
    tried   Megan read   the   book
    'Megan tried to read the book.'
(4) Rhoddodd Emrys y   llyfri i   Megan.
    gave   Emrys the   book to Megan
    'Emrys gave the book to Megan.'

9

Passives

9.1 Introduction

We can return now to some of the data that we introduced in Chapter 7. As we saw there, passives provide an important example of sentences involving a noncanonical complement or a noncanonical subject. In this chapter, we can look more closely as passives and consider how they can be analyzed. We will begin by looking at some relevant data. Then, we will consider how passives were analyzed within classical TG. Next, we will look at the rather different approach that has been developed within GB. Then, we will consider how passives can be analyzed within PSG. Finally, we will look at some Further data.

9.2 The data

A typical passive involves a subject, some form of the verb *be*, and what we can call a passive participle, which is identical in form to a past participle but different in its syntactic properties. In addition, in a typical passive, a post-verbal constituent is missing and the subject has the main properties of the missing constituent. If the post-verbal constituent must or can be a dummy, so must or can the subject. Thus, the data in (1) and (2) parallels that in (3) and (4).

(1) $\left\{ \begin{array}{l} \text{It} \\ \text{* Stefan} \end{array} \right\}$ is believed to be easy to annoy Fred.

(2) $\left\{ \begin{array}{l} \text{There} \\ \text{Stefan} \end{array} \right\}$ is believed to be a dragon in the wood.

(3) They believe $\left\{ \begin{array}{l} \text{it} \\ \text{* Stefan} \end{array} \right\}$ to be easy to annoy Ben.

(4) They believe $\left\{ \begin{array}{l} \text{there} \\ \text{Stefan} \end{array} \right\}$ to be a dragon in the wood.

Similarly, if the post-verbal constituent can be a clause, so can the subject. Here, the data in (5) parallels that in (6).

(5) That he is a fool is $\left\{ \begin{array}{l} \text{believed} \\ \text{* kicked} \end{array} \right\}$ by everyone.

(6) Everyone $\left\{ \begin{array}{l} \text{believes} \\ \text{* kicks} \end{array} \right\}$ that he is a fool.

Finally, if the post-verbal constituent can be understood as part of an idiom, so can the subject. Thus, *the cat* can be understood idiomatically in (7) just as it can in (8).

(7) The cat is believed to be out of the bag.
(8) They believe the cat to be out of the bag.

One further point that we should note here is that there are passive constructions without any form of *be*. The following illustrate:

(9) Stefan had Maja followed.
(10) Stefan got arrested.
(11) This is the book given to Maja.

In (9), *followed* is a passive participle with *Maja* as its subject. Within GB, these two expressions would be analyzed as a small clause. Within PSG, they would be analyzed as two separate complements of *had*. In (9), we have a passive participle as a complement of the verb *get*. Finally, in (11), we have a passive expression acting as a nominal adjunct.

9.3 The classical transformational approach

As we have seen, within TG the ordinary structure of a typical passive is derived from a more abstract structure involving a normal complement or a normal subject. Thus, we have derivations like the following:

(12)

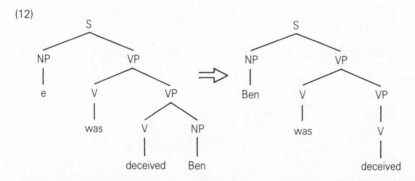

The obvious question to ask is: what allows such a derivation? We can look first at the answer that was given to this question within classical TG (the kind of transformational grammar that was assumed in the 60's). Then, we can consider the rather different answer that is given within modern TG, i.e. GB.

For classical transformational grammar, the derivation in (12) is possible because a rule known as the passive transformation says so. We can formulate this rule as follows:

(13) NP – *be* – V – NP
　　　1　　2　　3　　4 ⇒
　　　4　　2　　3　　ø

　　　OBLIGATORY

This rule consists of three components. The topmost line, which we can refer to as a 'structural description', identifies the type of tree to which the rule applies. It indicates that the rule applies to any tree that consists of an NP, immediately followed by a form of *be*, immediately followed by a V, immediately followed by an NP. Such a tree is said to satisfy the structural description of the rule. The next two lines, which we can call the 'structural change', indicate the change that the rule licences. Specifically, they indicate that the second NP replaces the first, leaving nothing in its original position. The final line of the rule indicates that it is obligatory, i.e. that it must apply to any tree that satisfies its structural description. ·

This analysis handles the basic facts quite well but there is an important objection to it. This is that there are a number of questions that the analysis raises but to which it can provide no interesting answers.

Firstly, we might ask the following question:

(14) Why do we have movement in passive structures?

To take a specific example, we might ask why *Ben* in the initial structure in (12) cannot remain in object position. If we assume that *it* is inserted in subject position, this would give the following:

(15) * It was deceived Ben.

The only answer we can give is just that the rule is obligatory and hence does not allow that. This is not a very satisfying answer.

Secondly, we might ask the following:

(16) Why can we not have movement in active structures?

In other words, why can we not have a derivation like the following:

(17)

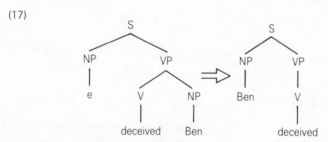

The only answer that we can give within classical TG is just that no rule allows this kind of movement. Again, this is not a very satisfying answer.

Finally, we might ask the following question:

(18) Why do we have just the kind of movement that we do have?

To make this more specific, we might ask why we can derive (19) but not (20) from the structure in (21).

(19) Stefan is believed to like Maja.

(20) * Maja is believed Stefan to like.
(21)

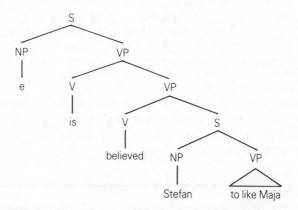

All we can say in answer to this is that the rule only allows the movement of the NP immediately following the verb which immediately follows the form of *be*. In other words, we cannot derive (20) from (21) because the rule doesn't allow it. Again, this is not a very illuminating answer.

Thus, although the classical transformational analysis of passives handles the basic facts fairly successfully, it cannot be regarded as a satisfactory analysis.

9.4 The GB approach

We can now turn to the GB approach to passives. As we will see, a central feature of this approach is that it does permit answers to the questions that we have just highlighted.

We can formulate the guiding assumption of classical TG as follows:

(22) A movement operation is possible iff some transformation explicitly allows it.

In other words, all movement operations are impossible except those that some rule allows. The GB framework adopts the following, very different guiding assumption:

(23) Any movement operation is possible unless it violates some constraint.

In other words, all movement operations are allowed except those that are ruled out by some constraint. This assumption is embodied in the idea first advanced in Chomsky (1980b) that there is a single transformational rule, which is standardly formulated as follows:

(24) Move α

This is essentially a license to move anything anywhere. It shows again that we cannot require categories in trees to be identical to the corresponding categories in rules. Movement is defined as either substitution or adjunction. One type of substitution in the movement of an NP to an empty NP position. This is known as NP-movement. Of course, it is not in fact possible to move any NP to any other NP position. For GB, this is because a variety of grammatical principles interact with this rule to allow just the kind of movement processes that in fact occur. This means that movement processes have much the same status in GB as local trees have in both GB and PSG. In both frameworks, whether or not a particular local tree is well-formed depends not on a single rule but on a number of different factors. In much the same way, whether or not a movement process is legitimate in GB depends not on a single rule but on a number of different factors.

We can look first at how GB permits an answer to the first of the three questions that we have raised: why do we have movement in passives? The answer crucially involves the notion of Case, traditionally invoked in connection with contrasts like the following:

(25) a. I saw Stefan.
     b. * Me saw Stefan.
(26) a. Stefan saw me.
     b. * Stefan saw I.

The standard explanation for such data is that we have nominative forms and hence *I* in subject position, but accusative or objective forms and hence *me* in object position.

Within GB, it is assumed that all NP's with phonetic content, i.e. which are not empty, have Case even if it is not reflected in some distinctive form. In fact, it is assumed that they must have Case. This is embodied in the Case filter, which we can formulate as follows:

(27) An NP with phonetic content must have Case.

A more specific assumption that is made about Case is the following:

(28) An active transitive verb assigns Case to an NP which it governs. The related passive participle does not.

To understand this, we need to know something about government. A variety of definitions of government have been proposed. It is not necessary, however, to go into these definitions. We can simply note that all of them have the following consequence:

(29) A lexical head governs a complement and the subject of an exceptional clause or small clause complement.

For GB, 'ordinary' clausal complements are 'extended' clauses with something like the following structure:

(30)

(We will introduce a slightly more complex structure in Chapter 12.) The COMP category may be filled by a complementizer (or subordinating conjunction) such as *that* or under certain circumstances may be empty. The S' category was introduced in Bresnan (1970). This structure prevents the subject of an ordinary clause from being governed from outside. Exceptional clauses and small clauses, however, are not extended clauses and so their subjects can be governed from outside.

Consider now the following, which are passives in which no movement has occurred:

(31) a. * It was deceived Ben.
   b. * It was considered Ben to be a genius.
   c. * It was considered Ben a genius.

In (31)a. the NP after the participle is a complement, in (31)b. it is the subject of an exceptional clause complement, and in (31)c. it is the subject of a small clause complement. Given (29), these NP's will be governed by the passive participles. However, given (28), the passive participles will not assign Case to these NP's. Hence, all these examples will violate the Case filter. Here, then, we have an explanation for the occurrence of movement in passives. Without movement, there is a violation of the Case filter.

An interesting feature of this approach is that it predicts that movement is not necessary if the constituent governed by the passive participle is not an NP. The following data suggests that this predication is correct:

(32) a. Everyone believes that Stefan is a spy.
   b. That Stefan is a spy is believed by everyone.
   c. It is believed by everyone that Stefan is a spy.

In (32)a., we have an active verb with a clausal complement. In (32)b. and (32)c., we have the related passive participle. In (32)b., the clause appears in subject position, but in (32)c., it remains in the post-verbal position.

We can turn now to the second of our three questions: why do we not have movement in active structures? The GB answer to this question crucially involves θ-roles, the semantic roles associated with lexical heads, which we discussed in chapters 5 and 6. The central assumption that is made here is the following:

(33) No NP can have more than one θ-role.

A more specific assumption about θ-roles is the following:

(34) Active transitive verbs have an external θ-role, i.e. assign a θ-role to their subjects. The related passive participles do not.

This is a second difference between passive participles and the related active verbs, or, as we might say, a second respect in which passive participles are 'defective'. It receives some support from the fact that dummy *it* appears in passive likes (32)c. in which no constituent is moved into subject position. As we noted in chapter 6, dummy *it* appears in a subject position to which no θ-role assigned.

Two further assumptions are relevant here. The first is the following, which has been an important part of TG since Chomsky (1973):

(35) Movement leaves a trace, an empty category coindexed with the moved category.

Various kinds of evidence have been advanced for this assumption, but the most important is the way that it permits an interesting account of certain restrictions on movement. It also allows one to assume that the Projection Principle, which we introduced in chapter 6, applies at all levels of syntactic representation and not just at D-structure. Given the assumption that movement leaves a trace, we will have the following surface structure for a typical passive.

(36)

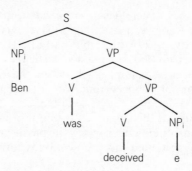

(We could if we wanted replace the *e* here by *t* for trace.) Similarly, we will have the following surface structure if we move an object into an empty subject position in a simple active sentence:

(37)

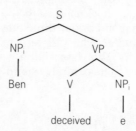

The final assumption that is relevant here is the following:

(38) An NP inherits a θ-role from its trace.

This accounts, for example, for the fact that *Stefan* is understood in the same way in (39) and (40).

(39) Stefan was chosen.
(40) Someone chose Stefan.

Consider now the implications of these assumptions. Given (38), the subjects in (36) and (37) will inherit θ-roles from their traces. Since passive participles do not assign a θ-role to their subjects, the subject in (36) will have just one θ-role and hence will conform to the constraint in (33). On the other hand, since active transitive verbs do assign a θ-role to their subjects, the subject in (37) will have two θ-roles. Hence, it will violate (33). Here, then, we have an explanation for the impossibility of movement in active structures. Such movement gives rise to NPs which violate (33).

There is one further point that we can note here. We noted in chapter 5 that it is assumed in GB that every complement has a θ-role. (33) interacts with this assumption to rule out movement to complement position. In fact, (33) places quite tight restrictions on movement.

Finally, we can return to the last of our three questions: why do we have just the kind of movement that we do have? Illustrating this, we noted in effect that the surface structure in (41) is possible but not the surface structure in (42). We can also note that the surface structure in (43) is not possible.

(41) Ben$_i$ is believed [s e$_i$ to like Maja]
(42) * Maja$_i$ is believed [s Ben to like e$_i$]
(43) * Ben$_i$ is believed [s' that [s e$_i$ likes Maja]]

Notice now that we have similar data with reflexives.

(44) Stefan$_i$ believes [s himself$_i$ to be clever]
(45) * Stefan$_i$ believes [s Maja to like himself$_i$]
(46) * Stefan$_i$ believes [s' that [s himself$_i$ is clever]]

(The indices here indicate that *Stefan* is the intended antecedent of *himself*.) In the light of this, the obvious suggestion is that traces have the same status as reflexives and that whatever restrictions account for the impossibility of (45) and (46) also account for the impossibility of (42) and (43).

In GB, reflexives are referred to as anaphors, and the following principle is assumed:

(47) An NP-trace, i.e. a trace left by NP-movement, counts as an anaphor.

Notice that this does not say that all traces count as anaphors, only that NP-traces do. We will see in chapter 12 that there are other traces which do not count as anaphors. For GB, the main restriction on anaphors is the following:

(48) An anaphor must be A-bound in its governing category.

To understand this we need to know what is meant by 'A-bound' and what is meant by a 'governing category'. We can define these notions as follows:

(49) A category is A-bound iff it is coindexed with a c-commanding category in an A-position (subject, object or object of a preposition).
(50) The governing category of an item is the minimal (i.e. smallest) NP or S containing the item and an item governing it.

Of course, (50) depends on what governs what. We have already noted that a lexical head governs a complement and the subject of an exceptional clause or small clause complement. All definitions of government also have the following consequence:

(51) The agreement features associated with a finite verb govern its subject.

It is assumed within GB that agreement features are only superficially associated with a finite verb. They are assumed to originate as part of an empty I (or INFL or INFLECTION) category, which also includes information about tense and which is some versions of the theory appears in structures like the following:

(52)

$$S$$

NP   I   VP

This element is combined with V on the surface either by movement of I to V or by movement of V to I.

We can now look at how (48) predicts the data in (41) – (46), which we repeat here.

(41) Ben$_i$ is believed [s e$_i$ to like Maja]
(42) * Maja$_i$ is believed [s Ben to like e$_i$]
(43) * Ben$_i$ is believed [s' that [s e$_i$ likes Maja]]
(44) Stefan$_i$ believes [s himself$_i$ to be clever]
(45) * Stefan$_i$ believes [s Maja to like himself$_i$]
(46) * Stefan$_i$ believes [s' that [s himself$_i$ is clever]]

First, we can consider (41) and (44). Here, the anaphors are governed by the preceding verb given the assumption that a lexical head governs the subject of an exceptional clause complement. Since this verb is in the main clause, the governing category for the anaphors is the main S. Hence, the anaphors are A-bound within their governing category, as (48) requires.

Next we can consider (42) and (45). Here, the anaphors are governed by the preceding verb given the assumption that a lexical head governs its complements. Since this verb is in the subordinate clause the governing category for the anaphors is the subordinate S. Hence, the anaphors are not A-bound within their governing category and we have a violation of (48).

Finally, we can consider (43) and (46). In these examples, the anaphors are not governed by the preceding verb because the complement is an S' and not just an S. Instead, they are governed by the agreement features of the following verb given the assumption that the agreement features of a finite verb governs its subject. Since this verb is in the subordinate clause the governing category for the anaphors is the subordinate S. Therefore, the anaphors are not A-bound within their governing category and we have another violation of (48).

A final point that we should note is that (43) is no better without the complementizer *that*. This is no problem as long as the complement of *believe* is an S' even when it does not contain a complementizer. It would be a problem, however, if the complement were just an S in this situation. If the complement were just an S, the trace in subject position would be governed by the higher verb and hence would be A-bound in its governing category.

It seems, then, GB permits interesting answers to all three of the questions that we have asked about passives. Firstly, certain assumptions about Case explain why we have movement in typical passives. Secondly, certain assumptions about θ-roles combined with the assumption that movement processes leave traces explain why we do not have movement in active structures. Finally, the assumption that traces left by NP-movement are anaphors permits an explanation for the impossibility of certain types of movement. Since it has answers to these questions, it seems fair to say that GB represents a clear advance on classical TG in this area. A final point that we should note is that we will be returning to the concepts that we have been concerned with here in the next chapter.

9.5 The PSG approach

We can now consider how passives can be accommodated within PSG. More precisely, we can look at how they can be analyzed within HPSG. There is an obvious sense in which the HPSG approach is simpler than the GB approach. It involves just a single level of structure, and there is no reference to traces, Case, θ-roles or conditions on anaphora. As we will see, however, it involves some rather complex categories.

Within PSG, passives have only the ordinary, obvious structure. Thus, (53) will have just the structure in (54).

(53) Stefan was sent to Bangor.

(54)

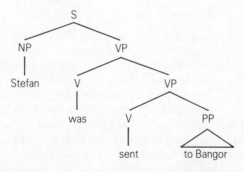

As we noted in chapter 7, if passives have just this structure, the passive participle must somehow be sensitive to the presence of a particular constituent higher up the tree. In this case, *sent* must somehow be sensitive to the presence of *Stefan*. It is in fact not difficult to achieve this.

We already have some of the machinery we need. Earlier, we noted that the following head-complement rule can be proposed within HPSG:

(55) X[SUBCAT,⟨⟩; SUBJ,Y] → X[SUBCAT,⟨. . .⟩; SUBJ,Y], C∗

Given this rule, if *sent* in the above structure is [SUBJ,NP[NFORM, NORM]], so will the immediately dominating VP be. Thus, we can expand the lower VP as follows:

(56)

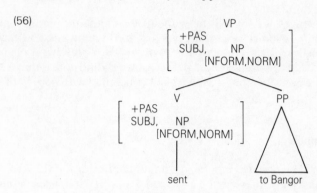

All we need, then, is some way of ensuring that the higher VP is also [SUBJ,NP[NFORM,NORM]]. We can do this by assigning *was* to the following category:

(57)

$$
\begin{bmatrix}
\text{V} \\
\text{SUBCAT},< \quad \begin{matrix} \text{VP} \\ \begin{bmatrix} +\text{PAS} \\ \text{SUBJ,Y} \end{bmatrix} \end{matrix} \quad > \\
\text{SUBJ,Y}
\end{bmatrix}
$$

The important point about this category is that the SUBJ feature within the value of SUBCAT has a variable as its value and the main SUBJ feature has the same variable as its value. When *was* appears in a tree, the Subcategorization Principle will ensure that the category within the SUBCAT list is identical to the complement and hence that it has the same value for SUBJ as the complement. In the present case, this means that the variable will be instantiated as NP[NFORM,NORM]. Since we have the same variable as the value of the main SUBJ feature, this too must be instantiated as NP[NFORM,NORM]. Hence, we will have the following category in the tree:

(58)

$$
\begin{bmatrix}
\text{V} \\
\text{SUBCAT},\langle \quad \begin{matrix} \text{VP} \\ \begin{bmatrix} +\text{PAS} \\ \text{SUBJ}, \quad \begin{matrix} \text{NP} \\ [\text{NFORM,NORM}] \end{matrix} \end{bmatrix} \end{matrix} \quad \rangle \\
\text{SUBJ}, \quad \begin{matrix} \text{NP} \\ [\text{NFORM,NORM}] \end{matrix}
\end{bmatrix}
$$

If *was* is [SUBJ,NP[NFORM,NORM]], the head-complement rule will ensure that the higher VP is as well. Hence, we will have the following structure in the middle of the tree:

(59)

$$
\begin{array}{c}
\text{VP} \\
\begin{bmatrix} \text{SUBJ}, \quad \begin{matrix} \text{NP} \\ [\text{NFORM,NORM}] \end{matrix} \end{bmatrix} \\
\diagdown
\end{array}
$$

$$
\begin{matrix}
\text{V} & \text{VP} \\
\begin{bmatrix} \text{SUBJ}, \quad \begin{matrix} \text{NP} \\ [\text{NFORM,NORM}] \end{matrix} \end{bmatrix} &
\begin{bmatrix} +\text{PAS} \\ \text{SUBJ}, \quad \begin{matrix} \text{NP} \\ [\text{NFORM,NORM}] \end{matrix} \end{bmatrix}
\end{matrix}
$$

Thus, it is not difficult to ensure that the VP that takes the passive subject has the same value for SUBJ as the passive participle.

This, however, ignores the fact that it is because the related active verb requires an NP[NFORM,NORM] as its first complement that the passive requires an NP[NFORM,NORM] as its subject. Thus, (60) is ungrammatical because (61) is.

(60) * That John was ill was sent to Bangor.
(61) * They sent that John was ill to Bangor.

In contrast, (62) is possible because (63) is.

(62) That John was ill was widely believed.
(63) They believed that John was ill.

We can make essentially the same point about the categories that we will have for the verbs in these sentences. For *sent* in (53) we will have the category in (64), and for the related active verb we will have the category in (65).

(64)
$$\begin{bmatrix} & V & \\ +PAS & \\ SUBCAT,\langle PP \rangle & \\ SUBJ, & NP & \\ & [NFORM,NORM] & \end{bmatrix}$$

(65)
$$\begin{bmatrix} & V & \\ SUBCAT,\langle PP, & NP & \rangle \\ & [NFORM,NORM] & \\ SUBJ, & NP & \\ & [NFORM,NORM] & \end{bmatrix}$$

(64) has NP[NFORM,NORM] as the value of SUBJ because the last category in the value of SUBCAT in (65) is NP[INFORM,NORM]. For *believed* in (62) we will have the category in (66), and for the related active verb in (63) we will have the category in (67).

(66)
$$\begin{bmatrix} & V & \\ +PAS & \\ SUBCAT,\langle \rangle & \\ SUBJ,S & \end{bmatrix}$$

(67)
$$\begin{bmatrix} & V & \\ SUBCAT,\langle S \rangle & \\ SUBJ, & NP & \\ & [NFORM,NORM] & \end{bmatrix}$$

(66) has S as the value of SUBJ because the one category in the value of SUBCAT in (67) is S.

We can capture these facts with a lexical rule, a rule deriving lexical entries from lexical entries. What we need is a rule deriving entries for passive participles from entries for the related active verbs. Ignoring the phonological and semantic components of the entries, we can formulate the rule as follows:

(68) $V[SUBCAT,\langle \ldots ,Y_{n-1} \rangle; SUBJ,Y_n] \Rightarrow V[+ PAS; SUBCAT,\langle \ldots \rangle; SUBJ,Y_{n-1}]$

This will derive (64) from (65) and (66) from (67).

We noted in chapter 5 that while the bracketed strings in the following are clauses for GB, they involve two separate constituents for PSG:

(69) Stefan considered [Ben to be a fool]
(70) Stefan considered [Ben foolish]
(71) Stefan considered [Ben a fool]

It follows, as noted in chapter 7, that the subjects of the related passives are not just abnormal subjects but also abnormal complements. We can now see why such examples are analyzed in this way. If we assume that we have two separate complements, we will have the category in (72) for *considered* in (69) and we will have similar categories for *considered* in (70) and (71):

$$
(72) \quad
\begin{bmatrix}
\text{SUBCAT,} \left\langle
\begin{array}{c}
V \\
VP \\
\begin{bmatrix}
+\text{INF} \\
\text{SUBJ,} \quad NP \\
\quad\quad [\text{NFORM,}\alpha]
\end{bmatrix}
\end{array}
\,,\,
\begin{array}{c}
NP \\
[\text{NFORM,}\alpha]
\end{array}
\right\rangle \\
\text{SUBJ, NP}
\end{bmatrix}
$$

Related to (69)–(71), we have the following passives:

(73) Ben was considered to be a fool.
(74) Ben was considered foolish.
(75) Ben was considered a fool.

For *considered* in (73), we will have the following category and we will have similar categories for *considered* in (74) and (75).

$$
(76) \quad
\begin{bmatrix}
V \\
+\text{PAS} \\
\text{SUBCAT,} \left\langle
\begin{array}{c}
VP \\
\begin{bmatrix}
+\text{INF} \\
\text{SUBJ,} \quad NP \\
\quad\quad [\text{NFORM, }\alpha]
\end{bmatrix}
\end{array}
\right\rangle \\
\text{SUBJ,} \quad NP \\
\quad\quad [\text{NFORM, }\alpha]
\end{bmatrix}
$$

We can derive this from (72) with the rule in (68). Consider now the situation if we assumed that examples like (69)–(71) involve single clausal complements. Given this assumption, we would have the following category for *considered* in (69):

$$
(77) \quad
\begin{bmatrix}
V \\
\text{SUBCAT,} \langle S \rangle \\
\text{SUBJ,NP}
\end{bmatrix}
$$

There is no way to derive (76) from this with the rule in (68). Thus, given the approach to passives that we have just outlined, there is no real alternative to the assumption that (69)–(71) involve two separate complements.

One point that we should note here is that we have no account of examples like the following:

(78) It is widely believed that Stefan is a fool.

Here, *believed* will have the following category:

(79)
$$
\begin{bmatrix}
V \\
+PAS \\
SUBCAT,\langle S\rangle \\
SUBJ, \quad NP \\
\quad\quad [NFORM,IT]
\end{bmatrix}
$$

We cannot derive this from (67) with the rule in (68). Hence, we must either introduce another lexical rule or simply list such categories.

We do, however, have an account of the impossibility of examples like the following:

(80) * Maja is believed Ben to like.
(81) * Ben is believed that likes Maja.

As we saw in 9.4 examples like these are ruled out by a condition on anaphors in GB. Within the analysis that we have just sketched, they would only be possible if the following active sentences were possible.

(82) * Stefan believes Maja Ben to like.
(83) * Stefan believes Ben that likes Maja.

Since they aren't, neither are (80) and (81).

Here, then, we have a detailed PSG analysis of passives. As we noted at the outset, there is an obvious sense in which it is simpler than the GB analysis. It does, however, involve rather complex categories.

9.6 Some further data

We have now seen how passive sentences can be analyzed within TG, and especially GB, and within PSG. In this section, we will look at some further relevant data.

We can begin by looking at the following sentences, which are commonly known as pseudo-passives:

(84) The scandal was talked about for days.
(85) Ben can be relied on.

They differ from normal passives in that the missing constituent is on the face of it not a complement of the verb but a complement of a preposition. We have the following related sentences:

(86) They talked about the scandal for days.
(87) You can rely on Ben.

Here, we seem to have prepositions with ordinary complements.

How, then, can we analyze pseudo-passives? It has been assumed quite widely that they are not in fact very different from ordinary passives. It has been proposed that the verb and the following preposition form a complex verb of the following form:

(88)

On this analysis, the missing constituent is in fact the complement of a verb just as it is in an ordinary passive. One thing that provides some support for this analysis is the fact that we cannot have an adverb between the verb and following the preposition in a pseudo-passive in the way that we can in other types of sentence. Thus (89) and (90) are ungrammatical but (91) and (92) are fine.

(89) * The scandal was talked repeatedly about for days.
(90) * Ben can be relied absolutely on.
(91) They talked repeatedly about the scandal for days.
(92) You can rely absolutely on Ben.

Of course, if we have a complex verb in pseudo-passives, we will also have a complex verb in the related actives. It is clear, however, that the related actives can involve a simple verb with a PP complement. (91) and (92) show this, and so do the following:

(93) It was about the scandal that they talked for days.
(94) They talked about the scandal and about who was to blame.
(95) It is on Ben that you can rely.
(96) You can rely on Ben and on Maja.

These show that *about the scandal* and *on Ben* can be constituents. It seems, then, that we must allow two different analyses for examples like (86) and (87), one involving a complex verb with an NP complement and one involving a simple verb with a PP complement. Within transformational grammar, it is generally assumed that the former is derived from the latter in the following way:

(97)

```
      VP                           VP
     /  \                         /  \
    V    PP        =>            V     NP
        /  \                    / \
       P    NP                 V   P
```

Here, we have a process that changes the structure of the VP but does not change the order of any of the lexical items. This is often referred to as a process of reanalysis.

We can turn next not to another class of sentences, but to a class of NP's, NP's containing deverbal nouns, nouns derived from verbs. We can look first at the following:

(98) a. the Vikings' destruction of the monastery
     b. the king's betrayal of the country

These NP's are similar in form and meaning to the following active sentences:

(99) a. The Vikings destroyed the monastery.
     b. The king betrayed the country.

It is natural, then, to call the NP's in (98) active NP's. Notice now that we also have the following NP's:

(100) a. the monastery's destruction by the Vikings
      b. the country's betrayal by the king

These are similar in form and meaning to the following passive sentences:

(101) a. The monastery was destroyed by the Vikings
      b. The country was betrayed by the king

It seems, reasonable, then, to call the NP's in (100) passive NP's. We also have a third type of NP, as the following illustrate:

(102) a. the destruction of the monastery by the Vikings
      b. the betrayal of the country by the king

Here, what look like related sentences are ungrammatical:

(103) a. * It was destroyed the monastery.
      b. * It was betrayed the country by the king.

It seems reasonable, however, to regard the NP's in (102) as passive NP's as well.

There has been little discussion of this sort of data within PSG, but it has been an important focus of interest within TG since Chomsky (1970). In GB, it has been proposed that nouns like *destruction* and *betrayal* have an NP complement in D-structure just like the related verbs. This means that (98)a. will have the following D-structure:

(104)

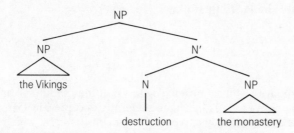

To derive the S-structure of (98)a. we have to insert *of*. If we assume that nouns cannot assign Case, we can see *of* insertion as a way of avoiding a violation of the Case filter.

For (100)a., we will have the following D-structure:

(105)

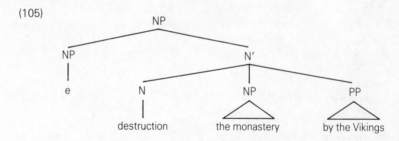

This is like (104) except that the specifier is an empty NP and we have the PP *by the Vikings*. To derive the S-structure of (100)a., we simply move the NP *the monastery* into the empty NP position. There is no need for *of*-insertion here because an NP-trace does not need Case.

Finally, for (102)a., we will have the following D-structure:

(106)

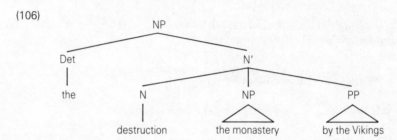

This is like (105) except that we have a determiner and not an empty NP as specifier. Here, we cannot move *the monastery* because there is no empty NP position to move it into. Hence, *of*-insertion is necessary to avoid a violation of the Case filter.

We can turn finally to what are known as unaccusative or ergative sentences. The following illustrate:

(107) The vase smashed.
(108) The ice melted.
(109) The ship sank.

These are very similar to the following passives:

(110) The vase was smashed.
(111) The ice was melted.
(112) The ship was sunk.

Given this similarity, it is natural to suggest that they should be analysed in the same way as passives. This has been generally accepted in GB, where it has been proposed that unaccusative verbs are basic verbs which like passive particles have a subject position to which they assign no θ-role and which take an NP complement to which they cannot assign Case. Given these properties, NP-movement is both possible and necessary as it with passives. Hence, (107) will have the following derivation:

(113)

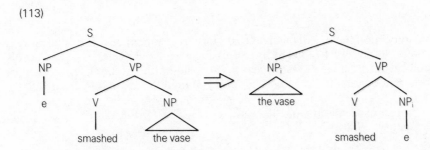

There are, of course, a number of differences between unaccusatives and passives. An obvious one is that passives but not unaccusatives allow a *by*-phrase expressing what we can refer to loosely as an 'agent'. Thus, we have the following contrasts:

(114) The vase was smashed by the ball.
(115) The ice was melted by the flame.
(116) The ship was sunk by a missile.
(117) * The vase smashed by the ball.
(118) * The ice melted by the flame.
(119) * The ship sank by a missile.

A more subtle one is illustrated by the contrast between the following:

(120) The vase was smashed intentionally.
(121) The vase smashed intentionally.

(120) is a perfectly natural sentence suggesting that the individual or individuals who smashed the vase did it intentionally. (121) is a rather odd sentence suggesting that the vase itself intended to smash. Such contrasts are standardly accounted for by saying that there is an implicit agent in a passive with no *by*-phrase, but no implicit agent in an unaccusative.

9.7 Summary

In this chapter, we have taken a closer look at passives, which provide an important example of sentences containing either an abnormal object or an abnormal subject. We began in 9.2 by taking a looking at the relevant data. Then we considered transformational approaches, first, in 9.3, the approach of classical TG, and then, in 9.4, the approach of GB. We criticized the former on the grounds that it raises certain questions to which it can provide no answers, and we showed how the latter can provide answers. We highlighted here the crucial role of Case, traces, θ-roles, and a condition on anaphora. In 9.5, we looked at how passives can be analyzed in PSG. We made crucial use here of a lexical rule deriving passive participles from the related active verbs. Finally, in 9.6, we looked at pseudo-passives, passive NP's and unaccusatives.

Notes

One important feature of passives that I largely ignore in this chapter is the fact that they allow a PP headed by *by* expressing what we can refer to rather loosely as an 'agent'. These phrases have had considerable attention in recent GB work. See especially Jaeggli (1986) and Baker, Johnson and Roberts (1989).

For extensive discussion of classical TG, see Horrocks (1987, 2.1.) and Newmeyer (1986, 3.).

Government is discussed at length in Aoun and Sportiche (1983) and Chomsky (1981, 3.2.1.). It is also a major concern of Chomsky (1986), who defines government in terms of a notion of barrier which is also relevant to the Subjacency Condition, which we discuss in chapter 13. For textbook dission, see Haegeman (1991, 2.4.).

Early arguments for the view that movement processes leave a trace were advanced in Wasow (1972) and Fiengo (1974).

It is assumed in GB that the agreement features associated with a finite verb assign Case to the subject of a finite clause and that a preposition assigns Case to its complement. It is assumed, however, that nouns and adjectives do not assign Case at all or that they assign a different sort of Case, which is realized as the preposition *of*. Either assumption will account for the fact that nouns and adjectives never have an NP complement in S-structure. For textbook discussion of GB assumptions about Case, see Haegeman (1991, 3.).

The standard formulation of the restriction on θ-roles is somewhat different from that in the text. It involves the notion of a chain, an NP together with any traces which it may have. It is proposed that θ-roles are assigned to chains and that no chain can have more than one θ-role. See Chomsky (1981, 6.).

Chomsky (1981) proposes that V and I are combined by movement of I to V by what he calls rule R. Chomsky (1986), following Koopman (1984), proposes that they are combined by movement of V to I. Pollock (1989) proposes that we have movement of V to I in the case of auxiliary *be* and *have* and movement I to V in the case of other verbs. Chomsky (1988) (which was written more recently) also adopts this position.

Given the definition of governing category in the text, the condition on anaphors will rule out a variety of grammatical sentences. It will correctly rule out (1), but it will also exclude (2).

(1) * Ben likes Debbie's pictures of himself.
(2) Ben likes pictures of himself.

In (1), the governing category for *himself* is the NP *Debbie's pictures of himself*. Hence, it is not bound within its governing category. In (2), the governing category for *himself* is the NP *pictures of himself*. Here too, then, it is not bound within its governing category. The condition will also exclude the following examples:

(3) Ben thought that a picture of himself would please Debbie.

(4) Ben thought that there was a picture of himself in the hall.

In both, the governing category for himself is the NP *a picture of himself.* Chomsky (1981, 3.2.3.) develops a more complex definition of governing category which does not exclude these examples. See Lasnik and Uriagereka (1988, 2.), for a textbook discussion of these matters.

Within GB, it is assumed that passive participles arise through a process that combines a passive element with an active verb. In some GB work this process is assumed to be lexical. However, Baker (1988) and Baker, Johnson and Roberts (1989) argue that the process is syntactic and that the passive element originates in INFL.

As we noted in Chapter 5, GPSG assumes a variety of different ID rules for active V' constituents. GPSG also needs a variety of different ID rules for passive V' constituents. The latter are derived from the former by a so-called metarule, a rule that derives ID rules from ID rules. See Gazdar *et al.* (1985, 4.) and for textbook discussion Horrocks (1987, 3.) and Sells (1985, 3.). A rather different GPSG analysis of passives is developed in Zwicky (1987), which treats them as more like the *wh*-dependency constructions discussed in Chapter 12.

The LFG approach to passives is discussed in Bresnan (1982b). The RG approach to passives is discussed in Perlmutter and Postal (1983). Passives are discussed within the related Arc Pair Grammar framework in Postal (1986).

The view that pseudo-passives involve a reanalysis process is advanced in van Riemsdijk (1978) and Hornstein and Weinberg (1981). This position is criticized in Koster (1987).

Williams (1982) argues contrary to the view presented in the text that NP-movement is limited to Ss and does not apply within NPs.

The term unaccusative was first used in Relational Grammar. See, for example, Perlmutter (1983). The term ergative was introduced into GB in Burzio (1986). For some discussion of the historical origins of the unaccusative/ergative analysis, see Pullum (1988).

We assumed in the text that passive participles are verbs. It is clear, however, that they often can and sometimes must be adjectives. Consider the following examples:

(5) He was very impressed by her work.

Here, the passive participle is preceded by *very*. This cannot precede a verb. Hence, (6) is ungrammatical.

(6) * Her work very impressed him.

Very, however, combines readily with adjectives. Thus, we have examples like the following:

(7) Her work was very impressive.

The obvious conclusion is that the passive participle in (5) is an adjective. Consider now (8).

(8) The island has been uninhabited for years.

Here, the passive participle includes the negative prefix *un-*. This can combine with some verbs. We have, for example, the verb *untie*. However, it does not combine with the verb *inhabit*, as the following illustrates:

(9) * People uninhabited the island for years.

It does, however, combine readily with adjectives, giving examples like the following:

(10) The island was uninhabitable.

Again, then, the obvious conclusion is that the passive participle in (8) is an adjective.

An important fact about adjectival passive participles is that they cannot appear in certain situations in which verbal passive participles can appear. Thus, we do not have (12) parallel to (11) or (14) parallel to (13).

(11) Ben is known to be unwell.
(12) * Ben is unknown to be unwell.
(13) Ben was expected to be late.
(14) * Ben was unexpected to be late.

Such restrictions have led proponents of TG to propose that there is no NP-movement with adjectival passive participles. For discussion, see Wasow (1977, 1980).

Exercises

Exercise 1

Discuss the following examples and show how they suggest that the complement of *need* is passive although it contains the 'ing' form of a verb.

(1) This needs mending.
(2) * This needs mending the shoe.
(3) * He mended.
(4) He mended the shoe.
(5) This needs investigating.
(6) * This needs investigating the problem.
(7) * They investigated.
(8) They investigated the problem.
(9) He needs talking to.
(10) * He needs talking to her.
(11) * He talked to.
(12) He talked to her.

Exercise 2

Each of the following examples is problematic for the passive transformation given in 9.2. Explain why.

(1) Ben was often deceived.
(2) She may have been impressed.
(3) That he annoyed her is regretted.
(4) They were not wanted.
(5) Whether he knew the truth was investigated.

Exercise 3

Consider each of the italicized NP's in the following sentences and say which if any of the GB Case marking conventions introduced in this chapter (including the notes) will assign Case to it. Assume that a verb is an active transitive verb if and only if it has a passive participle.

(1) *He* shot *himself*.
(2) *He* has *himself* talked to *her*.
(3) *Those men*, *they* can't be trusted.
(4) *She* is *a psychologist*.
(5) *He* is too old, *Ben*.

Exercise 4

The following sentences provide a problem for the GB account of passives presented in this chapter. Why?

(1) They believe under the bed to be a good place to hide.
(2) They consider by train to be the best way to travel.
(3) Under the bed is believed to be a good place to hide.
(4) By train is considered to be the best way to travel.
(5) * It is believed under the bed to be a good place to hide.
(6) * It is considered by train to be the best way to travel.

Exercise 5

Give the categories that the lexical rule introduced in 9.5 will derive from the following categories:

(1)
$$
\begin{bmatrix}
\text{V} \\
\text{SUBCAT,}\langle\text{PP,} \quad \underset{[\text{NFORM,NORM}]}{\text{NP}} \quad \rangle \\
\text{SUBJ,NP}
\end{bmatrix}
$$

(2)
$$
\begin{bmatrix}
\text{V} \\
\text{SUBCAT,}\langle\text{S,} \quad \underset{[\text{NFORM,NORM}]}{\text{NP}} \quad \rangle \\
\text{SUBJ,NP}
\end{bmatrix}
$$

(3)
$$
\begin{bmatrix}
\text{V} \\
\text{SUBCAT,}\langle \begin{bmatrix} \text{AP} \\ \text{SUBJ,} \quad \underset{[\text{NFORM,}\alpha]}{\text{NP}} \end{bmatrix} , \quad \underset{[\text{NFORM,}\alpha]}{\text{NP}} \quad \rangle \\
\text{SUBJ,NP}
\end{bmatrix}
$$

10

Raising sentences

10.1 Introduction

We saw in Chapter 7 that raising sentences provide an important example of
sentences involving a noncanonical subject. In this chapter, we will look more
closely at these sentences and consider how they can be analyzed. We will begin
by looking at some data. Then, we will consider how raising sentences can be
analyzed within transformational grammar and in particular within GB. Next,
we will consider how they can be analyzed within PSG. Finally, we will look at
some further examples of raising sentences. One point we can note immediately is that there will be few new ideas in this chapter. Most of the ideas
that are important here were introduced in the last chapter.

10.2 The data

We can distinguish two kinds of raising sentence. One type involves a subject,
one of a small class of verbs, which we can call raising verbs, and an infinitive
with no overt subject. The other type involves a subject, a form of *be*, one of a
small class of adjectives, which we can call raising adjectives, and an infinitive
with no overt subject. The first type is exemplified by (1) and (2) and the second
type by (3) and (4).

(1) Stefan seems to be irritating.
(2) Stefan tends to be irritating.
(3) Stefan is likely to be irritating.
(4) Stefan is certain to be irritating.

In both types, the subject functions as a subject of the infinitive. It is the
infinitive and not the raising verb or adjective which determines the character
of the subject. If the infinitive requires a dummy subject, the raising verb or *be*
will require a dummy subject. Thus, the data (5) and (6) parallels the data in
(7).

(5) $\left\{ \begin{array}{l} \text{It} \\ \text{* Stefan} \end{array} \right\}$ seems to be easy to annoy Maja.

(6) $\left\{ \begin{array}{l} \text{It} \\ \text{* Stefan} \end{array} \right\}$ is likely to be easy to annoy Maja.

(7) $\left\{ \begin{array}{l} \text{It} \\ \text{* Stefan} \end{array} \right\}$ is easy to annoy Maja.

Similarly, if the infinitive allows a dummy subject, so will the raising verb or *be*. The data in (8) and (9) parallels that in (10).

(8) $\left\{ \begin{array}{l} \text{There} \\ \text{Stefan} \end{array} \right\}$ seems to be a dragon in the wood.

(9) $\left\{ \begin{array}{l} \text{There} \\ \text{Stefan} \end{array} \right\}$ is likely to be a dragon in the wood.

(10) $\left\{ \begin{array}{l} \text{There} \\ \text{Stefan} \end{array} \right\}$ is a dragon in the wood.

If the infinitive allows a clausal subject, the raising verb or *be* will allow a clausal subject. Here, the data in (11) and (12) parallels that in (13).

(11) That he is a fool seems to be $\left\{ \begin{array}{l} \text{obvious} \\ \text{* obese} \end{array} \right\}$

(12) That he is a fool is likely to be $\left\{ \begin{array}{l} \text{obvious} \\ \text{* obese} \end{array} \right\}$

(13) That he is a fool is $\left\{ \begin{array}{l} \text{obvious} \\ \text{* obese} \end{array} \right\}$

Finally, if the infinitive allows a subject with an idiomatic interpretation, the raising verb will also allow such a subject. Thus, (14) and (15) parallel (16).

(14) The cat seems to be out of the bag.
(15) The cat is likely to be out of the bag.
(16) The cat is out of the bag.

10.3 The transformational approach

We can now consider how raising sentences can be analyzed within a transformational approach. As we have seen, within such an approach, they will be derived from more abstract structures by a movement process. If we assume with GB that movement processes leave behind traces, we will have the following derivations for (1) and (3):

(17)

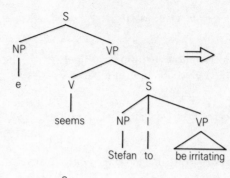

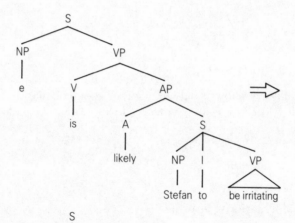

(18)

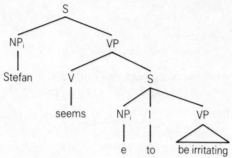

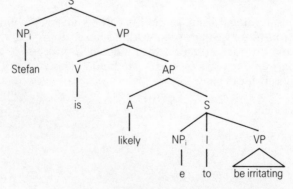

These structures involve the standard GB assumption that infinitival *to* is a member of the I category introduced in the last chapter. The question that we must ask is: why are such derivations possible? Within classical transformational grammar, they will be possible because a rule, which we can call the raising transformation, says so. The problem with this approach, like the similar approach to passives that we considered earlier, is that it raises various questions to which it can provide no illuminating answers.

Firstly, we might ask the following question:

(19) Why is movement possible in raising sentences?

The only answer we can give is that the raising transformation allows this. This is not a very interesting answer.

Secondly, we might ask the following:

(20) Why is movement necessary in raising sentences?

In other words, we might ask why we do not have sentences like the following:

(21) a. * It seems Stefan to be irritating.
b. * It is likely Stefan to be irritating.

All we can say in answer to this is that the raising transformation is an obligatory rule. Again, this is not a very satisfying answer.

Finally, we might ask the following:

(22) Why do we have just the kind of movement that we do?

More precisely, we might ask why we can derive the S-structure in (23) but not the S-structures in (24) and (25).

(23) Stefan$_i$ seems [$_s$ e$_i$ to like Maja]
(24) * Maja$_i$ seems [$_s$ Stefan to like e$_i$]
(25) * Stefan$_i$ seems [$_{s'}$ that [$_s$ e$_i$ likes Maja]]

All we can say is that the rule allows the movement that is involved in (23) but not the movement that is involved in (24) and (25). Once more, this is not a very satisfying answer.

Thus, the classical transformational approach to raising sentences is unsatisfactory in much the same way as the classical transformational approach to passives.

The GB approach to raising sentences is very similar to the GB approach to passive sentences. As we have seen, GB assumes a very general movement rule, move α, and a variety of grammatical principles that interact with it to determine what kinds of movement actually occur. All the principles that we considered in connection with passives are also relevant in connection with raising sentences.

We can look first at how GB answers the first of our questions: why is movement possible in raising structures? The crucial assumption here is the following:

(26) Raising verbs and adjectives have no external θ-role, i.e. do not assign θ-role to their subjects.

Some evidence for this assumption comes from the fact that raising sentences often have related sentences with a dummy *it* in subject position. Recall that dummy *it* appears in a subject position to which no θ-role is assigned. For example, parallel to (1) and (3), we have (27) and (28).

(27) It seems that Stefan is irritating.
(28) It is likely that Stefan will be irritating.

The assumption makes raising verbs and adjectives rather like passive participles and unaccusative verbs. It means that movement into subject position in a raising sentence, like movement into subject position in a passive or unaccusative sentence, will not result in an NP with two θ-roles. Hence, there will be no violation of the constraint that no NP can have more than one θ-role.

We turn now to our second question: why is movement necessary in raising structures? Here, the following assumption is crucial:

(29) Raising verbs and adjectives do not assign Case to an NP that they govern.

This makes raising verbs and adjectives even more like passive participles and unaccusative verbs. Given this assumption, the initial structures in (17) and (18) involve an NP with phonetic content in a position to which no Case is assigned. In both cases, then, movement is necessary to avoid a violation of the Case filter, the requirement that an NP with phonetic content must have Case.

Finally, we can consider our third question: why do we have the kind of movement that we do? More precisely, why can we derive the S-structure in (23) but not the S-structures in (24) and (25)? We repeat the crucial examples:

(23) Stefan_i seems [s e_i to like Maja]
(24) * Maja_i seems [s Stefan to like e_i]
(25) * Stefan_i seems [s' that [s e_i likes Maja]]

The important point to note is that these examples are just like the passive examples that we considered in the last chapter, i.e. the following:

(30) Ben_i is believed [s e_i to like Maja]
(31) * Maja_i is believed [s Ben to like e_i]
(32) * Ben_i is believed [s' that [s e_i likes Maja]]

We can explain (23)–(25) in just the same way as these examples. That is, we can attribute the facts to the following constraint:

(33) An anaphor must be A-bound in its governing category.

Remember that a category is A-bound if and only if it is coindexed with a c-commanding category in an A-position such as subject, object or object of a preposition, and that the governing category of an item is the minimal NP or S containing the item and an item governing it.

In (23), the trace is governed by the preceding verb given the assumption that a lexical head governs the subject of an exceptional clause complement. This verb is in the main clause. Hence, the governing category for the trace is the main S, and the trace is A-bound within its governing category, as (33) requires.

In (24), the trace is governed by the preceding verb given the assumption that a lexical head governs its complements. Since this verb is in the subordinate clause the governing category for the trace is the subordinate S. Hence, the trace is not A-bound within its governing category and we have a violation of (33).

Finally, in (25), the trace is not governed by the preceding verb because the complement is an S′ and not just an S. Instead, it is governed by the agreement features of the following verb given the assumption that the agreement features of a finite verb govern its subject. Since this verb is in the subordinate clause the governing category for the trace is the subordinate S. Therefore, the trace is not A-bound within its governing category and we have another violation of (33).

10.4 The PSG approach

We can now consider how raising sentences can be analyzed within PSG, more precisely within HPSG. Like the HPSG approach to passives, there is a sense in which this is simpler than the GB approach, but like the HPSG approach to passives, it involves some complex categories.

Within PSG, raising sentences have only the ordinary obvious structure. Thus, (1) and (3) will have just the structures in (34) and (35), respectively:

(34)

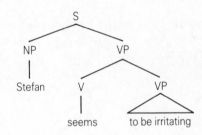

(35)

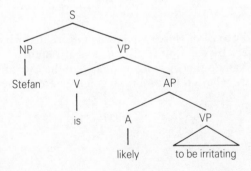

If raising sentences have just the ordinary, obvious structure, the infinitival VP's that they involve must somehow be sensitive to the presence of a particular constituent higher up the tree. In these examples, the VP *to be irritating* must somehow be sensitive to the presence of the NP *Stefan*. We have already in effect seen how this can be achieved.

We can begin by looking at (34). Here, all we have to do is to ensure that whatever category is required as subject by the infinitival VP is also required as a subject by the higher VP. We can do this by assigning *seems* to the same kind of category as passive *was* in the last chapter. Specifically, we can propose the following:

(36)
$$
\begin{bmatrix}
\text{SUBCAT, } \langle \quad \overset{\textstyle \text{V}}{\begin{bmatrix} \text{VP} \\ \text{+INF} \\ \text{SUBJ,Y} \end{bmatrix}} \quad \rangle \\
\text{SUBJ,Y}
\end{bmatrix}
$$

Here, as in the category that we proposed for passive *was*, the SUBJ feature within the value of SUBCAT and the main SUBJ feature have the same variable as their value. When *seems* appears in a tree, we will have a more specific category. In the present case, the variables will be instantiated as NP[NFORM,NORM]. Hence, instead of (36), we will have the following:

(37)
$$
\begin{bmatrix}
\text{SUBCAT,} \langle \quad \overset{\textstyle \text{V}}{\begin{bmatrix} \text{VP} \\ \text{+INF} \\ \text{SUBJ,} \quad \underset{\text{[NFORM,NORM]}}{\text{NP}} \end{bmatrix}} \quad \rangle \\
\text{SUBJ,} \quad \underset{\text{[NFORM,NORM]}}{\text{NP}}
\end{bmatrix}
$$

If *seems* is [SUBJ,NP[NFORM,NORM]], the head-complement rule will ensure that the higher VP is too. Thus, we will have the following structure in the middle of the tree in (34):

(38)
$$
\overset{\textstyle \text{VP}}{\begin{bmatrix} \text{SUBJ,} \quad \underset{\text{[NFORM,NORM]}}{\text{NP}} \end{bmatrix}}
$$

$$
\overset{\textstyle \text{V}}{\begin{bmatrix} \text{SUBJ,} \quad \underset{\text{[NFORM,NORM]}}{\text{NP}} \end{bmatrix}}
\qquad
\overset{\textstyle \text{VP}}{\begin{bmatrix} \text{+INF} \\ \text{SUBJ,} \quad \underset{\text{[NFORM,NORM]}}{\text{NP}} \end{bmatrix}}
$$

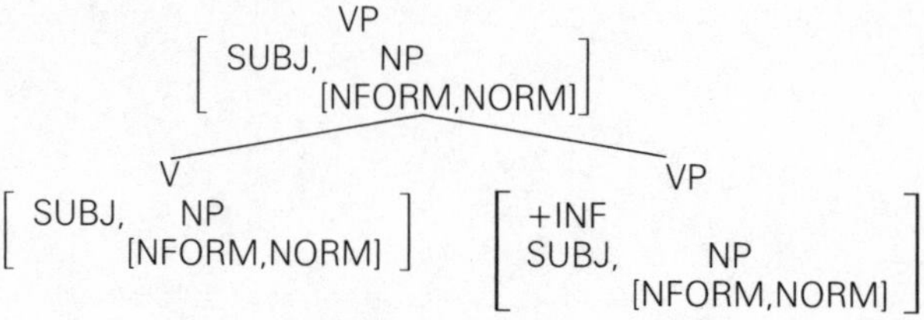

We can turn now to (35). Here, we have to ensure that whatever category is required as subject by the infinitival VP is also required as subject by the topmost VP. We can do this by assigning *likely* to the category in (39) and the various forms of *be* where it takes an AP complement to the category in (40)

(39)
$$
\begin{bmatrix}
\text{SUBCAT,} \langle \quad \overset{\textstyle \text{A}}{\begin{bmatrix} \text{VP} \\ \text{+INF} \\ \text{SUBJ,Y} \end{bmatrix}} \quad \rangle \\
\text{SUBJ,Y}
\end{bmatrix}
$$

(40)
$$
\begin{bmatrix}
\text{SUBCAT,} \langle \quad \overset{\textstyle \text{V}}{\begin{matrix} \text{AP} \\ \text{[SUBJ,Y]} \end{matrix}} \quad \rangle \\
\text{SUBJ,Y}
\end{bmatrix}
$$

Here again, the SUBJ feature within the value of SUBCAT and the main SUBJ feature have the same variable as their value. As before, when these categories appear in a tree, the variables will be instantiated as an actual category. Given (39), if the complement of *likely* is [SUBJ,NP[NFORM,NORM]], *likely* itself will be too, and the head-complement rule will ensure that the immediately dominating AP is as well. Similarly, given (40), if the complement of *is* is [SUBJ,NP[NFORM,NORM]], so will *is* itself be, and the head-complement rule will ensure that the immediately dominating VP is also. Hence, we will have the following structure in the middle of the tree in (35):

(41)
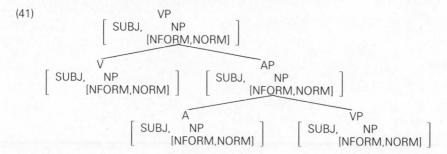

Thus, as in GB, we can accommodate raising sentences without any new mechanisms.

There is in fact an important similarity between the PSG approach and the GB approach. In GB, a raising verb has a subject which originates as the subject of a complement. We can say, then, that the raising verb inherits a subject from its complement. In PSG, a raising verb combines with a certain kind of subject because that is what its complement requires. Here, then, we can say that a raising verb inherits the requirement for a certain kind of subject from its complement. Thus, what are superficially very different approaches are in fact not as different as they appear.

10.5 Some further data

In this final section, we can look at some more data. In particular, we can consider what look like raising sentences with different kinds of complement. Within GB, the obvious analysis of these examples will involve the kind of movement that we discussed in 10.3, and within PSG the obvious analysis will involve the sort of category that we discussed in 10.4.

We can begin by considering the following examples:

(42) Stefan seemed intelligent.
(43) Ben appears devious.

These look rather like a reduced version of the following, which are ordinary raising sentences:

(44) Stefan seemed to be intelligent.
(45) Ben appears to be devious.

In these sentences, as in ordinary raising sentences, the complement determines what sort of subject appears. Thus, (46) and (47) parallel (48) and (49).

(46) It seems easy to fool Ben.
(47) It appears difficult to please Maja.
(48) It is easy to fool Ben.
(49) It is difficult to please Maja.

It seems, then, that sentences like (42) and (43) are very much the same kind of sentence as the ordinary raising sentences that we have been discussing. If this is so, then they should be analyzed in the same way.

Within GB, this means that they should involve the movement of a subordinate clause subject into an empty main clause subject position. We can propose derivations like the following:

(50)

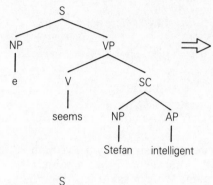

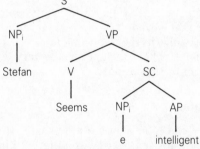

This is very similar to the derivation that we proposed for ordinary raising sentences. The only difference is that the complement is a small clause.

Within PSG, we should have the same sort of categories in these examples as in ordinary raising sentences. We can propose categories like the following:

(51)
$$\begin{bmatrix} V \\ \text{SUBCAT}\langle \quad \text{AP} \quad \rangle \\ \qquad \text{[SUBJ,Y]} \\ \text{SUBJ,Y} \end{bmatrix}$$

This is just like the category we proposed for *seem* as an ordinary raising verb except that we have AP instead of VP[+INF].

It is not just with *seems* that an AP complement determines what kind of subject appears. We have the same situation with *be*. Thus, it is because we have the adjective *strong* in (52) that we have a normal subject and because we have the adjective *likely* with a full clausal complement in (53) that we have a dummy *it* subject.

(52) Ben is strong.
(53) It is likely that Ben did it.

Within GB, this suggests that we again have movement of a subordinate subject into an empty main clause subject position, in other words that we have derivations like the following:

(54) e is [sc Ben strong] $\Rightarrow$ Ben$_i$ is [sc e$_i$ strong]

Within PSG, the data suggests that *be* too should be assigned to the category in (51) when it takes an AP complement. We in fact proposed this category for *be* when it takes an AP complement in the last section. Thus, we have already assumed that *be* is a raising verb in this situation.

A VP complement of *be* also determines what type of subject appears. Thus, in (55) we have a normal subject because that is what the verb *run* requires while in (56) we have a dummy *it* subject because that is what the verb *rain* requires.

(55) Ben is running.
(56) It is raining.

Within GB, this suggests that we have derivations like the following:

(57) e is [sc Ben running] $\Rightarrow$ Ben$_i$ is [sc e$_i$ running]

Within PSG, the facts suggests that we should assign *be* where it takes a VP complement to the following category:

(58)
$$\begin{bmatrix} V \\ SUBCAT\langle \begin{bmatrix} VP \\ +ING \\ SUBJ,Y \end{bmatrix} \rangle \\ SUBJ,Y \end{bmatrix}$$

I use [+ING] here to identify the VP as headed by the present participle or 'ing' form of a verb.

One of the main uses of *be* is, of course, in passives. It is natural to suggest that it should be analyzed in the same way here as in its other uses. We have in fact already treated passive *be* as a raising verb. In our discussion of how passives could be analyzed within PSG, we proposed the following category:

(59)
$$\begin{bmatrix} V \\ SUBCAT\langle \begin{bmatrix} VP \\ +PAS \\ SUBJ,Y \end{bmatrix} \rangle \\ SUBJ,Y \end{bmatrix}$$

If we analyze passive *be* as a raising verb within GB, we will have not one instance of NP-movement but two in a typical passive. We will have derivations like the following:

(60) e was [sc e arrested Ben] $\Rightarrow$ e was [sc Ben$_i$ arrested e$_i$] $\Rightarrow$ Ben$_i$ was [sc e$_i$ arrested e$_i$]

Here, we have movement from object position to subject position within a small clause, and then movement into the main clause subject position.

There is one further point we can make about *be*. Notice that we have pairs of sentences like the following:

(61) a. A man was running.
　　 b. There was a man running.
(62) a. A vase was broken.
　　 b. There was a vase broken.

Within GB, the subjects of the a. examples have been moved from a small clause subject position following *was*. It is natural, then, to suggest that the b. examples have the same analysis as the a. examples except that they involve insertion of *there* instead of movement from the small clause subject position. Of course, it is necessary here to explain why *there*-insertion is far less natural if the subject of the small clause is definite, why, that is, examples like the following are unnatural unless one is giving some sort of list:

(63) ∗ There is Ben running.

We will not, however, go into this matter.

There are two further matters that we should consider here, modals and infinitival *to*. Consider first the following:

(64) Ben $\left\{ \begin{array}{l} \text{may} \\ \text{must} \\ \text{will} \end{array} \right\}$ run.

(65) It $\left\{ \begin{array}{l} \text{may} \\ \text{must} \\ \text{will} \end{array} \right\}$ rain.

In (64) we have a normal subject because that is what *run* requires, while in (65) we have a dummy *it* subject because that is what *rain* requires. It looks, then, as if modals too are a kind of raising verb. Consider now the following:

(66) I expect Ben to run.
(67) I expect it to rain.

Here, the material following *expect* is an exceptional clause for GB, but two separate complements for PSG. In either case, however, *Ben* is subject of *to run* and *it* is subject of *to rain*. It is clear that we have a normal subject in the first case because that is what *run* requires, and a dummy *it* subject in the second case because that is what *rain* requires. It looks, then, as if infinitival *to* is a kind of raising verb.

Within PSG, we can implement the idea that modals and infinitival *to* are raising verbs by assigning the former to the category in (68) and the latter to the category in (69):

(68)
$$
\text{V} \\
\begin{bmatrix} +\text{FIN} \\ \text{SUBCAT}\langle \begin{bmatrix} \text{VP} \\ +\text{BASE} \\ \text{SUBJ,Y} \end{bmatrix} \rangle \\ \text{SUBJ,Y} \end{bmatrix}
$$

(69)
$$
\begin{bmatrix}
& & V \\
+\text{INF} & & \\
\text{SUBCAT}\langle & \begin{bmatrix} VP \\ +\text{BASE} \\ \text{SUBJ,Y} \end{bmatrix} & \rangle \\
\text{SUBJ,Y} & &
\end{bmatrix}
$$

These are identical except that (68) is [+FIN] while (69) is [+INF].

The idea that modals and infinitival *to* are raising verbs might seem problematic for GB since it is generally assumed in GB that they are members of the I category. We can assume, however, that I is a raising category, which takes a small clause complement whose subject is raised into an empty main clause subject position. Given this assumption, we will have something like the following derivation for the examples in (64):

(70)

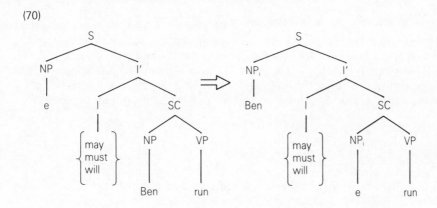

Similarly, we will have the following derivation for the post-verbal material in (65):

(71)

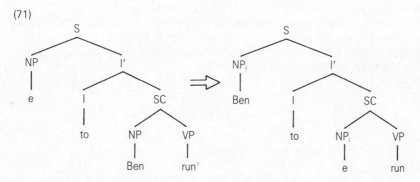

Notice that we are assuming in these analyses that I and its complement form an I'. Given this assumption, it is natural to analyze S as IP, and this is in fact the standard analysis within GB. I will continue, however, to use the label S in subsequent discussion.

10.6 Summary

In this chapter, we have taken a closer look at raising sentences, an important example of sentences containing an abnormal subject. We began in 10.2 by looking more closely at the data. Then in 10.3, we looked at transformational approaches. We noted that the classical transformational approach faces the same objection as the classical transformational approach to passives: it raises questions to which it can provide no answer. We then showed how the GB approach answers these questions. Here, we were concerned with essentially the same ideas as in Chapter 9. In 10.4, we looked at the PSG approach to raising sentences. Here, we made crucial use of a particular type of complex category. Finally, in 10.5, we considered some further examples of raising sentences, and considered how they could be analyzed both in GB and PSG.

Notes

The proposal that *be* and the modals are raising verbs has its origins in Ross (1969) and was argued for in some detail in Pullum and Wilson (1977). Within GB, *be* is analyzed as a raising verb in Stowell (1981, 4.) and Burzio (1986).

Examples like the following suggest that what is often known as perfective *have*, the *have* that combines with a past participle, is another raising verb:

(1) Stefan has run.
(2) It has rained.

This is the position of both Ross (1969) and Pullum and Wilson (1977).

The analysis of *there* subject sentences sketched in the text is proposed in Stowell (1978). It is criticized in Williams (1984a).

The proposal that INFL is a raising category has been advanced by a number of GB syntacticians. See, for example, Sportiche (1988). For textbook discussion, see Haegeman (1991, 6.). The proposal can be seen as a revival of the proposal of McCawley (1973) that tense is a raising verb.

Recent GB work has proposed that INFL should be replaced by two separate elements, a tense element (T) and an agreement (AGR), each of which has an associated maximal projection. In one version of this approach, an ordinary clause has the following structure:

(3)

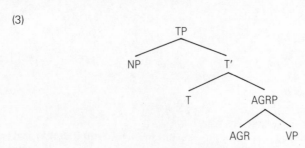

See Pollock (1989) and Chomsky (1988).

We noted in the last chapter that there are passive NP's as well as passive sentences. It seems, however, that there are no raising NP's. Thus, we do not have (6) and (7) corresponding to (4) and (5).

(4) Ben appears to be late.
(5) Ben is likely to be late.
(6) * Ben's appearance to be late
(7) * Ben's likelihood to be late

Exercises

Exercise 1

Show with appropriate use of related sentences that the following is a raising sentence. Note any differences between this and the raising sentences discussed in 10.2.

(1) She took three hours to solve the problem.

Exercise 2

Provide GB analyses for the following examples, giving D-structures, S-structures and intermediate structures, and taking into account the arguments of 10.5.

(1) She tends to appear nervous.
(2) He strikes me as a fool.
(3) They may seem to be intelligent.
(4) He is likely to seem arrogant.

Exercise 3

We assume in this chapter and the previous one that the GB condition on anaphora applies at S-structure. Show with appropriate tree diagrams how the following example supports this assumption.

(1) He seems to himself to be an ideal candidate for the job.

Exercise 4

Provide PSG categories of the kind given in the text for the italicized items in the following sentences. Assume that a VP headed by a past participle is marked [+ED].

(1) They are *sure* to be late.
(2) He *appeared* to her to be too old.
(3) He *has* seen the light.
(4) She *seemed* honest to me.

Exercise 5

We have seen in this chapter that auxiliaries are analyzed in both GB and PSG as heads of phrases taking complements of various kinds. A more traditional view is that they combine with the following ordinary verb to form a 'verb-group'. In other words, it is assumed that we have structures like the following:

(1)

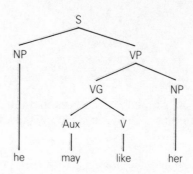

(2)

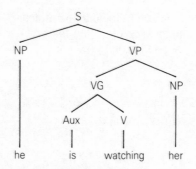

Discuss how the following examples provide evidence against this view of auxiliaries and in favour of the view presented in this chapter:

(3) He may like her and respect her.
(4) He is watching her and recording her movements.
(5) They say he may like her and like her he may.
(6) They say he is watching her and watching her he is.

11

Control

11.1 Introduction

We saw in the last chapter that raising sentences normally involve a subject, a verb, and an infinitive with no overt subject, or a subject, a form of *be*, an adjective, and an infinitive with no overt subject. It has been clear, however, since Rosenbaum (1967) that not all sentences of this kind are raising sentences. For example, the following are not:

(1) Stefan tried to please Maja.
(2) Stefan is eager to please Maja.

These are generally known as control sentences and the subject, which is understood as subject of the infinitive, is known as the controller. In this chapter we will look first at the basic properties of control sentences. Then we will consider how they can be analyzed, first within GB and then within PSG. Finally, we will look at some further relevant data.

11.2 The data

The first matter to consider is how sentences like (1) and (2) differ from raising sentences. The most important point is that such sentences only allow a normal NP in subject position. In other words, the subject cannot be a dummy NP, a clause or an NP with an idiomatic interpretation. In a raising sentence, all these can appear in subject position as long as they are compatible with the infinitive. Thus, if the infinitive requires or allows a dummy subject, the raising verb or *be* will require or allow a dummy subject. Hence, we have examples like the following:

(3) It seemed to be easy to please Maja.
(4) It is likely to be easy to please Maja.
(5) There seemed to be a flaw in the argument.
(6) There is likely to be a flaw in the argument.

There are no sentences like these with *try* and *eager*.

(7) * It tried to be easy to please Maja.
(8) * It is eager to be easy to please Maja.
(9) * There tried to be a flaw in the argument.
(10) * There is eager to be a flaw in the argument.

Similarly, if the infinitive in a raising sentence allows a clausal subject, the raising verb or *be* will allow a clausal subject. The following illustrate:

(11) That he is clever seems to be obvious.
(12) That he is clever is likely to be obvious.

Again, there are no comparable sentences with *try* and *eager*.

(13) * That he is clever tries to be obvious.
(14) * That he is clever is eager to be obvious.

Finally, if the infinitive in a raising sentence allows a subject with an idiomatic interpretation, the raising verb or *be* will also allow such a subject.

(15) The cat seems to be out of the bag.
(16) The cat is likely to be out of the bag.

Again, this is not possible with *try* and *eager*. The subject in the following does not have the idiomatic interpretation:

(17) The cat tried to be out of the bag.
(18) The cat was eager to be out of the bag.

It is fairly clear, then, that we have a different kind of sentence here.

Although some control sentences are superficially similar to raising sentences, not all are. Consider, for example, the following:

(19) Stefan persuaded Ben to be careful.
(20) Stefan appealed to Ben to go home.

In (19), the controller is an object, and in (20) it is the object of a preposition. These examples do not look like raising sentences. (19), however, is superficially similar to the following:

(21) Stefan believed Ben to be careful.

As we have seen, sentences like this are analyzed as involving a single clausal complement within GB and as involving separate NP and VP complements in PSG. It is clear, however, that sentences like (19) are rather different. With *believe*, any kind of NP can appear in post-verbal position as long as it is compatible with the infinitive. The following illustrates this:

(22) Stefan believed it to be easy to please Maja.

With *persuade*, on the other hand, we can only have a normal NP in post-verbal position, as the following illustrates:

(23) * Stefan persuaded it to be easy to please Maja.

It is clear, then, that we have a different kind of sentence in (19).

A further distinctive feature of control sentences is that the infinitive can sometimes be preceded by the complementizer *whether* or a *wh*-phrase. The following illustrate:

(24) Ben asked whether to do it.
(25) Ben asked what to do.

The infinitive in a raising sentence is never preceded by *whether* or a *wh*-phrase.

Another distinctive feature is that the controller can sometimes be separated from the infinitive by the boundary of a finite clause. The following, in which the finite clause boundaries are indicated, by brackets, illustrate this point:

(26) Ben wondered [if it was necessary to tickle himself]
(27) Ben thought [it would be easy to tickle himself]

Again, there are no comparable raising sentences.

A final distinctive feature of control sentences is illustrated by the following pairs:

(28) a. Ben hoped to be elected.
    b. Ben hoped that he would be elected.
(29) a. Ben is keen to be elected.
    b. Ben is keen that he should be elected.

The first member of each pair is a control sentence, and the second is a related sentence with an ordinary clause instead of the infinitive. The important point to note is that the second member of each pair has a normal NP in subject position. These pairs contrast with the following:

(30) a. Ben seemed to be late.
    b. It seemed that Ben was late.
(31) a. Ben is likely to be late.
    b. It is likely that Ben will be late.

Here, the first member of each pair is a raising sentence and the second is a related sentence with an ordinary clause instead of the infinitive. Here, we have dummy *it* in subject position.

11.3 The GB approach

We can now look at how control sentences are analyzed within GB. The fact that many control sentences have related sentences with an ordinary clause instead of the infinitive is important here. This is seen as evidence that the infinitive is in fact a clause with an empty subject. Also important is the fact that related sentences with an ordinary clause have a normal non-dummy NP in the position of the controller. This suggests that the position of the controller is one to which a θ-role is assigned. This means that the controller must have originated in its surface position since if it were moved there we would have an NP with two θ-roles. It seems, then, that there is no movement in control sentences and hence that the clause has an empty subject from the outset.

What sort of structures does this imply? Since infinitives in control sentences can sometimes be introduced by a complementizer, it is plausible to assume that they involve not just an S but an S′ as well. If so, we will have the structure in (32) for (1) and the structure in (33) for (19).

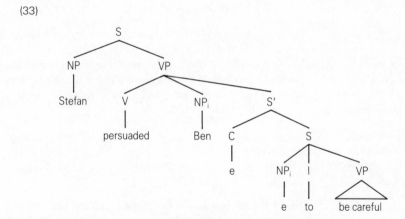

(32)

(33)

The obvious question to ask about these structures is: what exactly is the empty subject. If it is present from the outset, it cannot be a trace. This empty category is known as PRO, and we could if we wanted replace the e's in subject position in (32) and (33) by PRO. The following assumption is made about PRO:

(34) PRO is an anaphor and a pronominal.

This means that it has the central properties of both anaphors and of ordinary pronouns like *he*, *she* and *it*. What exactly are these properties? For GB, as we have seen in the last two chapters, the central property of anaphors is that they are subject to the following condition:

(35) An anaphor must be A-bound in its governing category.

Remember again that a category is A-bound if and only if it is coindexed with a c-commanding category in an A-position such as subject, object or object of a preposition, and that the governing category of an item is the minimal NP or S containing the item and an item governing it. The central property of pronominals is that they obey the following condition:

(36) A pronominal must be A-free in its governing category.

This is just like (35) except that it has 'A-free' instead of 'A-bound'. 'A-free' essentially means 'not A-bound'. We can define it as follows:

(37) A category is A-free iff it is not coindexed with a c-commanding category in an A-position.

We must look at the motivation for (36). Then, we can return to PRO.

The main motivation for (36) comes from data like the following, where the indices indicate that *Stefan* is the intended antecedent of the pronoun.

(38) a. * Stefan$_i$ likes him$_i$
b. * Stefan$_i$ believes [s him$_i$ to be a genius]
c. Stefan$_i$ believes [s Maja to like him$_i$]
d. Stefan$_i$ believes [s' that [s he$_i$ is a genius]]

In (38)a., *him* is governed by *likes* since a lexical category governs its complements. Its governing category is the only S that the sentence involves. Hence, it is not A-free in its governing category, and we have a violation of (36). In (38)b., *him* is governed by *believes* since a lexical category governs the subject of an exceptional clause complement. Its governing category is the main S. Therefore, it is not free in its governing category, and we have another violation of (36). In (38)c., *him* is governed by *like*. Hence, its governing category is the subordinate S and it is A-free in its governing category, as (36) requires. Finally, in (38)d., *he* is governed by the agreement features of *is* given the assumption that the agreement features of a finite verb governs its subject. Consequently, its governing category is the subordinate S and it is A-free in its governing category, as required.

We can return now to PRO. If PRO is both a pronominal and anaphor, it must be both free and bound in its governing category. Clearly, however, this is impossible. This might suggest that PRO is a rather useless element. There will, however, be no problem if PRO has no governing category and it will have no governing category if it is not governed. Hence, the consequence of analyzing PRO as both a pronominal and an anaphor is the following, which is commonly known as the PRO theorem:

(39) PRO must be ungoverned.

This essentially means that PRO can appear in just one position – subject position in a non-finite S within an S'. If it appears as the complement of a lexical head, it will be governed by it. If it appears as the subject of an exceptional clause or small clause complement, it will be governed by the lexical head of which the clause is a complement. Finally, if it appears as the subject of a finite S, it will be governed by the agreement features of the finite verb. Thus, all the following are correctly ruled out:

(40) Stefan likes PRO

(41) Stefan considers [s PRO to be a genius]
(42) Stefan considers [s PRO a genius]
(43) Stefan considers [s' that [s PRO is a genius]]

Thus, analysing PRO as both a pronominal and an anaphor seems to account for its distribution quite well.

There is a further question about PRO which we should consider here: why is it generally impossible to have a lexical NP in the same position? The answer is that no Case is assigned to this position so that a lexical NP will violate the Case filter. Examples like the following appear to suggest that PRO and a lexical NP can sometimes occupy the same position:

(44) Stefan wants to go home.
(45) Stefan wants Maja to go home.

The ungrammaticality of the following examples suggests that (44) is a control sentence, and hence, given GB assumptions, that it has a PRO subject:

(46) * It wants to be easy to please Maja.
(47) * That he is clever wants to be obvious.

On the face of it, then, we have here a position in which both PRO and a lexical NP can appear. There is evidence, however, that we have two rather different complement clauses here and hence two rather different subject positions. With (45), we have a related pseudo-cleft containing *for*:

(48) What Stefan wants is for Maja to go home.

We do not have this with (44).

(49) * What Stefan wants is for to go home.

In the light of these examples, it is plausible to suggest that (45) but not (44) contains a *for* complementizer, which governs and assigns Case to the following subject and is then deleted.

A final point that we should note is that this account says nothing about which NP is the controller in a control sentence. It says nothing, for example, about the fact that it is *Maja* and not *Stefan* that is the controller in (50).

(50) Stefan said Maja tried to tickle him.

Similarly, it says nothing about the fact that *Ben* is the controller in (51) while *Debbie* is the controller in the superficially similar (52).

(51) Ben persuaded Debbie to go home
(52) Ben promised Debbie to go home

Such facts are assumed to fall within the scope of a separate control theory. This, however, is largely undeveloped.

11.4 The PSG approach

We can now consider how control sentences can be analyzed within PSG, more precisely how they can be analyzed within HPSG.

Within HPSG, the infinitives in control sentences, like the infinitives in raising sentences, are analyzed as 'bare' VP's. This means that we have structures of the following form for (1) and (15).

(53)

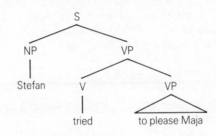

(54)

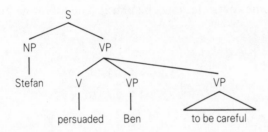

All we need in HPSG to allow these structure is appropriate categories for the verbs *tried* and *persuaded*. For *tried*, we can propose the following:

(55)
$$
\begin{bmatrix}
& V \\
\text{SUBCAT}\langle & \begin{bmatrix} VP \\ +\text{INF} \\ \text{SUBJ,} \quad \text{NP} \\ \quad\quad [\text{NFORM,NORM}] \end{bmatrix} \rangle \\
\text{SUBJ,} & \text{NP} \\
& [\text{NFORM,NORM}]
\end{bmatrix}
$$

This is like the category we proposed earlier for *seems* except that it has NP[NFORM,NORM] instead of a variable as the value of the two SUBJ features. It indicates that the verb's complement is an infinitival VP that requires a normal NP subject and that its requires a normal NP subject itself. Given this category, we will exclude examples like the following:

(56) ∗ Stefan tried to be easy to please Maja.

Here, we have an infinitival VP that requires a dummy *it* as its subject.

Turning to *persuaded*, we can propose the following category:

(57)

$$
\begin{bmatrix}
\text{SUBCAT}\langle
\begin{bmatrix}
V \\
VP \\
\text{+INF} \\
\text{SUBJ,} \quad NP \\
\qquad\qquad [\text{NFORM,NORM}]
\end{bmatrix}
,\;
\begin{matrix}
NP \\
[\text{NFORM,NORM}]
\end{matrix}
\;\rangle \\[4pt]
\text{SUBJ, } NP
\end{bmatrix}
$$

This is like the category we proposed in chapter 6 for *expect* that it has NP[NFORM,NORM] and not NP[NFORM,α] as the second item in the SUBCAT list and as the value of the SUBJ feature within the first item. It indicates that the verb's first complement is a normal NP and it's second complement an infinitival VP that requires a normal subject. With this category, examples like the following are excluded:

(58) * Stefan persuaded Ben to be easy to please Maja.

Here, as in (56), we have an infinitival VP that requires a dummy *it* as its subject as the second complement.

There is, however, a further complication here. If the infinitive requires a singular subject, the controller must be singular, and if the infinitive requires a plural subject, the controller must be plural. The following illustrate:

(59) $\left\{ \begin{matrix} \text{He} \\ \text{* They} \end{matrix} \right\}$ tried to be a gentleman.

(60) We persuaded $\left\{ \begin{matrix} \text{him} \\ \text{* them} \end{matrix} \right\}$ to be a gentleman.

(61) $\left\{ \begin{matrix} \text{They} \\ \text{* He} \end{matrix} \right\}$ tried to be gentlemen.

(62) We persuaded $\left\{ \begin{matrix} \text{them} \\ \text{* him} \end{matrix} \right\}$ to be gentlemen.

To accommodate this data, we can revise (55) and (57) as follows:

(63)

$$
\begin{bmatrix}
\text{SUBCAT}\langle
\begin{bmatrix}
V \\
VP \\
\text{+INF} \\
\text{SUBJ,} \quad
\begin{bmatrix}
NP \\
\text{NFORM,NORM} \\
\text{NUMB,}\alpha
\end{bmatrix}
\end{bmatrix}
\;\rangle \\[4pt]
\text{SUBJ,} \quad
\begin{bmatrix}
NP \\
\text{NFORM,NORM} \\
\text{NUMB,}\alpha
\end{bmatrix}
\end{bmatrix}
$$

(64)

$$
\begin{bmatrix}
\text{SUBCAT}\langle
\begin{bmatrix}
V \\
VP \\
\text{+INF} \\
\text{SUBJ,} \quad
\begin{bmatrix}
NP \\
\text{NFORM,NORM} \\
\text{NUMB,}\alpha
\end{bmatrix}
\end{bmatrix}
,\;
\begin{bmatrix}
NP \\
\text{NFORM,NORM} \\
\text{NUMB,}\alpha
\end{bmatrix}
\;\rangle \\[4pt]
\text{SUBJ, } NP
\end{bmatrix}
$$

In (63), we have added the feature specification [NUMB,α] to the value of the two SUBJ features, and in (64), we have added this feature specification to the second item within the value of SUBCAT and to the value of SUBJ within the first item. When these categories appear in trees, the α's will be instantiated as either SING or PLUR and the controller will be singular if the infinitive requires a singular subject and plural if the infinitive requires a plural subject.

(63) and (64) are quite complex, but they are rather minor modifications of categories that are required elsewhere. Thus, it is quite easy to accommodate the central cases of control within HPSG.

11.5 Some further data

As in the last two chapters, there is some further data that we should consider here.

In the last chapter, we saw that while typical raising sentences involve an infinitival complement, there are also raising sentences with other sorts of complement. Thus, many raising sentences that contain an infinitive have reduced counterparts with an AP. The following illustrate this:

(65) a. Stefan seemed to be popular.
  b. Stefan seemed popular.

Control sentences do not have reduced counterparts in this way. For example, we do not have (66)b. as a reduced counterpart of (66)a.

(66) a. Stefan tried to be popular.
  b. * Stefan tried popular.

We do, however, find control sentences with non-infinitival complements. Consider the following:

(67) Ben $\left\{ \begin{array}{l} \text{considered} \\ \text{remembered} \\ \text{imagined} \end{array} \right\}$ being late.

Notice that the following are impossible:

(68) * It $\left\{ \begin{array}{l} \text{considered} \\ \text{remembered} \\ \text{imagined} \end{array} \right\}$ being easy to please Maja.

It is clear, then, that we are not dealing with raising sentences here. Hence, it seems reasonable to regard these as control sentences.

In earlier discussion, we were concerned exclusively with controlled complements. There are also controlled adjuncts. Consider the bracketed strings in the following:

(69) Stefan came early [to get a good seat]
(70) Ben arrived [drunk]
(71) Debbie left [without saying anything]

In (69), it is understood that Stefan intended that he, Stefan, should get a good seat. Hence, *Stefan* is the controller. Similarly, in (70), we understand that it is Ben who was drunk. Here, then, *Ben* is the controller. Finally, in (71), we understand that it is Debbie who didn't say anything. Hence, *Debbie* is the controller.

In the above examples, we have VP adjuncts. It is also possible to have controlled NP adjuncts. Here, we have the following:

(72) We need someone [to look after the garden]
(73) He painted some men [playing cards]
(74) I know a man [wanted by the police]

In (72) the controller is *someone*, in (73) it is *some men*, and in (74) it is *a man*.

11.6 Summary

In this chapter, we have been concerned with control sentences, a type of sentence which sometimes looks very similar to raising sentences. We began in 11.2 by looking at the basic data, paying particular attention to the ways in which control sentences differ from raising sentences even when they look similar. Then, in 11.3, we looked at the GB approach to control sentences, highlighting the central role of the empty pronominal anaphor, PRO. In 11.4, we considered how control sentences can be analyzed within PSG. Here, as in our PSG account of raising sentences, we made crucial use of a particular type of complex category. Finally, in 11.5, we looked at some further data, including controlled adjuncts.

Notes

In Chapter 6, we cited *it* in examples like the following, which we might refer to as weather *it*, as an example of a dummy subject:

(1) It rained all day.

Notice now that we have sentences like the following:

(2) It tried to rain.

This is unexpected if weather *it* is a dummy. Compare example (7) in the text. Equally unexpected is the following cited in Chomsky (1981: 324):

(3) It sometimes rains after snowing.

Chomsky suggests on the basis of this example that weather *it* is a quasi-argument, an element with some of the properties of dummies and some of the properties of normal NP's.

Deciding whether a sentence is a raising sentence or a control sentence is sometimes more difficult than the discussion in the text suggests. Consider, for example, the following:

(4) Ben is certain to be late.

This seems to be related both to (5) and to (6).

(5) It is certain that Ben will be late.
(6) Ben is certain that he will be late.

The former suggests that (4) is a raising sentence, but the latter suggests that it is a control sentence. What can we make of this data? Notice that there is an important difference between (4) and (5) on the one hand and (6) on the other. (4) and (5) do not attribute certainty to Ben, but (6) does. Hence, while (7) and (8) are fine, (9) is unacceptable.

(7) Ben is certain to be late, but he doesn't know it.
(8) It is certain that Ben will be late, but he doesn't know it.
(9) * Ben is certain that he will be late, but he doesn't know it.

This suggests that (4) is in fact related to (5) and not to (6) and hence that it is a raising sentence. The following support this conclusion:

(10) It is certain to be easy to please Maja.
(11) There is certain to be a flaw in the argument.

It seems, then, that we have two rather different uses of *certain*.

A further point to note about *certain* is that it gives us sentences that look like counterexamples to the observation in the text that the infinitive in a raising sentence is never preceded by *whether* or a *wh*-phrase. We have examples like the following:

(12) Ben isn't certain whether to do it.
(13) Ben isn't certain what to do.

It is clear, however, that these are not raising sentences but sentences rather like (6). Notice that the following are impossible:

(14) * It isn't certain whether to be easy to please Maja.
(15) * It isn't certain what to be easy to please.

An important difference between verbs whose object is a controller and verbs whose subject is a controller is that the latter do not allow passives. Thus, while (16)a. has the passive counterpart in (16)b., (17)a. does not have (17)b. as a passive counterpart.

(16) a. Ben persuaded Debbie to do the shopping.
     b. Debbie was persuaded by Ben to do the shopping.
(17) a. Ben promised Debbie to do the shopping.
     b. * Debbie was promised by Ben to do the shopping.

The view that PRO is both an anaphor and a pronominal is not universally accepted within GB. An alternative view is that it is sometimes an anaphor and sometimes a pronominal but never both. Roughly, the proposal is that it is a pure anaphor in control sentences that resemble raising sentences or sentences that would be analyzed within GB as involving exceptional clauses, e.g. (1) and (2) and (19) in the text, and a pure pronominal in other kinds of control sentence. Important references here are Bouchard (1984), Koster (1984, 1986) and Manzini (1983). For textbook discussion of the GB approach to control, see Haegeman (1991, 5.).

The view that the superficially subjectless infinitives in raising and control sentences are 'bare' VP's was first advanced in Brame (1975, 1976). A number of arguments against this view and in favour of a clausal analysis are presented in Koster and May (1982). One of the main arguments involves the fact that superficially infinitives have a similar distribution to ordinary clauses. However, this is also expected on a bare VP analysis if S and VP are both V[SUBCAT,⟨⟩]. Borsley (1984) and Borsley (1986) argue for a bare VP analysis of the infinitives in Welsh control and raising sentences.

The HPSG approach to control is outlined in Pollard and Sag (forthcoming). The LFG approach to control is presented in Bresnan (1982c).

Ross (1969) suggested that the modals *may* and *must* are control verbs where they have a root or deontic interpretation, i.e. where they refer not to what is possible and what is necessary but to what is allowed and what is required. The following argue against this position:

(18) It may be admitted that we are behind schedule.
(19) It must be made clear that she isn't working hard enough.

Both these examples can have a root interpretation, but both are clearly raising sentences.

We observed in the notes to the last chapter that there are no NP's corresponding to raising sentences. There are, however, NP's corresponding to control sentences. For example, corresponding to the sentences in (20) and (21), we have the NP's in (22) and (23).

(20) Ben attempted to follow the instructions.
(21) Ben is eager to make a good impression.
(22) Ben's attempt to the follow the instructions.
(23) Ben's eagerness to make a good impression.

This is a further difference between raising sentences and control sentences.

Exercises

Exercise 1

Discuss using relevant data whether each of the following is a raising sentence or control sentence:

(1) They failed to come up to our expectations.
(2) We were pleased to be invited.
(3) She is sure to make a good impression.

(4) He intends to finish early.
(5) They were desperate to be successful.
(6) He proved to be a major problem.
(7) We planned to get away by 8.

Exercise 2

Discuss whether each of the following is a control sentence or the kind of sentence that is analyzed within GB as involving an exceptional clause.

(1) I may get him to read this book.
(2) We forced them to rethink their position.
(3) They allowed us to go home early.
(4) We asked them to leave us alone.
(5) We judged him to be the most promising newcomer.
(6) I expect them to work harder.
(7) We urged them to get on with it.

Exercise 3

We noted in 11.5 that there are control sentences with a complement involving the 'ing' form of a verb. There are also raising sentences with an 'ing' complement. Discuss which of the following are control sentences and which are raising sentences.

(1) Ben considered giving up.
(2) Debbie continued writing.
(3) I regretted talking to her.
(4) He liked watching old films.
(5) We began preparing the food.
(6) He resented being criticized.
(7) They stopped trying.

Exercise 4

We argued in the last chapter that modals, *be*, and aspectual *have* are raising elements. These are all auxiliaries, so one might suppose that all auxiliaries are raising verbs. However, this is not the case. Discuss which of the auxiliaries in the following are raising verbs and which are control verbs.

(1) We ought to look into this.
(2) I would go there often in my youth.
(3) I would rather stay in bed.
(4) You need not come in today.
(5) He dare not come any closer.
(6) You had better do something about this.

Exercise 5

Give three examples of control sentences and three examples of raising sentences from any language other than English for which you can obtain reliable data. Justify your classification with appropriate examples.

12

Wh-dependencies

12.1 Introduction

We noted in chapter 7 that *wh*-questions provide an important example of sentences involving a noncanonical complement or a noncanonical subject. *Wh*-questions are in fact one of a number of sentence types in which a complement or a subject is missing and in which there is a specific type of higher structure often but not always containing a *wh*-element. This was first emphasized in Chomsky (1977b). I will call the relation betwen the missing complement or subject and the higher structure a *wh*-dependency, and I will call the constructions *wh*-dependency constructions. We can look first at the basic properties of *wh*-questions. Then we can consider how they can be analyzed, first within GB and then within PSG. Finally, we can look at other *wh*-dependency constructions.

12.2 Wh-questions

The central feature of *wh*-questions is that they are much more varied than the other examples of sentences involving abormal complements and subjects that we have considered. One aspect of this is that the *wh*-phrase can have a variety of functions. In passives, the subject functions as the first complement of the passive participle or as the subject of an infinitival complement of the passive participle. (In the latter case, it functions as the first complement as well on PSG analyses.) In raising sentences, the subject functions as the subject of an infinitival complement of the raising verb or adjective. In *wh*-questions, the *wh*-phrase can function as an abnormal complement or an abnormal subject of various kinds. We can illustrate with the following:

(1) Who did Stefan see?
(2) Who did Stefan consider to be a fool?
(3) Who did Stefan give the book to?
(4) Who do you think saw Stefan?

In (1), *who* functions as the object of a verb in much the same way as the subject of a passive does. In (2), *who* functions as the subject of an infinitive, again like the subject of a passive. In (3), *who* functions as the object of a preposition in a way that is not possible with the subject of a passive. Finally, in (4), *who* functions as the subject of a finite VP, again in a way that is not possible with the subject of a passive. We have similar data with subordinate *wh*-questions, as the following illustrate:

(5) I asked who Stefan saw.
(6) I asked who Stefan considered to be a fool.
(7) I asked who Stefan gave the book to.
(8) I asked who you thought saw Stefan.

A second aspect of the varied nature of *wh*-questions is that whereas the subjects of passives and raising sentences are normally NP's, *wh*-phrases can easily be other categories. The following examples, in which the *wh*-phrases are bracketed, illustrate this:

(9) [Which man] did you talk to?
(10) [To which man] did you talk?
(11) [How ill] has Stefan been?
(12) [How frequently] did Stefan see Maja?

In (9) the *wh*-phrase is an NP, in (10) it is a PP, in (11) it is an AP, and in (12) it is an ADVP (Adverb Phrase). The fact that a *wh*-phrase can be both an NP and a PP means that there are often two different *wh*-questions that are equivalent. (9) and (10) illustrate this. The following provide a further illustration:

(13) Who does he rely on?
(14) On whom does he rely?

A further point that we should note is that there are both simple *wh*-questions involving a single clause and complex *wh*-questions involving more than one clause. In the complex cases, at least in English, any number of clause boundaries can intervene between the *wh*-phrase and the associated lexical head or predicate. The following illustrate:

(15) a. Who do you think Stefan saw?
     b. Who do you think Stefan said he saw?
     c. Who do you think Stefan said he imagined that he saw?

In (15)a. we have one clause boundary between the *wh*-phrase and the associated verb, in (15)b. we have two, and in (15)c. we have three. Clearly, we could have even more complex examples. Because of this, *wh*-dependencies are standardly known as unbounded dependencies within PSG.

12.3 The GB approach

We can now consider how *wh*-questions can be analyzed within GB. Within a transformational framework, the ordinary obvious structure of a *wh*-question will be derived from a more abstract structure by a movement process. This process is standardly referred to as *wh*-movement. If we assume that movement processes leave behind traces, we might have the following derivation for the subordinate clause in (5):

(16)

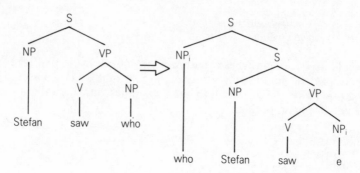

The GB derivation is, however, somewhat different. For recent GB, *wh*-movement is a case of substitution, i.e. movement into an empty 'landing site', just like NP-movement. Chomsky (1986) proposes that COMP is the head of S' and that it takes an S as its complement. Within this analysis, the fact that COMP precedes S is a consequence of the fact that heads precede their complements in English. Chomsky also proposes that COMP has an associated specifier position, comparable to the determiner position within NP's, and that this is a landing site for moved *wh*-phrases. Given these assumptions, we have not (16) but the following:

(17)

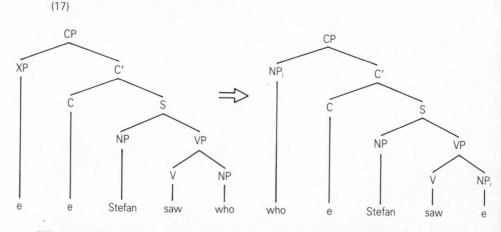

Why should we believe that clause-initial *wh*-phrases are in this CP-specifier position? The simplest evidence for this proposal comes from various languages in which a *wh*-phrase can be followed by an overt complementizer. The following illustrate:

(18) Es is no   ned G'wieß wea daß   kummt.
     it is yet   no sure   who that   comes
     'It is not yet sure who will come.'
        (Bavarian – Bayer 1983, 25)
(19) Ce   al   dhiol an   domhan?
     who   COMP   sold the   world
     'Who sold the world?'
        (Modern Irish – McCloskey 1979, 52)

(20) Jeg lurer pa hvem som   ser   mest svensk ut.
     I   wonder who that   looks   most Swedish
     'I wonder who looks most Swedish.'
     (Norwegian – Taraldsen 1978, 633)

It is also assumed in GB that pre-subject auxiliaries are in the COMP position. The main evidence for this is that they do not co-occur with complementizers. The following provide a partial illustration:

(21) He wondered
$\left\{ \begin{array}{l} \text{would she like him} \\ \text{whether she would like him} \\ \text{* whether would she like him} \end{array} \right\}$

(22)
$\left\{ \begin{array}{l} \text{If he had been there} \\ \text{Had he been there} \\ \text{* If had he been there} \end{array} \right\}$, I would have talked to him.

Thus, for GB the fronting of auxiliaries is a substitution process and not an adjunction process, as assumed in 8.4.

A further point we should note here is that it seems reasonable to assume that there is no θ-role associated with the CP specifier position. Given this assumption, *wh*-movement will not give rise to an NP with more than one θ-role and hence will not violate the principle, discussed in chapters 9 and 10, that no NP can have more than one θ-role.

One question we should ask here is what happens with examples like the following?

(23) Who saw Stefan?

It looks as if *who* is just an ordinary subject here. It is generally assumed, however, that the *wh*-phrases in such examples are moved just like the *wh*-phrases in the kind of example we considered earlier. Given GB assumptions, this means that we will have derivations like the following:

(24)

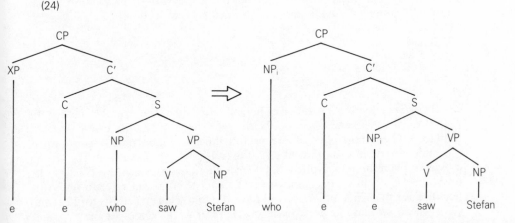

Here, we have a movement process which changes the structure of the sentence but does not change the linear order of the words it contains. It is rather like the reanalysis process introduced in 9.6. Such movement is termed 'vacuous movement'.

Another question that we should consider is: how should complex examples like those in (15) be analyzed? There are two possibilities. Either the *wh*-phrase is moved directly to its surface position or it is via the initial position in each containing clause. In the case of (15)a., the two possibilities can be represented as follows:

(25) Who$_i$ do [s you think [cp [s Stefan saw e$_i$]]]

(26) Who$_i$ do [s you think [cp e$_i$ [sStefan saw e$_i$]]]

Which is the right analysis? For various reasons, one of which we will highlight in the next chapter, it is assumed within GB that the second analysis is the right one. This is standardly known as the successive cyclic analysis.

A final question that we should ask is: what is the status of the traces in *wh*-questions? We saw earlier that traces in passives and raising sentences, which are known as NP-traces, are analyzed as anaphors. It is clear that the traces in *wh*-questions, which are known as *wh*-traces (or variables), cannot be anaphors. This is because they are not A-bound in their governing category, as anaphors are required to be. In (17), the trace is governed by the preceding verb given the assumption that a lexical head governs its complements. Hence, the governing category is the single S. In (24), the trace is governed by the agreement features of the following verb given the assumption that the agreement features of a finite verb governs its subject. Again, then, the governing category is the single S. Thus, in both (17) and (24), the trace is not A-bound in its governing category. In fact, in both examples, it is not A-bound at all. In both, the trace is coindexed with the *wh*-phrase, but the *wh*-phrase is not in an A-position. Rather, it is in what is known as a non-A- or Ā (pronounced A-bar) position.

If *wh*-traces are not anaphors, what are they? The answer is that they are grouped together with non-pronominal NP's as a class of 'R-expressions'. The following examples provide motivation for this classification:

(27) Who thinks he is clever?
(28) Stefan thinks he is clever.
(29) Who does he think is clever?
(30) He thinks Stefan is clever.

In (27), *who* and *he* can be the same person, and so can *Stefan* and *he* in (28). In (29), however, *who* and *he* cannot be the same person, and nor can *Stefan* and *he* in (30). The impossibility of interpreting the *wh*-element and the pronoun as the same person in examples like (29) is commonly referred to as the strong crossover phenomenon. Notice that the *wh*-element has been moved across the pronoun. How can we account for these facts? If NP's that refer to the same person have the same index, we will have the following structures for (27) and (28), where *who* and *he* and *Stefan* and *he* refer to the same person:

(31) Who$_i$ [se$_i$ thinks [cp [s he$_i$ is clever]]]
(32) Stefan$_i$ thinks [cp [s he$_i$ is clever]]

One point to note about these structures is that *he* is A-bound by the trace in (31) and by *Stefan* in (32). Both the trace and *Stefan* are c-commanding categories in an A-position. Turning to (29) and (30), if *who* and *he* and *he* and *Stefan* referred to the same person, we would have the following structures:

(33) Who$_i$ does [$_S$ he$_i$ think [$_{CP}$ [$_S$ e$_i$ is clever]]]
(34) He$_i$ thinks [$_{CP}$ [$_S$ Stefan$_i$ is clever]]

The important point about these structures is that the trace is A-bound by *he* in (33) and *Stefan* is A-bound by *he* in (34). In both, *he* is a c-commanding category in an A-position. We can rule out the structures in (33) and (34) and thus explain why the crucial interpretations are not possible by assuming the following principle:

(35) An R-expression must be A-free.

Remember that a category is A-free if and only if it is not coindexed with a c-commanding category in an A-position such as subject, object or object of a preposition. (35) and the conditions on anaphors and pronominals introduced in chapters 9, 10 and 11 constitute what is known as Binding theory, one of the main components or subtheories of GB.

With the introduction of *wh*-trace, we now have four different empty NP's: *pro*, NP-trace, PRO and *wh*-trace. These can be classified in terms of the features p (pronominal) and a (anaphoric) as follows:

(36)

	+p	−p
+a	PRO	NP−t
−a	*pro*	*wh*−t

One point we should note is that all these empty NP's except PRO have overt counterparts. The overt counterparts of NP-trace are reflexives, the overt counterparts of *pro* are ordinary pronouns, and the overt counterparts of *wh*-trace are non-pronominal NP's.

There is one further point that we should highlight here. This is that *wh*-movement is only possible from positions to which Case is assigned. The following illustrate:

(37) Who$_i$ was e$_i$ arrested e$_i$?
(38) Who$_i$ e$_i$ seemed e$_i$ to be best?
(39) * Who$_i$ was it arrested e$_i$?
(40) * Who$_i$ did it seem e$_i$ to be best?

In (37) and (38), we have NP-movement and then *wh*-movement from a position to which Case is assigned. In (39) and (40), we have just *wh*-movement from positions to which no Case is assigned. Why is this impossible? The obvious suggestion is that it is a consequence of the Case filter, discussed in chapters 9 and 10. This requires an NP with phonetic content to have Case. Suppose now that we make the following assumption:

(41) A *wh*-NP inherits Case from its trace.

Given this, the *wh*-NP's in (37) and (38) will have Case since their traces are in positions to which Case is assigned, but those in (39) and (40) will not since their traces are in positions to which no case is assigned and will therefore violate the Case filter. Here, then, we seem to have a straightforward account of the restriction of *wh*-movement to positions to which Case is assigned. We will see, however, in section 5 that this is not entirely satisfactory.

12.4 The PSG approach

Within PSG, sentences have only the ordinary obvious structure. But what exactly is the ordinary obvious structure of a *wh*-question? It is not assumed in PSG that *wh*-questions are CP's. However, it has generally been assumed that they involve empty categories like the traces of GB. Given these assumptions, we will have something like the following structure for the subordinate clause in (5):

(42)

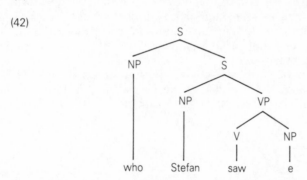

Assuming such a structure, we need to somehow make the empty category sensitive to the presence of the *wh*-phrase higher up the tree. Within both versions of PSG, a feature called SLASH is employed for this purpose. (The name arises from the fact that early work uses categories of the form X/Y in this context.) In GPSG, this feature takes a category as its value and indicates that a constituent contains an empty category of some kind. Assuming this feature, we can expand the above tree as follows:

(43)

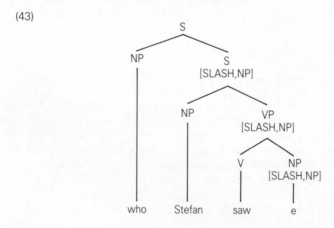

Here, we have a chain of SLASH feature specifications connecting the *wh*-phrase with the associated empty category. One point to note is that it is not only the constituents that contain an empty category that are marked [SLASH,NP]. The empty category itself is also marked in this way.

How can we allow structure like (43)? It is quite easy to provide for the top and bottom of the chain of SLASH features. For the top of the chain, all we need is the following rule:

(44) S → Y, S[SLASH,Y]

This is rather like the rule proposed in chapter 6 for subject-predicate structures. For the bottom of the chain, we can propose the following:

(45) XP[SLASH,XP] → e

This will allow not just empty NP's but also empty PP's, AP's and AdvP's, which are necessary for examples like (10)–(12).

The middle of the chain of SLASH features is a more complex matter. Here, we have the following local trees:

(46)

(a)
```
          S
      [SLASH,NP]
       /\
   NP      VP
        [SLASH,NP]
```

(b)
```
         VP
     [SLASH,NP]
      /\
   V      NP
       [SLASH,NP]
```

We need to allow trees like these but we need to rule out trees like the following:

(47)

(a)
```
        S
      /\
   NP      VP
        [SLASH,NP]
```

(b)
```
        VP
      /\
   V      NP
       [SLASH,NP]
```

(48)

(a)
```
          S
      [SLASH,NP]
       /\
    NP      VP
```

(b)
```
          VP
      [SLASH,NP]
       /\
    V      VP
```

In (47)a. and b., a daughter is identified as containing an empty NP but the mother is not identified as containing an empty NP. In (48)a. and b., the mother is identified as containing an empty NP but none of the daughters is identified as containing an empty NP. We can rule out structures like these by adopting the following principle:

(49) a. If a SLASH feature specification appears within some category, then it must also appear within its mother.
b. If a SLASH feature specification appears within some category, then it must also appear within one of its daughters.

(49)a. rules out trees like those in (47) while (49)b. rules out trees like those in (48).

As it stands, however, the principle is not satisfactory. The first clause rules out the topmost local tree in (43), which is the following:

(50)

How can we allow this while ruling out the trees in (47)? It is in fact quite easy to distinguish the two cases. Notice that the SLASH feature specification in (50) is required to be there since it is present in the licensing rule, (44). This is not the case with the SLASH feature specifications in the trees in (47). (47)a. is a subject-predicate structure and (47)b. is a head-complement structure. Neither the subject-predicate rule nor the head-complement rule requires a daughter in the structures that it licenses to have a SLASH feature specification. Thus, we can allow (50) while ruling out the trees in (47) if we revise the first clause of (49) as follows:

(51) If a SLASH feature specification appears within some category, then it must also appear within its mother unless it is required by the licensing rule.

With the first clause revised in this way, the principle provides a largely satisfactory account of the distribution of SLASH feature specifications.

An obvious question here is: is there any other feature that behaves like SLASH? The answer to this is yes. The evidence comes from *wh*-phrases. We can look at the following:

(52) To whom did you talk?

The *wh*-phrase is *to whom* and it is a *wh*-phrase because it contains the *wh*-word *whom*. If we mark *wh*-elements as [+WH], it will contain the following local tree:

(53)

We need to allow this but not trees like the following:

(54)

(55)

With trees like (54) we would be failing to identify phrases that contain a *wh*-element as *wh*-phrases, and with trees like (55) we would be identifying phrases that do not contain a *wh*-element as *wh*-phrases. We can allow trees like (53) while ruling out trees like (54) and (55) if we extend the principle to WH. It is easy quite easy to do this. Following GPSG, we can call SLASH and WH FOOT features. We can then reformulate the principle as follows:

(56) a. If a FOOT feature specification appears within some category, then it must also appear within its mother unless it is required by the licensing rule.
 b. If a FOOT feature specification appears within some category, then it must also appear within one of its daughters.

We can call this the FOOT Feature Principle.

There are two further points that we should note about the PSG approach to *wh*-questions. The first concerns examples like (23), which involve vacuous movement in GB. In PSG, it has generally been assumed that these do not involve an empty category, i.e. that we have structures like (57) and not structures like (58).

(57)

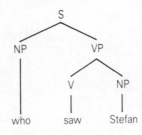

(58)

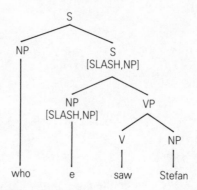

The second point concerns examples like (15). For PSG, there are no intermediate empty categories in such examples. (15)a. will involve something like
the following structure:

(59)

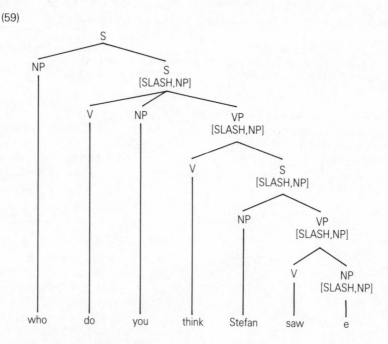

12.5 Other *wh*-dependency constructions

We noted at the outset that *wh*-questions are just one of a number of what can
be called *wh*-dependency constructions. We can turn now to some other
examples.

We can look first at relative clauses and in particular at the bracketed strings
in the following:

(60) the man [who Stefan saw]

(61) the man [who Stefan considered to be a fool]
(62) the man [who Stefan gave the book to]
(63) the man [who I thought saw Stefan]

These examples are identical to the subordinate *wh*-questions in (5)–(8). As in the *wh*-questions, we have a *wh*-element with a variety of functions. Within GB, the natural assumption is that they involve movement in just the same way as *wh*-questions. Within PSG, the natural assumption is that they involve a chain of SLASH feature specifications just like *wh*-questions.

We can look next at the bracketed strings in the following:

(64) the man [that Stefan saw]
(65) the man [that Stefan considered to be a fool]
(66) the man [that Stefan gave the book to]
(67) the man [that I thought saw Stefan]

In these examples, there is no *wh*-element. *That* appears to play the same role here as the *wh*-element in (60)–(63). There is evidence, however, that it is a rather different element. A *wh*-word can be part of a larger *wh*-phrase, as the following illustrate:

(68) the man [to whom we talked]
(69) the man [on whose help we relied]

This is not possible with *that*, as the following show:

(70) * the man [to that we talked]
(71) * the man [on that's help we relied]

Because of such contrasts, it is generally accepted that *that* in relative clauses is not an element like *who* but a complementizer, i.e. that it is the same element as *that* in an example like (71).

(72) I think that Ben saw him

If this view is accepted, then the examples in (64)–(67) do not involve any overt element that functions as an abnormal complement or an abnormal subject.

How, then, should these examples be analyzed? Within GB, it is proposed that such examples involve movement of an empty *wh*-element (often referred to as an empty operator). Thus, (64) has the S-structure in (73).

(73) the man [CP ei that [S Stefan saw ei]]

Within PSG, there is no need for a specific category to appear at the top of the chain of SLASH feature specifications. Hence, there is no need to assume that there is an empty *wh*-element in these examples.

A further type of relative clause is exemplified by the following:

(74) the man [Stefan saw]
(75) the man [Stefan considered to be a fool]
(76) the man [Stefan gave the book to]
(77) the man [I thought saw Stefan]

These are just like (64)–(67) except that they lack the *that* and they can be analyzed in the same way.

Other sentences that involve a *wh*-dependency are clefts and pseudo-clefts. The following are typical clefts:

(78) It is Ben [who she loves]
(79) It is Ben [that she loves]
(80) It is Ben [she loves]

The bracketed strings in these examples are identical to relative clauses. Within GB, we will have movement of an overt *wh*-element in (78) and movement of an empty *wh*-element in (79) and (80). Within PSG, we will have a chain of SLASH feature specifications, with a *wh*-element at the top in (78) but not in (79) and (80). The following is a typical pseudo-cleft:

(81) [What she likes] is beer.

The bracketed string in this example is identical to a subordinate *wh*-question. Again, then, the obvious assumption within GB is that we have movement of a *wh*-element, and the obvious suggestion in PSG is that we have a chain of SLASH feature specifications.

A final class of sentences that we can consider are what are known as 'tough' sentences since they involve one of a small class of adjectives, including *tough*. The following illustrate:

(82) Ben is easy to like.
(83) Ben is easy to talk to.

In (82), the complement of *like* is missing, and in (83), *to* has no complement. The following show that not just any adjective can appear in this construction.

(84) * Ben is certain to like.
(85) * Ben is certain to talk to.

Again within GB, we will have movement of an empty *wh*-element giving us the following S-structures:

(86) Ben is easy [CP e$_i$ [S PRO to like e$_i$]]
(87) Ben is easy [cp e$_i$ [S PRO to talk to e$_i$]]

Again within PSG, we will have a chain of SLASH feature specifications. There is, however, something of a problem here. At the top of the chain, we will have the following local tree:

(88)

AP
├── A
└── VP
    [SLASH,NP]

This is a head-complement structure and the head-complement rule does not require a SLASH feature specification to appear on a daughter in the structures it licenses. It seems, then, that we have a violation of the first clause of the FOOT Feature Principle, which we repeat here.

(89) If a FOOT feature specification appears within some category, then it must also appear within its mother unless it is required by the licensing rule.

It is, however, fairly easy to eliminate this problem. *Easy* is an item that requires a VP[SLASH NP] as its complement. It will have something like the following category:

(90)
$$
\begin{bmatrix} \text{SUBCAT,} \langle & \overset{A}{\underset{[\text{SLASH,NP}]}{\text{VP}}} & \rangle \end{bmatrix}
$$

Given this category, the Subcategorization Principle will require the SLASH feature specification in (88). Hence, we can allow this structure if we revise the first clause of the FOOT Feature Principle as follows:

(91) If a FOOT feature specification appears within some category, then it must also appear within its mother unless it is required by the licensing rule or the Subcategorization Principle.

There is a further matter that we should consider here. We noted in our discussion of the GB approach in section 3 that *wh*-movement is only possible from positions to which Case is assigned and we showed that the Case-filter seems to offer a simple explanation for this fact. We can now see that this is too simple. Consider the following:

(92) the man [$_{CP}$ e$_i$ that [$_s$ e$_i$ was arrested e$_i$]]
(93) the man [$_{CP}$ e$_i$ that [$_{CP}$ e$_i$ seemed e$_i$ to be best]]
(94) * the man [$_{CP}$ e$_i$ that [$_s$ it was arrested e$_i$]]
(95) * the man [$_{CP}$ e$_i$ that [$_s$ it seemed e$_i$ to be best]]

For GB, these examples involve movement of an empty *wh*-element. In (92) and (93) we have NP-movement and then *wh*-movement from a position to which Case is assigned, while in (94) and (95) we have just *wh*-movement from positions to which no Case is assigned. Since the moved element is empty, the contrast between (92) and (93) and (94) and (95) cannot be a consequence of the Case filter. How, then, can we explain the contrast. One possibility is that the Case-filter should be replaced by the following:

(96) An NP that has a θ-role must have Case.

If the empty *wh*-element in various constructions has a θ-role, then it must have Case even though it has no phonetic content. Hence, (96) will account for the contrast between (92) and (93) and (94) and (95). (96), however faces some problems. Consider firstly the following:

(97) Ben tried to please Debbie.

The infinitive here will have a PRO subject. This will have a θ-role, but it has no Case. As we saw in chapter 11, a notable feature of PRO is that it appears in a position to which no Case is assigned. On the face of it, then, this violates the revised Case filter. Consider now the following:

(98) * It seems it to be raining.

Here, the second *it* is a dummy *it* in a position to which no Case is assigned. Since dummy *it* does not have a θ-role, the revised Case filter will not require it to have Case. Hence, it will fail to rule out this example. It seems, then, that this is something of a problem area for GB.

12.6 Summary

We have been concerned in this chapter with *wh*-questions and more generally with what we have called *wh*-dependency constructions. We began in 12.2 by looking at the basic properties of *wh*-questions. Then, in 12.3, we looked at the GB approach, highlighting in particular the successive cyclic analysis of complex *wh*-questions and the assumption that *wh*-traces are R-expressions. Next, in 12.4, we considered the PSG approach. Here, we introduced the SLASH feature and the FOOT Feature Principle which governs its distribution. Finally, in 12.5, we looked at some other *wh*-dependency constructions and discussed how they could be handled in both GB and PSG.

Notes

An important feature of some *wh*-dependencies in some languages are what are known as resumptive pronouns, pronouns occupying positions where one would expect a gap. They play a limited role in English, but the following example, in which the resumptive pronoun is italicized, is acceptable for some speakers.

(1) That is a problem which we wondered whether *it* would ever be solved.

Resumptive pronouns play a much fuller role in some other languages. Thus, the following, in which the resumptive pronoun is again italicized, is an ordinary Welsh example:

(2) y   dyn   na   welais   i *ef*
    the man   NEG saw-1SG I he
    'the man that I didn't see'

The view that pre-subject auxiliaries are in COMP stems from den Besten (1978), Koopman (1983) and Chomsky (1986).

A number of arguments for successive cyclicity are summarized in Radford (1988, 10.8.). Postal (1972) argues against successive cyclicity on the grounds that it predicts that sentences like (5) should be possible as well as sentences like (3) and (4).

(3) Who do you think they talked to?

(4) To whom do you think they talked?
(5) * Whom do you think to they talked?

In (3) we have moved *who* to clause-initial position, and in (4) we have moved *to whom*. On the successive cyclic analysis, both have been moved via initial position in the subordinate clause. Postal points out that it is not clear why it should not be possible to move *to whom* to initial position in the subordinate clause and then to move just *whom* to initial position in the main clause leaving *to*. For one possible response to this argument, see Hornstein and Weinberg (1981).

An important question within GB is what determines whether an empty NP is *pro*, NP-trace, PRO, or *wh*-trace. This question has had considerable attention. For textbook discussion, see Lasnik and Uriagereka (1988, 3.)

The term crossover, introduced in 12.3, originates in Postal (1971), in which a variety of ungrammatical strings were ruled out by a principle restricting the movement of certain phrases over certain other phrases.

Although it is not generally assumed in PSG that *wh*-questions contain empty complementizers, Borsley (1989) shows that the GB view that COMP is the head of S' and that clause-initial *wh*-phrases occupy a pre-COMP specifier position can be incorporated into a version of HPSG.

SLASH and WH are called BINDING features in Pollard and Sag (1988) and the principle that governs their distribution is called the Binding Inheritance Principle. They are called NONLOCAL features in Pollard and Sag (forthcoming) and the principle is called the NONLOCAL Feature Principle. The HPSG approach to *wh*-dependencies is set out in detail in Pollard and Sag (forthcoming).

The LFG approach to *wh*-dependencies is discussed in Kaplan and Zaenen (1989).

For detailed discussion of relative *that*, see Van der Auwera (1985).
Two other important *wh*-dependency constructions are topicalization sentences and comparative and equative complements. (6)–(8) illustrate the former, and (9)–(12) illustrate the latter.

(6) That man nobody can stand.
(7) That man nobody will talk to.
(8) That man nobody thinks will do it.
(9) He is more intelligent [than she was]
(10) He is more intelligent [than they say she was]
(11) He is as intelligent [as she was]
(12) He is as intelligent [as they say she was]

'Tough' sentences differ from other *wh*-dependency sentences in important ways. Most notably, the dependency cannot cross the boundary of a finite clause. Thus, while (13) and (14) are fine, (15) and (16) are ungrammatical:

(13) Who do you think that Maja likes.
(14) Who do you think likes Maja.

(15) * Stefan is easy to think that Maja likes.
(16) * Stefan is easy to think likes Maja.

The GB approach to 'tough' sentences is subjected to critical scrutiny in Jones (1983).

For discussion of the attempt to link Case with θ-roles introduced in 12.5, see Bouchard (1984), Davis (1986) and Lasnik and Uriagereka (1988, 6.1.).

Exercises

Exercise 1

Provide GB derivations with D-structures, S-structures and intermediate structures for the following examples:

(1) Who did you say reported the crime?
(2) Which book do you think that he looked at?
(3) What do they expect that he will do?

Exercise 2

Provide PSG trees involving the feature SLASH for each of the following examples:

(1) Who is she talking to?
(2) What are you trying to do?
(3) What did he give to her?
(4) How long do you think the book is?
(5) What did he expect to break?

Exercise 3

We assume in Chapters 9, 10 and 11 that the GB condition on anaphora applies at S-structure. Show how the following example poses a problem for this assumption:

(1) Which picture of himself does Ben like most?

Exercise 4

The following Polish examples contain relative clauses introduced by a word which we can translate as 'what'. Discuss how these relative clauses differ from English relative clauses introduced by a *wh*-expression, and consider whether they should be analyzed in terms *wh*-movement.

(1) ten student, co   pojechał do Warszawy
     the student what   went to Warsaw
     'the student who went to Warsaw'
(2) ten student, co   go   wszyscy bardzo lubią
     the student what   him everyonemuch like
     'the student that everyone likes'

(3) ten student, co   o   nim wszyscy rozmawiali
     the student what about   him everyone talked
     'the student that everyone talked about'
(4) ten student, co   go   chcę   spotkać
     the student what   him   want-1SG   meet
     'the student that I want to meet'
(5) ten student, co   chcę   z   nim porozmawiać
     the student what   want-1SG   with him talk
     'the student that I wanted to talk to'

Exercise 5

The Norwegian examples in (1)–(4) (from Maling (1978)) and the Middle English examples in (5)–(10) (from Grimshaw (1974)) are problematic for the assumption that *wh*-dependencies with no overt *wh*-element involve just the same mechanisms as *wh*-dependencies with an overt *wh*-element. Explain why.

(1) Det er melodien, som ingen visste, hvem skrev.
     'This is the song that noone knew who wrote.'
(2) * Hva visste ingen hvem skrev?
     'What did noone know who wrote?'
(3) Det er melodien, som Jan spurte, hvem skrev.
     'This is the song that Jan asked who wrote.'
(4) * Hva spurte jan hvem skrev?
     'What did John ask who wrote?'
(5) this bok which (that) I see
(6) * this bok which (that) I make mencioun of
(7) this bok of which I make mencioun
(8) this bok that I see
(9) this bok that I make mencioun of
(10) * this bok of that I make mencioun

13

Island constraints

13.1 Introduction

We saw in the last chapter that an important feature of *wh*-questions and *wh*-dependency constructions in general is that they allow a gap in a variety of positions. The following provide a partial illustration:

(1) What did you say?
(2) Who did you talk to?
(3) Who do you think did this?
(4) What do you think he did?

In (1) the gap is in object position, in (2) it is in prepositional object position, in (3) it is in subject position in a subordinate clause, and in (4) it is in object position a insubordinate clause. Although there is this variety, some things are not possible. The gap cannot appear absolutely anywhere. The restrictions are generally known as island constraints and have been a major concern of syntactic theory for almost thirty years. The earliest discussion was in Chomsky (1964) and the first detailed exploration was in Ross (1967). In this chapter, we will look first at the main constraints that have been discussed. Then, we will consider how they have been analyzed, first within GB and then within PSG. Next, we will look at what are known as parasitic gaps, a phenomenon closely related to island constraints. Finally, we will introduce the notion of LF or logical form, an important element of GB.

13.2 The data

We can illustrate one important island constraint by considering *wh*-questions related to the following declarative sentences:

(5) He saw a picture of someone.
(6) A picture of someone was on the table.

Related to (5) we have the following *wh*-question:

(7) Who did he see a picture of?

But we cannot form a *wh*-question related in the same way to (6).

(8) * Who was a picture of on the table?

What is the difference between these two examples? In (7) the gap is within a complement but in (8) it is within a subject. We find a similar contrast when we consider *wh*-questions related to the following declaratives:

(9) It is likely that Stefan saw someone.
(10) That Stefan saw someone is likely.

Related to (9) we have (11), but related to (10) we have the ungrammatical (12).

(11) Who is it likely that Stefan saw?
(12) * Who is that Stefan saw likely?

In (11) the gap is within a complement clause but in (12) it is within a subject clause. It looks, then, as if we cannot have a gap within a subject. However, this is not quite right. Consider the following:

(13) What he did is unknown.

Here, we have a subordinate *wh*-question in subject position. Since it is in subject position, the gap that it contains is within a subject. The difference between this and the earlier ungrammatical examples is that the *wh*-element is also within the subject. In other words, the *wh*-dependency does not cross the boundary of the subject. It seems, then, that it is the crossing of the boundary of a subject that is impossible. We can state this as follows:

(14) A *wh*-dependency cannot cross the boundary of a subject.

Following standard practice, we can call this the Subject Condition.

We can illustrate a second important island constraint by considering *wh*-questions related to the following declarative sentences:

(15) I believe that Stefan saw something.
(16) I believe the claim that Stefan saw something.
(17) I know the man who saw something.

Related to these, we have the following:

(18) What do you believe that Stefan saw?
(19) * What do you know the man who saw?
(20) * What do you believe the claim that Stefan saw?

(18) is similar to (4) and (11) and not surprisingly is perfectly acceptable. Both (19) and (20), however, are quite unacceptable. In both, we have a *wh*-dependency which crosses the boundary of clause and an NP that contains it. In (19), the clause is a relative clause, while in (20) it is a complement. We can state the restriction as follows:

(21) A *wh*-dependency cannot cross the boundary of a clause and an NP that contains it.

Again following standard practice, we can call this the Complex NP Constraint.

We can illustrate another island constraint with the following examples:

(22) I wonder what he did to her.
(23) * Who do you wonder what he did to?

In (22) we have a declarative, and in (23) we have a related *wh*-question. The ungrammaticality of (23) suggests that the following restriction holds.

(24) A *wh*-dependency cannot cross the boundary of a subordinate *wh*-question.

This is generally known as the *Wh*-Island Condition.
A further constraint is illustrated by the following examples:

(25) He criticized Chomsky without reading *Aspects*.
(26) * What did he criticize Chomsky without reading?

Again, in (25) we have a declarative and in (26) we have a related *wh*-question. It seems, then, that we have the following restriction:

(27) A *wh*-dependency cannot cross the boundary of an adverbial expression.

This is normally known as the Adjunct Island Condition.
A rather different constraint is highlighted by the following examples:

(28) I think that Stefan dislikes someone and that Maja hates Ben.
(29) * Who do you think that Stefan dislikes and that Maja hates Ben?

Once more, we have a declarative and a related *wh*-question. The ungrammaticality of (29) suggests that a *wh*-dependency cannot cross the boundary of a coordinate structure. There is evidence, however, that this is too simple. Consider the following:

(30) Who do you think Stefan likes and Maja hates?

This also is a *wh*-question related to (28). Here, however, we have gaps in both conjuncts, whereas in (29) only one conjunct contains a gap. It seems, then, that a *wh*-dependency can cross the boundary of a coordinate structure as long as it affects every conjunct. We can summarize the facts as follows:

(31) A *wh*-dependency cannot cross the boundary of a coordinate structure unless it affects every conjunct.

Following standard practice, we can call the basic restriction the Coordinate Structure Constraint and refer to examples like (30) as across-the-board exceptions to the constraint.
The final constraint that we will consider is rather different from all the others. It was first discussed in Perlmutter (1971). It is highlighted by the following examples:

(32) Who do you think saw Stefan?
(33) * Who do you think that saw Stefan?

(32) is similar to (3). (33) is just like (32) except that the subordinate clause is a introduced by a complementizer. We can describe the situation as follows:

(34) A *wh*-dependency gap cannot appear in subject position in a clause introduced by a complementizer.

I will call this the Complementizer Gap Constraint. It is different from the other constraints in that it rules out gaps in a specific position whereas the others rule out *wh*-dependencies across various boundaries. One point to note about this constraint is that it incorrectly rules out an example like the following if it contains a gap in subject position:

(35) The man that saw Stefan

In the preceding discussion, we have illustrated island constraints with *wh*-questions. We could, however, have illustrated them with any of the *wh*-dependency constructions. We can conclude this section by looking at some relevant relative clauses.

Firstly, we can consider the following contrast:

(36) the girl who/that he saw a picture of
(37) * the girl who/that a picture of was on the table

This resembles the contrast between (7) and (8). In much the same way, the following contrast resembles that between (11) and (12):

(38) the girl who/that it's likely that he saw
(39) *the girl who/that he saw is likely

Here, then, we have some further evidence for the Subject Condition.

Next we can look at the following examples, which are very similar to (18)–(20):

(40) the girl who/that I believe that Stefan saw
(41) * the girl who/that I know the man who saw
(42) * the girl who/that I believe the claim that Stefan saw

The contrast between (40) on the one hand and (41) and (42) on the other provides further evidence for the Complex NP Constraint.

We can turn now to the following, which are similar to (23) and (26):

(43) * the girl who/that I wonder what he did to
(44) * the book which/that he criticized Chomsky without reading

(43) provides further evidence for the *Wh*-island Condition, and (44) provides further evidence for the Adjunct island Condition.

We can look next at the following, which are very similar to (29) and (30):

(45) * the man who/that I think Stefan dislikes and Maja hates Ben
(46) the man who/that I think Stefan dislikes and Maja hates

These provide further evidence for the Coordinate Structure Constraint.

Finally, we can consider the following examples, which are similar to (32) and (33):

(47)　the man who/that I think saw Stefan
(48)　* the man who/that I think that saw Stefan

These provide further evidence for the Complementizer Gap Constraint.

Thus, we can illustrate the island constraints just as well with relative clauses as with *wh*-questions. One point that should be stressed is that there is no difference between relative clauses with an overt *wh*-element and relative clauses without. Island constraints operate in just the same way in both.

13.3　The GB approach

We can now look at the main elements of the GB approach to island constraints. Two principles are crucial here: the Subjacency Condition and the Empty Category Principle (ECP). The former provides an account of the Subject Condition, the Complex NP Constraint, the *Wh*-island Condition, and the Adjunct Island Condition. The latter provides an account of the Complementizer Gap Constraint. The Coordinate Structure Constraint has had little attention within GB.

The Subjacency Condition is superficially quite simple. We can formulate the it as follows:

(49)　A movement operation cannot cross the boundary of more than one bounding node/barrier.

In earlier work the term bounding node is used. In more recent work this is replaced by the term barrier. Obviously, what effects the condition has depends on what the bounding nodes or barriers are. Chomsky (1986) develops a complex definition of barrier. We cannot go into the details of this definition, but we will have something of the flavour of this approach if we define a barrier as follows:

(50)　A maximal projection other than VP is a barrier unless it is the complement of a verb or adjective.

Maximal projection here includes both S' (or CP) and S.

We can look first at (7) and (8). Here, we will have the following derivations:

(51)　Who$_i$ did [$_S$ he see [$_{NP}$ a picture of e$_i$]]

(52)　Who$_i$ was [$_S$ [$_{NP}$ a picture of e$_i$] on the table]

In (51) the NP is not a barrier because it is the complement of a verb, but in (52) the NP is a subject and hence a barrier. In both, the S is a barrier. It is not the complement of a verb because the preceding auxiliaries are just surface occupants of the C position. It follows that we have movement across one barrier, S, in (51) but movement across two barriers, NP and S, and hence a violation of Subjacency in (52).

We can handle the contrast between (11) and (12) in much the same way. (11) will have the derivation in (53) and (12) will have the derivation in (54).

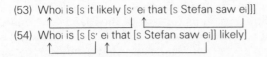

(53) Who$_i$ is [s it likely [s' e$_i$ that [s Stefan saw e$_i$]]]

(54) Who$_i$ is [s [s' e$_i$ that [s Stefan saw e$_i$]] likely]

In (53), the S' is not a barrier because it is the complement of an adjective, but in (54) the S' is a subject and hence a barrier. In both, both Ss are barriers. Given this, each movement operation in (53) crosses just one barrier, an S, but in (54), although the first movement operation crosses just one barrier, an S, the second crosses two, an S' and an S, and thus violates Subjacency.

Next we can look at (18), (19) and (20). Here, we will have the following derivations:

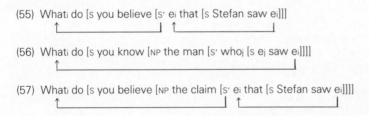

(55) What$_i$ do [s you believe [s' e$_i$ that [s Stefan saw e$_i$]]]

(56) What$_i$ do [s you know [NP the man [s' who$_j$ [s e$_j$ saw e$_i$]]]]

(57) What$_i$ do [s you believe [NP the claim [s' e$_i$ that [s Stefan saw e$_i$]]]]

In (55), each movement operation crosses just one barrier, an S, and hence there is no violation of Subjacency. Notice that Subjacency would be violated if *what* were moved directly from the subordinate object position to initial position in the main clause. Thus, Subjacency forces us to assume that such examples involve successive cyclic movement. In (56), *what* is moved directly from the subordinate object position to initial position in the main clause. It cannot be moved in two steps because the clause-initial position is occupied by *who*. The movement operation crosses two S's, both of which are barriers, and hence violates Subjacency. Finally, in (57), *what* is moved in two steps because nothing else occupies clause-initial position in the subordinate clause. The first movement crosses a single barrier, but the second crosses two, the S', which is a barrier because it is the complement not of a verb or an adjective but of a noun, and the S. Hence, we have another violation of Subjacency.

We can turn now to the *Wh*-island Condition example, (23). Here, we will have the following derivation:

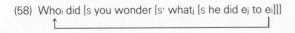

(58) Who$_i$ did [s you wonder [s' what$_j$ [s he did e$_j$ to e$_i$]]]

As in (56), *who* is moved in a single step because clause-initial position in the subordinate clause is occupied by *what*. This movement crosses two S's, both of which are barriers, and again we have a violation of Subjacency.

The Adjunct Island Condition example, (26), is quite straightforward. We will have the following derivation:

(59) What$_i$ did [s he criticize Chomsky [PP without reading e$_i$]]

Here, the PP is a barrier because it is an adjunct. The S is also a barrier. Hence, we have movement across two barriers and Subjacency is violated.

Thus, the Subjacency Condition accounts for four of the island constraints that we introduced in the last section. Remember, however, that we have assumed a simplified definition of barrier, and hence have only given the flavour of Chomsky's (1986) approach, ignoring a number of complexities.

We can look now at how the ECP accounts for the Complementizer Gap Constraint. (32) and (33) will have the following derivations:

(60) Who$_i$ do [s you think [s' e$_i$ [s e$_i$ saw Stefan]]]

(61) Who$_i$ do [s you think [s' e$_i$ that [s e$_i$ saw Stefan]]]

The ECP is formulated as follows:

(62) A trace must be properly governed.

To understand this, we need to know what is meant by proper government. We can define this as follows:

(63) α properly governs β iff (a) β is a complement to which α assigns a θ-role or (b) β is governed by and coindexed with α.

In the first situation, β is said to be θ-governed. In the second, it is said to be antecedent-governed. How does the ECP work? Given the assumption that a head always assigns a θ-role to its complements, traces in complement position are properly governed by the associated head, but traces in subject position are only properly-governed if they are governed by a coindexed category. If the trace in subject position in (60) is governed by the clause-initial trace while the trace in subject position in (61) is not, the ECP will allow (60) but will rule out (61).

One point that we noted in connection with the Complementizer Gap Constraint is that it seems to incorrectly rule out an example like (35), repeated here as (64).

(64) the man that saw Stefan

Is there any way to allow such examples? One proposal is that the complementizer *that* can be coindexed with a following trace when it introduces a relative clause, though not when it introduces a clausal complement. Given this coindexing, the trace in an example like (64) will be antecedent governed and hence will not violate the ECP.

Thus, Subjacency and the ECP provide an account of all but one of the island constraints that we identified in the previous section. One point that we should stress is that they account for island constraints in constructions without an overt *wh*-element just as much as in constructions in which there is an overt *wh*-element. As we have seen, for GB, these constructions involve movement of an empty *wh*-element. Hence, they will be affected by Subjacency and the ECP in just the same way as constructions containing an overt *wh*-element.

There are two further points that we should note about Subjacency. First, Subjacency will apply not just to *wh*-movement but also to NP-movement. However, this is not really of any importance because the examples that it rules out are also ruled out by the requirement that a trace must be A-bound in its governing category. We can consider the following example:

(65) Stefan₍ᵢ₎ seems [s' that [s it is likely [s' that [s Maja likes e₍ᵢ₎]]]]

Here, *Stefan* has been moved directly from object position in the most deeply embedded S to subject position in the main clause. In the process, it has crossed the boundaries of two Ss, neither of which is the complement of a verb or an adjective, and hence we have a violation of Subjacency. The trace, however, will be governed by the verb *likes*. Hence, its governing category will be the most deeply embedded S and it will not be A-bound in its governing category. Thus, (65) is ruled out independently of Subjacency.

Secondly, Subjacency will not affect dependencies which are not the result of movement. One is the control dependency between a controller and a PRO subject. Here, we have examples like the following:

(66) Stefan wondered [s' if [s it was necessary [s' [s PRO to do it]]]]

Here, the boundaries of two Ss intervene between the controller *Stefan* and PRO and neither is the complement of a verb or adjective.

A final question that one might raise is whether there is any further motivation for the ECP. It is a principle of some complexity. If its only function was to account for the Complementizer Gap Constraint, one might think that it was rather dubious. It also rules out examples like the following:

(67) * Stefan, is believed [s' that [s e₍ᵢ₎ likes Maja]]

As we saw in chapter 9, however, examples like this are also ruled out by the requirement that a trace must be A-bound in its governing category. The situation is different in the following example:

(68) * Stefan₍ᵢ₎ was tried [s' [s e₍ᵢ₎ to leave]]

This is also ruled out by the ECP. Here, however, the trace is in an ungoverned position. Hence, it has no governing category and the requirement that a trace must be A-bound in its governing category is irrelevant. Here, then, we have some further motivation for the ECP. We will see some additional motivation in 13.6.

13.4 The PSG approach

We can now turn to PSG approach to island constraints. Here, as in GB, we can account for a number of constraints with a single principle.

The principle that we need in PSG can be called the SLASH Principle and can be formulated as follows:

(69) If a SLASH feature specification appears within a category it must appear within a head daughter or a complement daughter.

This will account for the Subject Condition, part of the Complex Noun Phrase Constraint, and the Adjunct Island Condition.

We can look first at the Subject Condition. Here, we need to rule out structures of the following form:

(70)

```
(a)          S                    (b)            S
        [SLASH,NP]                         [SLASH,NP]
          /\                                 /    |    \
        /    \                              /     |      \
      NP      VP                           V     NP      VP
   [SLASH,NP]                                [SLASH,NP]
```

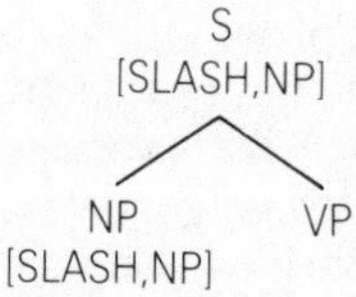

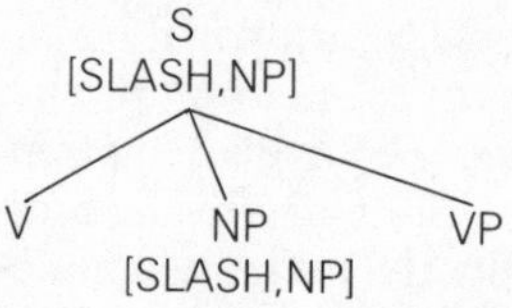

These conform to the FOOT Feature Principle, but they violate the SLASH principle because a SLASH feature specification appears within the mother but not within a head daughter or a complement daughter.

Next, we can look at the Complex NP Constraint. In the case where the clause is a relative clause, we can assume the following structure:

(71)

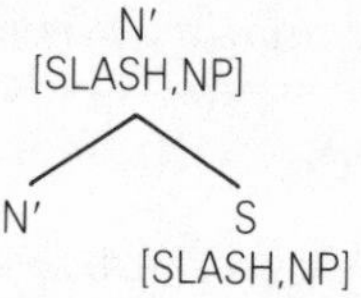

```
                    N'
                [SLASH,NP]
                  /\
                /    \
              N'      S
                  [SLASH,NP]
```

Again, we have a structure which conforms to the FOOT Feature Principle but violates the SLASH Principle because we have a SLASH feature specification within the mother but not within a head daughter or a complement daughter. In the case where the clause is a complement, we have the following structure:

(72)

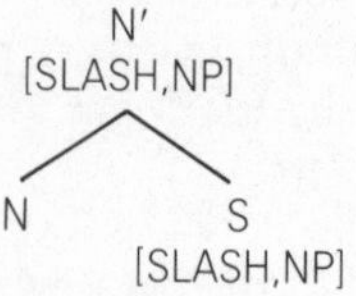

```
                    N'
                [SLASH,NP]
                  /\
                /    \
              N        S
                  [SLASH,NP]
```

Here, there is no violation of the SLASH Principle because we have a SLASH feature specification within a complement daughter. It seems, then, that we need some additional constraint to rule out structures like this.

Finally, we can consider the Adjunct Island Condition. Here, it is structures like the following that we need to rule out:

(73)

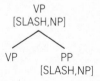

This is a straightforward violation of the SLASH Principle since the SLASH feature specification that appears within the mother does not appear within a head daughter or a complement daughter.

We can turn now to the coordinate structure constraint. We can account for this with the following principle.

(74) All components of a coordinate structure must have the same SLASH feature specifications.

This will rule out structures like the following:

(75)

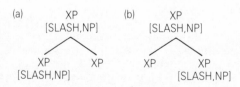

In both, the components of the coordinate structure do not have the same SLASH feature specifications.

There are two other constraints that we need to consider: the *Wh*-Island Condition and the Complementizer Gap Constraint. PSG offers a simple account of the former. At the heart of the PSG approach to *wh*-dependencies is the SLASH feature, which takes as its value a single category. This means that constituents can only involve a single *wh*-dependency. In our *Wh*-island Condition example, (23), the subordinate S involves two *wh*-dependencies. Hence, PSG will not allow such an example.

Turning to the Complementizer Gap Constraint, it has generally been assumed that this is a consequence of the fact that an unbounded dependency cannot terminate in subject position. We might formulate this as follows:

(76) An empty XP[SLASH,XP] cannot appear in subject position.

But what about the examples in which an unbounded dependency appears to terminate in subject position, e.g. (32)? Here, it has generally been assumed that we have not an S[SLASH NP] with an empty category in subject position but a 'bare' VP. Given this assumption, we will have something like the following structure for (32).

(77)

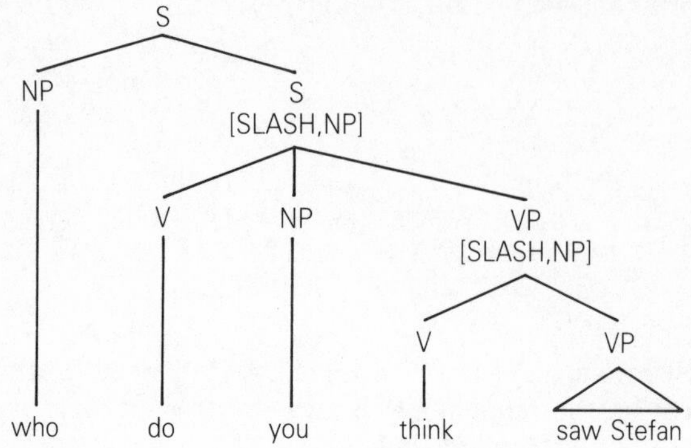

We will need some special mechanism to allow structures like this. However, I will not go into this.

Here, then, we have an account of all the island constraints that we identified in the first section. One point that we should note is that the account will apply to constructions without an overt *wh*-element in just the same way as constructions with an overt *wh*-element since all involve the SLASH feature.

13.5 Parasitic gaps

An important feature of *wh*-dependency constructions, closely related to island constraints, is the possibility of what are known as parasitic gaps, a phenomenon first noted in Ross (1967) and first discussed in detail in Engdahl (1983). In this section, we will look briefly at this phenomenon and consider how it can be handled within GB and PSG.

We noted earlier that examples like the following exemplify what is known as the Adjunct Island Constraint example.

(78) * Which book did he criticize Chomsky without reading?

Notice now that the following, rather similar sentence is grammatical:

(79) Which book did he criticize without reading?

Whereas (78) has just a gap following *reading*, this has a gap following *criticize* as well. The gap following *criticize* is an ordinary *wh*-dependency gap, but the gap following *reading* is a rather special sort of gap since it is only possible because the other gap is present. It is dependent or parasitic upon the other gap. Hence, we can call it a parasitic gap.

In (78), we have a non-finite adverbial expression. Similar examples with a finite adverbial expression are ungrammatical, as the following illustrates:

(80) * Which book did he criticize Chomsky before he read?

Again, however, a related sentences with an ordinary gap outside the adverbial expression is grammatical.

(81) Which book did he criticize before he read?

Again, then, we see that we can have a parasitic gap inside an adverbial expression.

For some speakers, it is also possible to have a parasitic gap inside a subject. Consider first the following:

(82) ∗ Which book did the reviewers of criticize Chomsky unmercifully?

This exemplifies the Subject Condition. Consider now the following:

(83) Which book did the reviewers of criticize unmercifully?

This is just like (82) except that it contains an ordinary gap following *criticize*. Here, then, the gap within the subject is a parasitic gap. Some speakers find examples like these fairly good. Others find them rather dubious. They are certainly far less natural than examples like (79) and (81).

Before we consider how parasitic gaps should be analyzed, there are two further points that we should note. The first is that it is only a *wh*-dependency gap that will allow or 'license' a parasitic gap. Passive sentences can be said to involve a gap and within GB they involve an empty category just like *wh*-dependency sentences. However, the following shows that a passive gap does not license a parasitic gap:

(84) ∗ The book was criticized after we read.

The second point to note is that not all *wh*-dependency gaps can license a parasitic gap. Consider the following:

(85) ∗ Who did you say was bothered by our talking to?

Here, we have a gap before *was* and another after *to*. How exactly does this example differ from the acceptable examples? One might suggest that the crucial point is that the first gap is in subject position. However, the following suggests that this is not the case:

(86) Who did he suggest was a fool while ostensibly praising?

Here, we have a gap before *was* and another after *praising*. The first is in subject position. Hence, we need some other explanation for the un-grammaticality of (85). One suggestion is that the problem with (85) is that the first gap c-commands the second. In (85), we have the structure in (87) and in (86) we have the structure in (88).

(87) Who did you say [s e [vp was bothered by our talking to e]]
(88) Who did he suggest [s e was a fool] while ostensibly praising e

In both the ordinary gap is in subject position within the subordinate clause. In

(87), the parasitic gap is within the VP of the subordinate clause and hence is c-commanded by the ordinary gap. In (88), the parasitic gap is within an adverbial expression in the main clause and hence is not c-commanded by the ordinary gap.

How, then, should parasitic gaps be analyzed? Within GB, two approaches have been proposed. In one developed in Chomsky (1982), the parasitic gap is an empty category throughout the derivation, which is coindexed with the trace that is the ordinary gap. On this approach, (79) is analyzed as follows:

(89) Which book$_i$ did [$_S$ he criticize e$_i$ [$_{PP}$ without reading e$_i$]]

In the other approach outlined in Chomsky (1986), the parasitic gap is a trace left by the movement of an empty *wh*-element, which is coindexed with the main trace. On this approach, (79) is analyzed as follows:

(90) Which book$_i$ did [$_S$ he criticize e$_i$ [$_{PP}$ without [e$_i$ reading e$_i$]]]

I will not review the arguments for these approaches. The important point to note is that neither analysis involves movement out of a PP to initial position in the containing clause. Hence, neither involves a violation of Subjacency. Within both of these analyses, explanations have been advanced for the fact that parasitic gaps only appear in sentences containing an ordinary *wh*-dependency gap in an appropriate position, but I will not go into this here.

To allow parasitic gap examples within PSG, we simply need to allow structures of the following form:

(91)

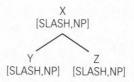

In fact, we already allow such structures. The SLASH Principle says that if a SLASH feature specification appears within some category, then it must also appear within a head daughter or a complement daughter. It does not say that it cannot appear in other types of daughter as well. If it does, we will have a parasitic gap. Thus, parasitic gaps are only to be expected within the PSG analysis. Various proposals have been advanced to ensure that the ordinary gap is correctly located but we will not go into these proposals here.

13.6 LF

It is appropriate at this point to introduce a further important GB concept, LF or Logical Form. This is a further level of structure derived from S-structure by processes rather like *wh*-movement. It was introduced in Chomsky (1976b) and is discussed in detail in May (1985) and Hornstein (1984). It is motivated in part by semantic considerations, but the main argument for its existence is that it permits an account of certain syntactic facts.

For many types of sentence, LF is identical to S-structure. However, there are two main types of sentence where there is a difference. One is sentences in which a *wh*-phrase appears in a clause-internal position at S-structure. (92) is an example.

(92) Who annoyed who?

Here, both *who*'s have the same semantic function. Hence, it is natural to assume that they should occupy the same position at whatever level of structure is relevant to semantic interpretation. If LF is this level, then it is natural to suggest that the second *who* should appear in clause-initial position at LF. In other words, it is natural to propose that it undergoes a process like *wh*-movement in the derivation of LF from S-structure. May (1985) proposes that this process adjoins a *wh*-expression to the *wh*-expression that is already in clause-initial position. In the case of (92), this will derive (94) from the S-structure in (93).

(93)

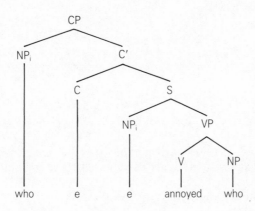

(94)

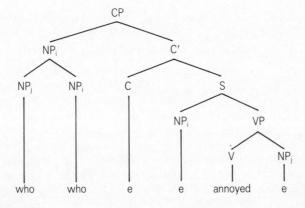

The second type of sentence in which there is a difference between LF and S-structure is sentences involving NP's containing a so-called quantifier, words like *all*, *every*, *each* and *some*. Such NP's differ semantically from proper names in various ways and as a result are standardly treated rather differently by logicians. The standard logical formulae for (95) and (96) are (97) and (98), respectively.

(95) Stefan likes Maja.
(96) Stefan likes everyone.
(97) L(s,m)
(98) $\forall x(L(s,x))$

'$\forall$' is known as a universal quantifier, and '$\forall x$' can be interpreted as 'for all x'. If we think that logicians are right to distinguish NP's containing quantifiers from other NP's, we can propose that such NP's also undergo a process like *wh-movement* in the derivation of LF. If we assume that this adjoins a quantified NP to S, we will have the following LF for (96):

(99)

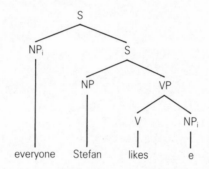

Although a level of LF is motivated in part by semantic considerations, the main evidence that has been advanced for its existence is syntactic in nature and much of it involves the ECP.

We can look first at the following examples:

(100) Who thought that he did what?
(101) * Who thought that who did it?

For many speakers, there is a clear contrast between these two examples. How can we explain it? Consider their structures. We will have the S-structures in (102) and (103) and the LF representations in (104) and (105).

(102) who$_i$ [s e$_i$ thought [s' that [s he did what]]]
(103) who$_i$ [s e$_i$ thought [s' that [s who did it]]]
(104) what$_j$ who$_i$ [s e$_i$ thought [s' that [s he did e$_j$]]]
(105) who$_j$ who$_i$ [s e$_i$ thought [s' that [s e$_j$ did it]]]

In (104) the second trace is in object position, but in (105) it is in subject position preceded by a complementizer. (105) is very much like the sort of overt *wh*-movement structure that is ruled out by the ECP. Just like such structures, then, it will be ruled out by the ECP. It seems, then, that we can attribute the contrast between (100) and (101) to the ECP if we assume a level of LF.

We can look now at the following sentences:

(106) Who said what?
(107) * What did who do?

While (106) is fine, (107) is only acceptable as an echo-question, a question which echoes someone's statement. (We referred to such questions in 7.4.) here, we will have the S-structures in (108) and (109) and the LF representations in (110) and (111).

(108) who$_i$ [s e$_i$ said what]
(109) what$_i$ did [s who do e$_i$]
(110) what $_j$ who$_i$ [s e$_i$ said e$_j$]
(111) who$_j$ what $_i$ did [s e$_j$ do e$_i$]

Both (110) and (111) have a trace in subject position. In (110) the coindexed *wh*-element is adjacent, but this is not the case in (111). This makes it plausible to suggest that the trace is antecedent governed in (110) but not in (111). If this right, (111) will violate the ECP. Again, then, we have a contrast which can be attributed to the ECP if we have a level of LF. Of course, we need some explanation for why (107) is acceptable as an echo-question. Thus, there is more to be said about this data.

It seems, then, that the assumption that there is a level of LF, allows us to attribute the ungrammaticality of certain kinds of sentence to the ECP. We could not do this, if we did not assume a level of LF. Here, then, we have some interesting evidence for this level of structure.

Some further evidence for LF comes from a rather different source. We can look first at the following examples:

(112) Who loves his mother?
(113) Who does his mother love?

There is an important contrast here. In (12) *his* can mean *who*, but in (113) this is not possible. This is commonly referred to as the weak crossover phenomenon. As in sentences which exemplify the strong crossover phenomenon, a *wh*-element has been moved across a pronoun. Here, however, the pronoun does not c-command the position from which the *wh*-element has been moved. How can we explain this contrast? To answer this question, we must look at the S-structures of these sentences, which are as follows:

(114) who$_i$ [s e$_i$ loves his mother]
(115) who$_i$ does [s his mother love e$_i$]

We can explain the contrast between (112) and (113) if we make the following assumptions (following in essence Chomsky (1976b)):

(116) A *wh*-NP cannot be the antecedent of a pronoun.
(117) A trace cannot be the antecedent of a preceding pronoun.

In (114), the pronoun follows the trace, and hence can have the trace as its antecedent. In (115), however, the pronoun precedes the trace, and hence the trace cannot be its antecedent.

Having accounted for the contrast between (112) and (113), we can now consider the following examples:

(118) Every man loves his mother.
(119) His mother loves every man.

Again, we have a contrast. In (118) *he* can mean *every man*, but in (119) this is not possible. How can we explain this? It is in fact quite easy to explain if we assume LF. For these sentences, we will have the following LF representantions:

(120) every man$_i$ [s e$_i$ loves his mother]
(121) every man$_i$ [s his mother loves e$_i$]

These representations are very similar to the S-structures in (114) and (115) and they will allow us to account for the contrast in just the same way given the following assumption:

(121) A quantified NP cannot be the antecedent of a pronoun.

This could in fact replace (116) if *wh*-NP's are regarded as a kind of quantified NP.

One further question that it is natural to ask here is: does LF-movement obey Subjacency? It seems that the answer is no. Chomsky (1981: 235) cites the following example in this context:

(122) I wonder who heard the claim that John had seen what.

Here, *what* will be moved to a position adjacent to *who*. If LF movement were subject to Subjacency, this would be ruled out just like the *wh*-movement in the following:

(123) * I wonder what he heard the claim that John had seen.

There is one further matter that we can consider here. We have seen that for GB English has *wh*-movement both in the derivation of S-structure from D-structure and in the derivation of LF from S-structure. There is evidence that some languages have just one or other type of *wh*-movement. There are some languages in which all *wh*-expressions must be in clause-initial position in S-structure. An example is Polish, where we have sentences like the following:

(124) Kto   co   zrobił?
      who   what   did-3SGM
      'Who did what.'

Here, the two *wh*-words are in clause-initial position. The following is not possible (except as an echo-question):

(125) * Kto zrobił co?

The following is also impossible:

(126) * Co zrobił kto?

Thus, *wh*-expressions must appear in clause-initial position in Polish. Here, then, we can say that *wh*-movement only applies in the derivation of S-structure from D-structure.

There are also languages in which *wh*-expressions appear in the same positions in S-structure as the related non-*wh*-expressions. An example is Chinese, where we have sentences like the following from May (1985):

(127) Zhangsan xiang-zhidao [ta   muqin   kanjian shei]
      Zhangsan wonder   his mother see   who
      'Zhangsan wondered who his mother.'

Here, the bracketed string is a subordinate *wh*-question, but the *wh*-word *shei* appears in an ordinary NP position and not in clause-initial position. Here, then, we must say that *wh*-movement only applies in the derivation of LF from S-structure.

13.7 Summary

In this chapter, we have looked at what are known as island constraints, various restrictions on *wh*-dependencies. We began in 13.2, by introducing the main island constraints that have been distinguished. In 13.3, we looked at the GB account of island constraints, introducing the Subjacency Condition and the Empty Category Principle, and in 13.4, we considered how island constraints could be handled within PSG, introducing the SLASH Principle. Then, in 13.5, we looked at so-called parasitic gaps, a phenomenon closely related to island constraints. Finally, in 13.6, we looked at the GB assumption that there is a level of LF or logical form derived from S-structure by processes like *wh*-movement. As we saw, this assumption is motivated in part by the way that it interacts with the Empty Category Principle.

Notes

The island constraints discussed in the text are not the only important restrictions on *wh*-dependencies. One important type of restriction is illustrated by the following Polish string:

(1) * Kim   Jan rozmawiał z?
      whom Jan talked   with
      'Who did Jan talk with?'

Here, the *wh*-phrase is an NP and the object of a preposition is missing from the following S. This is ungrammatical. The only way to express the intended meaning of (1) is the following:

(2) Z   kim   Jan rozmawiał?
    with whom Jan   talked
    'With whom did you talk?

Here, the *wh*-phrase is a PP and a PP is missing from the following S. (1) is said to involve preposition stranding, and while this is perfectly acceptable in English it is impossible in most languages.

Another important type of restriction is illustrated by the following contrast:

(3) Whose brother did you meet?
(4) * Whose did you meet brother?

In (3), the *wh*-phrase functions as the object of a verb, and this is fine. In (4), it functions as the specifier of the object of a verb, and this is ungrammatical. We have a similar contrast in the following:

(5) How tall are you?
(6) * How are you tall?

In (5) the *wh*-phrase functions as a complement, and in (6) it functions as the specifier of a complement. It seems, then, that a *wh*-dependency cannot terminate in specifier position in English. This restriction is commonly known as the Left Branch Condition (since specifiers appear on the left of larger expressions). Essentially the same restriction is found in many languages. The following show, however, that there is no such restriction in Polish.

(7) Czyjego brata   spotkałeś?
     whose   brother   met-2SG
     'Whose brother did you meet?'
(8) Czyjego spotkałeś brata?
     whose   met-2SG   brother
(9) Jaki wysoki jesteś?
     how   tall   are-2SG
     'How tall are you?'
(10) Jaki jesteś   wysoki?
     how   are-2SG tall

We suggest in the text that NP complements unlike NP subjects are not islands. However, some NP complements are islands. The following is a relevant example:

(11) * Who did you destroy a book about?

Many languages obey the Complementizer Gap Constraint, but many others do not. Perlmutter (1971) suggested that a language obeys the constraint unless it is a null subject language. Thus, French, which is not a null subject language obeys the constraint, as (12) illustrates, but the closely related Italian, which is a null subject language, does not, as (13) illustrates.

(12) * Qui crois-tu que   viendra?
         who think you that   will come
         'Who do you think will come?'
(13) Chi credi   che   viene?
       who you-think that   comes

However, some non-null-subject languages do not obey constraint. Thus, the following from Maling and Zaenen (1978) is grammatical in Icelandic, which is not a null-subject language.

(14) Hver sagðir þu, að   væri kominn til Reykjavikur?
     who said   you   that   was come   to Reykjavik
     'Who did you say had come to Reykjavik?'

It is generally accepted within GB that the barriers for Subjacency can vary somewhat from language to language. See Rizzi (1982) for the proposal that the barriers for Subjacency in Italian differ from those in English. Although the Coordinate Structure Constraint has had little attention within GB, a GB account is developed in Goodall (1987).

An important simplification in our discussion of Subjacency is the assumption that VP is not a barrier. In fact, for Chomsky (1986), VP is a barrier but adjunction provides a way of escaping certain barriers. A consequence of this is that the bracketed clause in (15) is derived not as in (16) but as in (17) with adjunction to VP.

(15) I asked [who Ben saw]
(16) who$_i$ [$_S$ Ben [$_{VP}$ saw e$_i$]]
     ⌐_____⌐

(17) who$_i$ [$_S$ Ben [$_{VP}$ e$_i$ [$_{VP}$ saw e$_i$]]]
     ⌐_____⌐. ⌐_____⌐

For further discussion of Chomsky's proposals, see Haegeman (1991, 10.).

The ECP was first proposed in Chomsky (1980b) but it can be seen as a descendant of a condition called the Nominative Island Condition (NIC) proposed in Chomsky (1980). The current version of the ECP owes much to the discussion of Lasnik and Saito (1984).

The original version of the ECP has a rather different first clause, which can be formulated as follows:

(18) α governs β and α is lexical (i.e. N, V, A or P but not the agreement features associated with a finite verb).

In this situation, β is said to be lexically governed. The difference between lexical government and θ-government can be illustrated with the following example:

(19) Ben$_i$ seems [$_S$ e$_i$ to like Debbie]

Here, the trace is lexically-governed by *seems* but it is not θ-governed since it is not a complement to which *seems* assigns a θ-role. Thus, in the current version of the ECP, but not in earlier versions, it is necessary to assume that the trace in such examples is antecedent-governed.

Kayne (1981) argues that an extended version of the ECP eliminates the need for Subjacency, but Kayne (1983) withdraws this claim. Aoun (1985) argues that the ECP should be replaced by a generalized version of binding theory. Aoun *et al.* (1987) propose that it should be replaced by two separate conditions. Lasnik and Uriagereka (1988, 4.) and Haegeman (1991, 8.) provide textbook introductions to the ECP.

For discussion of how structures like (77) can be allowed, see Pollard and Sag (forthcoming).

'Tough' sentences pose a problem for both GB and PSG approaches to island constraints. Consider the following example:

(20) Which violin are these sonatas easy to play on?

Here, the *wh*-phrase is associated with the preposition *on* within the complement of *easy*. For both GB and PSG, the complement of *easy* is comparable to a subordinate *wh*-question. For GB both involve *wh*-movement, and for PSG both involve a chain of SLASH feature specifications. We have seen, however, that a *wh*-dependency cannot cross the boundary of a subordinate *wh*-question. The following reinforces this point:

(21) * Which violin do you wonder which sonatas they played on?

For both frameworks, then, it is quite surprising that examples like (20) are grammatical.

For textbook discussions of parasitic gaps, see Lasnik and Uriagereka (1988, 3.2) and Haegeman (1991, 8.5).

For an introduction to logic especially as it relates to linguistics, see Allwood, Andersson and Dahl (1977). For textbook discussion of LF, see Riemsdijk and Williams (1986, 13.) and Haegeman (1991, 9.). The phenomena that have been seen in GB as supporting a level of LF, have generally been seen in PSG as semantic phenomena, but ones that necessitate a weakening of the relation between syntax and semantics. See Cooper (1983).

A number of approaches to the weak crossover phenomenon have been developed within GB. See, for example, Koopman and Sportiche (1982) and Safir (1984). For textbook discussions of the phenomenon, see Lasnik and Uriagereka (1988, 6.3).

Languages in which all *wh*-expressions appear in clause-initial position in S-structure are discussed in Rudin (1988). Languages in which all *wh*-expressions appear in the same position as the related non-*wh*-expressions are discussed in Huang (1982).

Exercises

Exercise 1

Identify the island constraints that are violated in the following examples.

(1) * Where did you consider the possibility that he put the book?
(2) * Which man is whether or not she met important?

(3) * Which book didn't you understand syntax until you read?
(4) * Who did you ask whether Stefan annoyed and Ben infuriated Debbie?
(5) * What were you asked how he did?
(6) * Which murder is a film about going to be made?
(7) * What did you see the boy who damaged?
(8) * Who is what she meant to a matter of controversy?

Exercise 2

Provide examples which show that the *wh*-dependencies in (a) clefts and (b) pseudo-clefts obey island constraints.

Exercise 3

In early GB work, it is assumed that certain categories are barriers in all circumstances. What predictions will Subjacency make about the following examples if NP and S are barriers in all circumstances and S' is never a barrier:

(1) * Which picture did you meet the man who painted?
(2) * Who was a story about in the paper?
(3) * Which book is that we read essential?
(4) Which book do you think he gave to her?
(5) Who did you read a book about?

Exercise 4

Identify the parasitic gaps and the ordinary gaps that license them in the following examples:

(1) Who did John send his book to in order to impress?
(2) This is a country which unless you've visited you'll never understand.
(3) Which carpet did he damage while rolling up?
(4) He is man who anyone who meets is impressed by.
(5) Which professor did you persuade some students of to write to?

Exercise 5

In the following examples, *he* and *John* cannot be the same person. Show with appropriate trees that this means that the condition on R-expressions introduced in the last chapter must apply at S-structure and not at LF.

(1) Who thinks that he read which book that John likes?
(2) He liked every book that John read.

14

Concluding remarks

14.1 Introduction

In this final chapter, I will draw together various strands in the earlier discussion. In particular, I will try to give a clear overall picture of the two approaches that have figured most prominently, and to identify the main similarities and differences. I will also offer some remarks on the future development of syntactic theory.

14.2 GB

The most basic point about GB is that it is a multistratal framework and in particular a transformational framework in which the ordinary, obvious structure of a sentence (the S-structure) is derived from a more abstract structure (the D-structure). We noted in the last chapter that it is also assumed in GB that there is a level of LF (Logical Form) derived from S-structure by certain movement processes. The phonetic representation of a sentence, or, as it is known in GB, its PF or Phonetic Form, is also derived from S-structure. Thus, for GB, a sentence has four main structures related as follows:

(1)

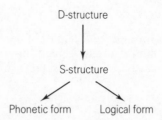

It is sometimes suggested that S-structure is more abstract than the characterization of it is as the ordinary, obvious structure suggests. We noted in chapter 11 that it is generally assumed within GB that examples like the following involve a *for* complementizer:

(2) Stefan wants Maja to go home.

It is also generally assumed that this *for* complementizer is present at S-structure and is only deleted in the mapping from S-structure to PF. It is also

202

commonly suggested that so-called extraposition processes apply in the mapping from S-structure to PF. These processes are illustrated by the following examples:

(3) a. A new book by Chomsky has just appeared.
     b. A new book has just appeared by Chomsky.
(4) a. The possibility that he did it never occurred to me.
     b. The possibility never occurred to me that he did it.
(5) a. A man who looked just like me was in the room.
     b. A man was in the room who looked just like me.

In (3)a. we have a PP within the subject NP, and in (3)b. the same PP appears at the end of the sentence. Similarly, in (4)a. we have a clausal complement within the subject NP, and in (4)b. it appears at the end of the sentence. Finally, in (5)a. we have a relative clause within the subject, and in (5)b. it appears at the end of the sentence. All three b. examples are assumed within GB to involve an extraposition process. If these processes apply in the mapping to PF, then the b. examples will have exactly the same S-structures as the corresponding a. examples.

Apart from the fact that it is a multistratal framework, the most important fact about GB is that it is a modular framework. This means that it is a framework in which various distinct systems of rules and principles interact. As we have noted earlier, the various systems are commonly referred to as subtheories. It is appropriate at this point to run through the various systems and to remind ourselves of their function.

Firstly, GB assumes a number of category-neutral immediate dominance rules. These are commonly referred to as principles of X-bar theory. Their role is to define the basic types of syntactic structure.

Next, there is Case theory, which consists of various case-marking rules and the Case filter. It's main function is to determine which NP positions can be occupied by overt NP's on the surface. It ensures that NP-movement is obligatory in passive and raising structures, and that only a PRO subject is possible in certain infinitives. Thus, it rules out examples like the following:

(6) * It was seen Stefan.
(7) * It seems Stefan to be late.
(8) * Stefan tried Maja to do it.

We discussed these matters in Chapters 9, 10 and 11. It is also commonly assumed that Case theory accounts for certain ordering facts. If we assume that English verbs and prepositions can only assign Case to the right, then we can explain why we have (9)a. and (10)a. and not (9)b. and (10)b.

(9) a. Stefan likes Maja.
     b. * Stefan Maja likes.
(10) a. Stefan looked at Maja.
     b. * Stefan looked Maja at.

It we also assume that a verb can only assign Case to an adjacent NP, we can account for why we have (11)a. but not (11)b.

(11) a. Stefan saw Maja yesterday.
     b. * Stefan saw yesterday Maja.

Then there is θ-theory, whose main element is the requirement, introduced in Chapter 9, that no NP can have more than one θ-role. Its main function is to limit the positions to which movement is possible, or, in other words, the landing sites for movement. Essentially, it ensures that movement is only possible to subject position in a passive, unaccusative or raising structure (NP-movement) and to clause-initial position (*wh*-movement).

A more complex system is binding theory. As we have seen, this consists of three different conditions, formulated as follows:

(12) a. An anaphor must be A-bound in its governing category.
     b. A pronominal must be A-free in its governing category.
     c. An R-expression must be A-free.

(12)a., which we introduced in Chapter 9, requires reflexives to have antecedents that are sufficiently close, ruling out examples like the following:

(13) a. * Stefan thinks himself is a genius.
     b. * Stefan expects Maja to like himself.

It also restricts NP-movement, ruling out examples like the following:

(14) a. * Stefan$_i$ is thought e$_i$ is a genius.
     b. * Stefan$_i$ is expected Maja to like e$_i$

(12)b., which was introduced in Chapter 11, prevents ordinary pronouns from having antecedents that are too close. For example, it prevents *Stefan* from being understood as the antecedent of *him* in the following:

(15) a. Stefan saw him.
     b. Stefan expects him to be popular.

(12)a., and b, together ensure that PRO can only appear in subject position in certain infinitives. Finally, (12)b., which was introduced in Chapter 12, prevents *he* in (16) from meaning *Stefan* and prevents *he* in (17) from meaning *who*.

(16) He thinks Stefan did it.
(17) Who does he think did it?

The two other systems are Subjacency, sometimes referred to as Bounding theory, and the Empty Category Principle, sometimes known as Government theory. Both were discussed in Chapter 13. The former restricts movement and accounts for the main island constraints. The latter restricts the positions from which movement is possible. Its main function is to account for the impossibility of extracting the subject from a clause introduced by a complementizer, but it also accounts in conjunction with the assumption with there is a level of LF for certain facts about sentences in which a *wh*-phrase appears in a clause-internal position.

One further element of GB should be mentioned, the Projection Principle, which we have formulated as follows:

(18) Syntactic representations are projections of the lexicon in that they observe the subcategorization properties of lexical items.

The Principle ensures that lexical heads have the right complements, and if we assume that it applies at S-structure as well as at D-structure, it will ensure that movement processes leave behind traces.

A further point that should be stressed about GB is that it is an evolving body of ideas, which includes a variety of different positions. We can conclude this section with a look at this diversity.

We have just identified D-structure and LF as important features of GB. There are, however, proponents of GB who reject both these levels of representation. Notable works here are Koster (1986) and Williams (1986). For the former, the only level of representation is S-structure. For the latter, there is an additional level of representation called NP-structure. This is a level identical to the output of NP-movement in 'standard' GB. We can illustrate with the following example:

(19) Who was sacked?

For 'standard' GB, this will have the D-structure in (20).

(20) e [s e was sacked who]

NP-movement will move *who* into the empty subject position, giving (21).

(21) e [s who$_i$ was sacked e$_i$]

Then, *wh*-movement will move *who* into the empty clause-initial position, giving (22).

(22) who$_i$ [s e$_i$ was sacked e$_i$]

In Williams' theory, (21) is the most basic structure of (19) and is not derived from (20).

We have also identified Subjacency and the ECP as important components of GB. There are, however, GB critics of both. The most important reference is again Koster (1986). Subjacency, however, is also rejected in Hoekstra (1984), and the ECP is replaced by a generalized version of binding theory in Aoun (1985).

Finally, we have identified as an important feature of GB the idea that control sentences involve an empty category which is both an anaphor and a pronominal. There are, however, proponents of GB who argue that the empty category is either an anaphor or a pronominal but never both. Roughly, the proposal is that it is a pure anaphor in control sentences that resemble raising sentences and a pure pronominal in other kinds of control sentence. The main references here are Bouchard (1984) and Koster (1984, 1986).

4.3 PSG

The most obvious feature of PSG is that it is a monostratal approach. Equally important, however, is the fact that for PSG all grammatical rules and principles are strictly local in the sense that they never affect anything larger than a local tree consisting of a category and its daughters.

PSG can also be seen as modular theory. HPSG especially is like GB in assuming a small number of category-neutral ID rules which interact with various linear precedence rules and a number of general principles. We have mentioned three principles: the Subcategorization Principle, the FOOT Feature Principle, and the SLASH Principle. The first of these ensures that a lexical head has the right complements. The second captures the basic properties of the FOOT features, SLASH and WH. The last imposes an additional restriction on SLASH and accounts for a range of island constraints. Recent work in HPSG has also involved a version of binding theory, though one that affects trees indirectly by affecting the internal makeup of categories.

Another important feature of PSG is the central role that syntactic categories play. Especially in HPSG, categories incorporate information about what other categories they combine with, and in particular, about what complements they take and what kind of subject they require. As we saw in Chapter 10, this makes it quite easy to handle raising expressions, which are essentially expressions which require as a subject whatever category their complement requires as a subject. Categories also incorporate information about what *wh*-dependency gaps they contain. As we saw in Chapters 12 and 13, this makes possible an interesting account of *wh*-dependencies. Lexical categories are particularly important within PSG since the character of phrasal categories is largely determined by their lexical heads. In some cases, the makeup of some lexical categories is predictable from the makeup of other lexical categories. In this situation, the former can be derived from the latter by lexical rules. We highlighted this possibility in connection with passives in Chapter 9.

One important feature of PSG, which we have ignored in earlier discussion, is that syntactic analyses have generally been allied to explicit semantic analyses. GPSG has drawn here on the ideas of Montague Semantics, an approach originally developed in the 60's by the logician Richard Montague. HSPG has drawn on the ideas of Situation Semantics, an approach developed during the 80s by the mathematician Jon Barwise, the philosopher John Perry, and the linguist Robin Cooper.

A final point that we should stress is that PSG like GB incorporates a variety of different positions. We have in fact already made this quite clear. We have indicated that PSG includes both GPSG and the more recent HPSG, and we have also noted (in Chapter 6) that two rather different approaches to subjects have been advanced within HPSG.

14.4 The relation between GB and PSG

In summarizing the central features of GB and PSG, we have already identified some of the main differences and similarities. There is, however, more to be said, so it seems appropriate to devote a section to this topic.

There are two major differences between GB and PSG. The first is very simple and can be summarized as follows:

(23) For GB, the syntactic structure of a sentence is a number of trees.

For PSG, the syntactic structure of a sentence is a single tree. The second is a little more complex. We can summarize it as follows:

(24) For GB, grammatical statements can refer to structures larger than a local tree consisting of a category and its daughters. Hence a tree can be ill-formed even if every local tree is well-formed.

For PSG, no grammatical statement can refer to anything larger than a local tree consisting of a category and its daughters. Hence, a tree is well-formed if and only if every local tree is well-formed.

These are important differences. It may be, however, that they are not quite as important as they seem. As we have noted, Koster (1986) develops a version of GB which like PSG assumes that the syntactic structure of a sentence is a single tree.

The two differences between GB and PSG that we have just highlighted are probably the most important differences. There are, however, a number of other differences that we should note. For example, there are different assumptions about empty categories. For GB, there are empty categories in passives, raising and control sentences, and in clause-initial position in complex *wh*-dependency sentences. As far as PSG is concerned, none of these empty categories exist. Thus, GB assumes all the empty categories in the following examples, but for PSG only the second empty category in (28) exists.

(25) Stefan$_i$ was sent e$_i$ to Coventry.
(26) Maja$_i$ seems e$_i$ to know the truth.
(27) Ben$_i$ tried e$_i$ to sleep.
(28) What$_i$ do you think e$_i$ Stefan did e$_i$?

There are also different assumptions about structures. One point that we have stressed is that strings like those italicized in the following are analyzed as clauses within GB but as two separate constituents in PSG:

(29) Stefan considered *Maja to be intelligent*.
(30) Stefan considered *Maja intelligent*.
(31) Stefan considered *Maja a genius*.
(32) We wanted *him out of the room*.
(33) We saw *him do it*.

Another point that we have noted is that complementizers are analyzed as heads of S′ (which is therefore CP) within GB, and clause-initial *wh*-phrases are seen as occupying a pre-complementizer specifier position. PSG makes neither of these assumptions. GB also assumes an I category which is not assumed within PSG.

A further difference between GB and PSG relates to semantics. As noted in the last section, syntactic analyses in PSG have generally been allied to explicit semantic analyses. Various elements of GB, notably θ-theory and Binding theory, provide a basis for an account of various semantic facts but proponents have GB have generally not been concerned to develop explicit semantic analyses in the way that proponents of PSG have. Some would see this as an important weakness of GB.

A final difference between the two frameworks has to do with research priorities. One thing that should be clear from the preceding chapters is that formalism looms larger in PSG analyses than in GB analyses. It should also be clear that GB appeals to abstract notions rather more than PSG. These differences reflect different priorities in research. Proponents of PSG place great emphasis on attaining the standards of precision and explicitness that are implied by the term generative. Proponents of GB, on the other hand, place more emphasis on developing analyses which can be seen as going beyond mere description and offering an explanation for the facts. This is an important difference although perhaps not as important as is sometimes suggested.

Although there are a number of important differences between GB and PSG, there are also some important similarities. As we have indicated, both are modular theories. Both also assume separate immediate dominance and linear precedence statements. GB and HPSG are also similar in assuming a small number of category-neutral immediate dominance rules, and the Projection Principle of GB and the Subcategorization Principle of HPSG are very similar. There is also a considerable measure of agreement about what the most important phenomena are and how they are like and unlike each other. For both approaches, the sentence-types considered here are of central importance and there is broad agreement on what the fundamental properties of these sentence-types are.

Thus, although there are major differences between GB and PSG, it is important not to exaggerate the differences.

14.5 Final remarks

In this book, I have tried to introduce a body of ideas that play a major role in more or less all approaches to syntax and to look at how they have been developed within two broad frameworks: GB and PSG. The ideas introduced here are likely to play an important role in syntactic theory for some time to come. It may be, of course, that other ideas not discussed here will also be influential, but an understanding of the ideas we have considered here should be a good basis for grappling with other ideas, including ones not yet developed.

One way to conclude a book of this nature would be to offer some predictions about how syntactic theory will develop in the coming years. However, it would be foolhardy to do this. Science in general is inherently unpredictable and syntactic theory is no exception. All I will do, therefore, is highlight three factors that are likely to be quite influential in the future development of theories of syntax.

One is how well they can accommodate languages which differ in important ways from English. Syntactic theory has always been applied to languages other than English, but it is probably fair to say that it is only over the last ten years or so that they have had a major influence. This influence is likely to increase in the future.

The obvious question to ask here is: what exactly do we mean by languages which differ in important ways from English? One point we can make is that differences of word order are not necessarily important differences. We noted in Chapter 1 that it seems that all six logically possible orders of subject, verb and object occur in human languages. It is doubtful, however, whether languages with different orders from English are particularly important. Subject – object – verb, verb – object – subject, and object – verb – subject sentences can probably be analyzed as subject – predicate structures much like those in English, and object – subject – verb sentences can probably be analyzed along the same lines as the verb-initial sentences of English and other languages, which we looked at briefly in Chapter 8. There are also languages, which differ from English in that they have postpositions, preposition-like elements which follow their complements. Presumably, however, these elements really are prepositions and do not differ in any fundamental way from ordinary prepositions, which precede their complements. (If one is unhappy about using the term preposition for elements that follow their complements as well as elements that precede, one can substitute the term adposition.)

There is, however, more to be said about word order. Many languages have a much freer word order than English. In some languages, the word order is remarkably free. Such languages are commonly known as non-configurational languages. A particularly notable example is the Australian Aborigine language Warlpiri. Here, we find examples like the following from Simpson and Bresnan (1983):

```
(34) Ngarrka     ka     wirnpirli-mi     kuluparnta.
     man-ABS     PRES   whistle -NPST    bellicose-ABS
     'The bellicose man is whistling.'
```

The important point about this example is that words which in English and other languages would form an NP are not adjacent and hence cannot form a constituent given standard assumptions about constituent structure.

Another important feature of certain languages, which poses a major challenge to theories of syntax is exemplified by the following sentences from the American Indian language, Mohawk:

```
(35) Ka-rakv         ne      sawatis hrao-nuhs   -a.
     3N-be-white DET  John    3M- house-SUF
     'John's house is white.'
(36) Haro-nuhs -rakv      ne    sawatis.
     3M-  house be-white DET John
     'John's house is white.'
     (Postal, 1962; cited in Baker, 1988)
```

(35) is not very different from English although the subject follows the verb. (36), however, differs from English in a rather major way. Here, the noun that means 'house' is combined with the verb that means 'be white' and is separated from the modifying expression that is translated as 'John'. Sentences like this are found in a number of languages and are generally described as examples of noun incorporation. A detailed GB analysis of such sentences has been developed in Baker (1988), while Sadock (1985) has outlined an analysis within a version of PSG.

Here, then, we have a variety of syntactic phenomena which appear to be unlike anything in English and related languages. Such 'exotic' phenomena are likely to be of considerable importance for the future development of theories of syntax.

A second factor that is likely to be important is how readily they can be incorporated into theories about how human beings process language, how speakers produce utterances and how hearers understand them. Proponents of a number of frameworks have argued that the approaches they favour receive some support from what is known about how humans process language. Such arguments have been particularly prominent in the literature of the LFG framework, which we looked at briefly in Chapter 8, but they have also been advanced in connection with GB and PSG.

A final factor that is likely to be of some importance in the future development of theories of syntax is how readily they can be exploited in the computer processing of ordinary language, which, as we noted in Chapter 1, is a rapidly expanding field. No syntactician would think that any theory should stand or fall on the basis of how useful it is in a computational context, but theories which cannot be readily exploited are likely to be seen as seriously deficient. There has in fact been considerable PSG-based computational work, and also much work based on the LFG framework. There has been rather less GB-based work.

It seems likely that these three factors will have considerable influence in the future development of theories of syntax. What exactly will happen, however, I will not try to predict.

14.6 Summary

In this Chapter, I have brought together some of the main elements of earlier discussion. In 14.2, I summarized the various components of GB, and in 14.3, I did the same thing for PSG. Then, in 14.4, I considered the main differences and similarities between these two frameworks. Finally, in 14.5, I commented on the future of syntactic theory.

Notes

For discussion of extraposition sentences, see Gueron and May (1984) and Culicover and Rochemont (1990). For textbook discussion of extraposition processes, see Radford (1988, 8.7).

Koster argued against the need for D-structure in Koster (1978a) before the emergence of GB. NP-structure was first proposed in van Riemsdijk and Williams (1981). For textbook discussion, see van Riemsdijk and Williams (1986, 19.5.).

For textbook discussion of Aoun's Generalized binding theory, see Lasnik and Uriagereka (1988, 5.1.).

The HPSG version of binding theory is presented in Pollard and Sag (1990, forthcoming).

Further differences between GB and PSG involve their LP constraints. Firstly, the LP rules of PSG simply require precedence whereas the LP constraints of GB include adjacency or immediate precedence requirements. Secondly, the LP rules of PSG only affect constituents that are sisters whereas the LP constraints of GB can affect non-sisters. For example, they require *him* to be adjacent to *consider* in *I consider him to be intelligent* even though for GB they are not sisters. It should be noted, however, that Ojeda (1988) suggests within GPSG that both immediate precedence rules and LP rules affecting non-sisters are necessary.

Montague's papers are published in Montague (1974). Dowty, Wall and Peters (1981) provide a textbook introduction to Montague semantics. Situation semantics is introduced in Barwise and Perry (1983). For a textbook introduction, see Cooper (forthcoming). Although GB syntactic analyses have generally not been allied to precise semantic analyses, Larson (1988a) combines GB assumptions with Montague semantics and Larson (1988b) combines GB assumptions with Situation semantics.

For some discussion of non-configurational languages, see the papers in Maracz and Muysken (1989).

For textbook discussion of Baker's ideas, see Spencer (1991. Chapter 7). For textbook discussion of Sadock's proposals, see Spencer (1991, Chapter 11).

For further discussion of the relation between current theories, see Horrocks (1987, 5.), and McCloskey (1988).

For a recent survey of research on human language processing, see Frazier (1988).

Grover *et al.* (1988) presents a large-scale GPSG-based computational grammar of English and Borsley (1990) describes a large-scale HPSG-based computational grammar. GB-based computational work is discussed in Berwick (1988).

Exercises

Exercise 1

Identify which subtheories of GB are violated in each of the following schematic S-structures:

(1) * She$_i$ is said [s' that [s t$_i$ is mistaken]]
(2) * It is likely [s her to be a success]
(3) * He$_i$ believes [s PRO$_i$ to be popular]]
(4) * They persuaded him$_i$ [s' [s t$_i$ to visit them]]
(5) * He wondered [s' whether [s him to go home]]
(6) * Which house$_i$ did he ask [s' whether [s t$_i$ was sold t$_i$]]

Exercise 2

Provide GB S-structures and PSG structures for each of the following sentences. Make use of the features SUBJ and SLASH in the PSG structures.

(1) They are likely to be in bed.
(2) She is considered a genius.
(3) What do you think he talked about?

Exercise 3

Provide ungrammatical sentences which are ruled out by each of the following:

(1) The rule that a lexical category in English precedes a phrasal category that is its sister

(2) The Case filter
(3) The SLASH Principle
(4) The principle that an R-expression must be free
(5) The rule that an S follows all its sisters
(6) The Subcategorization Principle
(7) The principle that an anaphor must be bound in its governing category
(8) The PRO theorem
(9) The principle that no NP can have more than one θ-role
(10) The principle that a trace cannot be the antecedent of a preceding pronoun

Exercise 4

The following sentences illustrate a process often known as *wanna*-contraction, which reduces infinitival *to* and combines it with a preceding a verb. These examples suggest that one of the empty categories assumed within GB blocks the process while some others do not. Identify the empty category which blocks the process and the others which do not. Then explain why this data might be seen as providing evidence against GB assumptions and in favour of PSG assumptions.

(1) a. Who do you want to go to London?
     b. * Who do you wanna go to London?
(2) a. Who do you want to eat the beefburger?
     b. * Who do you wanna eat the beefburger?
(3) a. I want to go to bed.
     b. I wanna go to bed.
(4) a. What do you want to drink?
     b. What do you wanna drink?
(5) a. You ought to read this.
     b. You oughta read this.
(6) a. It ought to be easy to read this.
     b. It oughta be easy to read this.
(7) a. We are going to see him.
     b. We are gonna see him.

Exercise 5

Polish word order is less free than Warlpiri word order but much freer than English word order. Thus, all of the following sentences are possible ways of saying 'Stefan read this book'. Discuss how each sentence might be analyzed either within GB or within PSG, and indicate what differences you are assuming between the grammar of Polish and the grammar of English.

(1) Stefan przeczytał tę   książkę.
    Stefan read   this book
(2) Stefan tę   książkę przeczytał.
    Stefan this book   read.
(3) Tę   książkę Stefan przeczytał.
    this   book   Stefan read
(4) Tę   Stefan przeczytał kaiążkę.
    this   Stefan read   book
(5) Tę   Stefan książkę przeczytał.
    this   Stefan book   read
(6) Stefan tę   przeczytał książkę.
    Stefan this   read   book

Bibliography

ABNEY S, (1987). *The English Noun Phrase in its Sentential Aspect*. Ph.D. dissertation, MIT.

ALLWOOD J, L-G ANDERSSON and O DAHL, (1977). *Logic in Linguistics*. Cambridge University Press: Cambridge.

ANDERSON JM, (1971). *The Grammar of Case: Towards a Localistic Theory*. Cambridge University Press: Cambridge.

ANDERSON JM, (1977). *On Case Grammar*. Croom Helm: London.

AOUN J, (1985). *The Grammar of Anaphora*. MIT Press: Cambridge, Mass.

AOUN J, N HORNSTEIN, D LIGHTFOOT and A WEINBERG, (1987). Two types of locality. *Linguistic Inquiry*: **18**; 537–577.

AOUN J and D SPORTICHE, (1983). On the formal theory of government. *The Linguistic Review*: **3**; 211–235.

BAKER CL, (1989). *English Syntax*. MIT Press: Cambridge, Mass.

BAKER MC, (1988). *Incorporation: A Theory of Grammatical Function Changing*. University of Chicago Press, Chicago and London.

BAKER MC, K JOHNSON and I ROBERTS, (1989). Passive arguments raised. *Linguistic Inquiry*: **20**; 219–251.

BARKER C and GK PULLUM, (1990). A theory of command relations. *Linguistics and Philosophy*: **13**; 271–295.

BARWISE J and J PERRY, (1983). *Situations and Attitudes*. MIT Press: Cambridge, Mass.

BAYER J, (1983). Towards an explanation of certain *that*-t phenomena: the COMP node In Bavarian. In *Sentential Complementation*. W de Geest and Y Putseys (eds.). Foris: Dordrecht.

BENNIS H, (1986). *Gaps and Dummies*. Foris: Dordrecht.

BERWICK R, (1988). *Principle-Based Parsing*. Technical Report 972. MIT Artificial Intelligence Lab. Camb: Mass.

BEUKEMA F and T HOEKSTRA, (1984). 'Extraction from *with*-constructions', *Linguistic Inquiry*: **15**; 689–698.

BEVER T, (1974). The psychology of language and structuralist investigations of nativism. In *On Noam Chomsky: Critical Essays*. G Harman (ed.). Anchor.

BLAKE BJ, (1990). *Relational Grammar*. Routledge: London.

BORSLEY RD, (1980). In defence of single mothers. *Journal of Linguistics*: **16**; 95–101.

BORSLEY RD, (1984). VP complements: evidence from Welsh. *Journal of Linguistics*: **20**; 277–302.

BORSLEY RD, (1986). Prepositional complementizers in Welsh. *Journal of Linguistics*: **22**; 67–84.

BORSLEY RD, (1987). Subjects and complements in HPSG. CSLI Report: **107**.

213

BORSLEY RD, (1989). Phrase structure grammar and the *Barriers* conception of clause structure. *Linguistics*: **27**; 843–863.

BORSLEY RD, (1990). *A Category-Driven Computational Grammar of English*. IBM UKSC Report: **223**.

BORSLEY RD, (forthcoming). Subjects, complements and specifiers in HPSG. To appear in *Readings in Information-Based Syntax and Semantics*. C Pollard and IA Sag (eds.). CSLI: Stanford.

BOTHA RP, (1989). *Challenging Chomsky: The Generative Garden Game*. Basil Blackwell: Oxford.

BOUCHARD D, (1984). *On the Content of Empty Categories*. Foris: Dordrecht.

BRAME MK, (1975). On the abtractness of syntactic structure: the VP controversy. *Linguistic Analysis*: **1**; 191–203.

BRAME MK, (1976). *Conjectures and Refutations in Syntax*. Elsevier North-Holland: New York.

BRAME MK, (1978). The base hypothesis and the spelling prohibition. *Linguistic Analysis*: **4**; 1–30.

BRESNAN J, (1970). On complementizers: toward a syntactic theory of complement types. *Foundations of Language*: **6**; 297–321.

BRESNAN J, (1976). Nonarguments for raising. *Linguistic Inquiry*: **7**; 485–502.

BRESNAN J, (1978). A realistic transformational grammar. In *Linguistic Theory and Psychological Reality*. M Halle, J Bresnan and G Miller (eds.). MIT Press: Cambridge, Mass.

BRESNAN J (ed.), (1982a). *The Mental Representation of Grammatical Relations*. MIT Press: Cambridge, Mass.

BRESNAN J, (1982b). The passive in lexical theory. In Bresnan (1982a).

BRESNAN J, (1982c). Control and complementation. In Bresnan (1982a).

BURZIO L, (1986). *Italian Syntax: A Government-Binding Approach*. Kluwer: Dordrecht.

CHOMSKY NA, (1957). *Syntactic Structures*. Mouton: The Hague.

CHOMSKY NA, (1964). *Current Issues in Linguistics*. Mouton: The Hague.

CHOMSKY NA, (1965). *Aspects of the Theory of Syntax*. MIT Press: Cambridge, Mass.

CHOMSKY NA, (1970). Remarks on nominalization. In *Readings in English Transformational Grammar*. R Jacobs and PS Rosenbaum (eds.). Ginn and co.: Waltham, Mass.

CHOMSKY NA, (1972). *Language and Mind*. Harcourt Brace Jovanovich: New York.

CHOMSKY NA, (1973). Conditions on transformations. In *Festschrift for Morris Halle*. S Anderson and P Kiparsky (eds.). Holt, Rinehart and Winston: New York. Reprinted in Chomsky (1977a).

CHOMSKY NA, (1974). The Amherst Lectures. Unpublished lecture notes distributed by Documents Linguistiques University of Paris VII.

CHOMSKY NA, (1976a). *Reflections on Language*. Fontana: London.

CHOMSKY NA, (1976b). Conditions on rules of grammar. *Linguistic Analysis*: **2**; 303–351. Reprinted in Chomsky (1977a).

CHOMSKY NA, (1977a). *Essays on Form and Interpretation*. Elsevier North Holland: Amsterdam.

CHOMSKY NA, (1977b). On *wh*-movement. In *Formal Syntax*. P Culicover, T Wasow, A Akmajian (eds.). Academic Press: New York. Reprinted in Chomsky (1977a).

CHOMSKY NA, (1980a). *Rules and Representations*. Basil Blackwell: Oxford.

CHOMSKY NA, (1980b). On binding. *Linguistic Inquiry*: **11**; 1–46.

CHOMSKY NA, (1981). *Lectures on Government and Binding*. Foris: Dordrecht.

CHOMSKY NA, (1982). *Some Concepts and Consequences of the Theory of Government and Binding*. MIT Press: Cambridge, Mass.

CHOMSKY NA, (1985). *Knowledge of Language*. Praeger: New York.

CHOMSKY NA, (1986). *Barriers*. MIT Press: Cambridge, Mass.

CHOMSKY NA, (1987). *Language and Problems of Knowledge: The Managua Lectures*. MIT Press: Cambridge, Mass.

CHOMSKY NA, (1988). Some notes on economy of derivation and representation. Unpublished paper. MIT.

CHOMSKY NA, R HUYBREGTS and H VAN RIEMSDIJK, (1982). *The Generative Enterprize*. Foris: Dordrecht.

COOPER R, (1983). *Quantification and Syntactic Theory*. D Reidel: Dordrecht.

COOPER R, (forthcoming). *Introduction to Situation Semantics*.

CULICOVER PW and MS ROCHEMONT, (1990). Extraposition and the complement principle. *Linguistic Inquiry*: **21**; 23–47.

DAVIS L, (1986). Remarks on the θ-criterion and Case. *Linguistic Inquiry*: **17**; 564–568.

DEN BESTEN H, (1978). On the interaction of root transformations and lexical deletive rules. Paper presented at the 1978 GLOW conference: Amsterdam.

DIK S, (1978). *Functional Grammar*. North Holland: Amsterdam.

DIK S, (1980). *Studies in Funcational Grammar*. Academic Press: London.

DOWTY D, (1982). Grammatical relations in Montague grammar. In *The Nature of Syntactic Representation*. P Jacobson and GK Pullum (eds.). D Reidel: Dordrecht.

DOWTY D, RE WALL and S PETERS, (1981). *Introduction to Montague Semantics*. D Reidel: Dordrecht.

EMONDS J, (1970). *Root and Structure-Preserving Transformations*. Ph.D. dissertation. MIT.

ENGDAHL E, (1983). Parasitic gaps. *Linguistics and Philosophy*: **6**; 5–34.

FIENGO R, (1974). Semantic conditions on surface structure. Ph.D. dissertation. MIT.

FILLMORE CJ, (1968). The case for case. In *Universals in Linguistic Theory*. E Bach and RT Harms (eds.). Holt, Rinehart and Winston: New York.

FILLMORE CJ, (1977). The case for case reopened. In *Syntax and Semantics*: **8**. P Cole and J Sadock (eds.). Academic Press: New York.

FLYNN M, (1983). A categorial theory of structure building. In *Order, Concord and Constituency*. G Gazdar, E Klein and GK Pullum (eds.). Foris: Dordrecht.

FRAZIER L, (1988). Grammar and language processing. In *Linguistics: The Cambridge Survey*: **II**; *Linguistic Theory: Extensions and Implications*. FJ Newmeyer (ed.). Cambridge University Press: Cambridge.

GAZDAR G, (1981). Unbounded dependencies and coordinate structure. *Linguistic Inquiry*: **12**; 155–184.

GAZDAR G, (1982). Phrase structure grammar. In *The Nature of Syntactic Representation*. P Jacobson and GK Pullum (eds.). D Reidel: Dordrecht.

GAZDAR G, E KLEIN, G PULLUM and I SAG, (1985). *Generalized Phrase Structure Grammar*. Basil Blackwell: Oxford.

GAZDAR G and C MELLISH, (1987). Computational linguistics. In *New Horizons in Linguistics*: **2**; J Lyons, R Coates, M Deuchar and G Gazdar (eds.). Penguin: London.

GAZDAR G and C MELLISH, (1989). *Natural Language Processing in PROLOG: An Introduction to Computational Linguistics*. Addison Wesley: New York.

GEORGE A (ed.), (1989). *Reflections on Chomsky*. Basil Blackwell: Oxford.

GOODALL G, (1987). *Parallel Structures in Syntax*. Cambridge University Press: Cambridge.

GRIMSHAW J, (1974). 'Evidence for relativization by deletion in Chaucerian Middle English', *Proceedings of NELS 5*, 216–224.

GRIMSHAW J, (1979). Complement selection and the lexicon. *Linguistic Inquiry*: **10**; 279–326.

GROVER C, T BRISCOE, J CARROLL and B BOGURAEV, (1988). *The Alvey Natural Language Tools Project Grammar: A Wide-Coverage Computational Grammar of English*. Lancaster Papers in Linguistics: **23**.

GRUBER J, (1965). *Studies in Lexical Relations*. Ph.D. dissertation. MIT.

GUERON J and R MAY, (1984). Extraposition and logical form. *Linguistic Inquiry*: **15**; 1–31.

GUNJI T, (1987). *Japanese Phrase Structure Grammar: A Unification-Based Approach*. Reidel, Dordrecht.

HAEGEMAN L, (1991). *Introduction to Government and Binding Theory*. Basil Blackwell: Oxford.

HALVORSEN PK, (1988). Computer applications of linguistic theory. In *Linguistics: The Cambridge Survey. Vol* **11**; *Linguistic Theory: Extensions and Implications*. FJ Newmeyer (ed.). Cambridge University Press: Cambridge.

HARMAN G, (1963). Generative grammars without transformational rules: a defense of phrase structure. *Language*: **39**; 597–616.

HARRIS ZS, (1951). *Methods in Structural Linguistics*. University of Chicago Press: Chicago.

HENY F, (1979). Review of Noam Chomsky, *Logical Structure of Linguistic Theory*. *Synthese*: **40**; 317–352.

HOEKSTRA T, (1984). *Transitivity: Grammatical relations in Government Binding Theory*. Foris: Dordrecht.

HORNSTEIN N and A WEINBERG, (1981). Case theory and preposition stranding. *Linguistic Inquiry*: **12**; 55–91.

HORNSTEIN N, (1984). *Logic as Grammar*. MIT Press: Cambridge, Mass.

HORROCKS G, (1987). *Generative Grammar*. Longman: London.

HUANG J, (1982). *Logical Relations in Chinese and the Theory of Grammar*. Ph.D. dissertation. MIT.

HUCK CJ and AE OJEDA (eds.), (1987). *Syntax and Semantics*: **20**. Academic Press: New York.

HUDDLESTON R, (1984). *Introduction to the Grammar of English*. Cambridge University Press: Cambridge.

HUDSON R, (1972). Evidence for ungrammaticality. *Linguistic Inquiry*: **3**; 227.

HUDSON R, (1984). *Word Grammar*. Basil Blackwell: Oxford.

HUDSON R, (1990). *English Word Grammar*. Basil Blackwell: Oxford.

HUKARI T, (1989). The domain of reflexivization. *Linguistics*: **27**; 207–244.

JACKENDOFF RS, (1972). *Semantic Interpretation in Generative Grammar*. MIT Press: Cambridge, Mass.

JACKENDOFF RS, (1977). *X-Syntax: A Study of Phrase Structure*. MIT Press: Cambridge, Mass.

JACKENDOFF RS, (1983). *Semantics and Cognition*. MIT Press, Cambridge, Mass.

JACKENDOFF RS, (1985). Multiple subcategorization and the θ-criterion: the case of *climb*. *Natural Language and Linguistic Theory*: **3**; 271–295.

JACKENDOFF RS, (1987). The status of thematic relations in linguistic theory. *Linguistic Inquiry*: **18**; 369–411.

JACKENDOFF RS, (1990). On Larson's treatment of the double object construction. *Linguistic Inquiry*: **21**; 427–456.

JACOBSON P, (1987). Phrase structure, grammatical relations, and discontinuous constituents. In Huck and Ojeda (eds.), (1987).

JAEGGLI O, (1986). Passive. *Linguistic Inquiry*: **17**; 587–622.

JAEGGLI O and K SAFIR, (1989). *The Null Subject Parameter*. Kluwer Academic Publishers: Dordrecht.

JESPERSEN O, (1909–1949). *A Modern English Grammar on Historical Principles*, Allen and Unwin, London.

JOHNSON D and PM POSTAL, (1980). *Arc Pair Grammar*. Princeton University Press: Princeton.

JONES M, (1983). Getting 'tough' with *wh*-movement, *Journal of Linguistics*: **19**; 129–159.

JOOS M, (1957). *Readings in Linguistics*. American Council of Learned Societies: Washington.

KAPLAN R and A ZAENEN, (1989). Long distance dependencies, constituent structure and functional uncertainty. In *Alternative Conceptions of Phrase Structure*. MR Baltin and AS Kroch (eds.). University of Chicago Press: Chicago.

KARTUNNEN L, (1984). Features and values. *Proceedings of Coling*: 28–33.

KAYNE RS, (1981). ECP extensions. *Linguistic Inquiry*: **12**; 93–133.

KAYNE RS, (1981). Unambiguous paths. In *Levels of Syntactic Representation*. R May and J Koster (eds.). Foris: Dordrecht.

KAYNE RS, (1983). Connectedness. *Linguistic Inquiry*: **14**; 223–249.

KOOPMAN H, (1983). ECP effects in main clauses. *Linguistic Inquiry*: **14**; 346–350.

KOOPMAN H, (1984). *The Syntax of Verbs*. Foris: Dordrecht.

KOOPMAN H and D SPORTICHE, (1982). Variables and the bijection principle. *The Linguistic Review*: 2.2.

KORNAI A and GK PULLUM, (1990). The X-bar theory of phrase structure. *Language*: **66**; 24–50.

KOSTER J, (1978a). *Locality Principles in Syntax*. Foris: Dordrecht.

KOSTER J, (1978b). Why subject sentences don't exist. In *Recent Transformational Studies in the European Languages*. SJ Keyser (ed.). MIT Press: Cambridge, Mass.

KOSTER J, (1984). On binding and control. *Linguistic Inquiry*: **15**; 417–459.

KOSTER J, (1986). *Domains and Dynasties: The Radical Autonomy of Syntax*. Foris: Dordrecht.

KOSTER J and R MAY, (1982). On the constituency of infinitives. *Language*: **58**; 116–143.

KRUISINGA E, (1925). *A Handbook of Present Day English*. Kemink en Zoon: Utrecht.

LAKOFF G and JR ROSS, (1976). A criterion for verb phrase constituency. In *Syntax and Semantics, Vol. 7: Notes from the Linguistic Underground*. J McCawley (ed.), (1976). Academic Press: New York.

LANGENDOEN DT and T BEVER, (1973). Can a not unhappy person be called a sad one? In A Festschrift for Morris Halle. S Anderson and P Kiparsky (eds.). Holt, Rinehart and Winston: New York.

LARSON R, (1988a). On the double object construction. *Linguistic Inquiry*: **19**; 335–391.

LARSON R, (1988b). Scope and comparatives. *Linguistics and Philosophy*: **11**; 1–27.

LARSON R, (1988c). Implicit arguments in situation semantics. *Linguistics and Philosophy*: **11**; 169–201.

LASNIK H and M SAITO, (1984). On the nature of proper government. *Linguistic Inquiry*: **15**; 235–289.

LASNIK H and J URIAGEREKA, 1988). *A Course in GB Syntax: Lectures on Binding and Empty Categories*. MIT Press: Cambridge. Mass.

LYONS J, (1968). *Introduction to Theoretical Linguistics*. Cambridge University Press: Cambridge.

MALING J, (1978). An asymmetry with respect to *wh-islands*. *Linguistic Inquiry*: **9**; 75–88.

MALING J and A ZAENEN, (1978). The nonuniversality of a surface filter. *Linguistic Inquiry*: **9**; 475–497.

MCCAWLEY J, (1968). Concerning the base component of a transformational grammar. *Foundations of Language*: **4**; 243–269.

MCCAWLEY J, (1971). Tense and time reference in English. In *Studies in Linguistic Semantics*. CJ Fillmore and DT Langendoen (eds.). Holt, Rinehart and Winston: New York.

MCCAWLEY J, (1982). Parentheticals and discontinuous constituent structure. *Linguistic Inquiry*: **13**; 91–106.

MCCAWLEY J, (1987). Some additional evidence for discontinuity. In *Syntax and Semantics. Vol. 20: Discontinuous Constituency*. GJ Huck and AE Ojeda (eds.). Academic Press: New York.

MCCLOSKEY J, (1979). *Transformational Syntax and Model-Theoretic Semantics*. D. Reidel: Dordrecht.

MCCLOSKEY J, (1988). Syntactic theory. In *Linguistics: The Cambridge Survey. 1. Linguistic Theory: Foundations*. FJ Newmeyer (ed.). Cambridge University Press: Cambridge.

MANASTER-RAMER A and M KAC, (1990). The concept of phrase structure. *Linguistics and Philosophy*: **13**; 325–362.

MANZINI MR, (1983). On control and control theory. *Linguistic Inquiry*: **14**; 421–426.

MARACZ L and P MUYSKEN (eds.), (1989). *Configurationality: The Typology of Asymmetries*. Foris: Dordrecht.

MARANTZ A, (1984). *On the Nature of Grammatical Relations*. MIT Press: Cambridge, Mass.

MATTHEWS P, (1981). *Syntax*. Cambridge University Press: Cambridge.

MAY R, (1985). *Logical Form: Its Structure and Derivation*. MIT Press: Cambridge, Mass.

MILLER G and N CHOMSKY, (1963). Finitary models of language users. In *Handbook of Mathematical Psychology*, **Vol. II**. P Luce, R Bush and E Galanter (eds.). Wiley: New York.

MONTAGUE R, (1974). *Formal Philosophy*. (ed.) and with an introduction by RH Thomason. Yale University Press: New Haven.

MUYSKEN PC and HC VAN RIEMSDIJK (eds.), *Features and Projections*. Foris: Dordrecht.

NEWMEYER FJ, (1983). *Grammatical Theory: Its Limits and Possibilities.* Chicago University Press: Chicago.

NEWMEYER FJ, (1986). *Linguistic Theory in America.* Second Edition. Academic Press: New York.

OEHRLE RT, E BACH and D WHEELER (1988). *Categorial Grammars and Natural Language Structures.* D. Reidel: Dordrecht.

OJEDA AE, (1987). Discontinuity, multidominance, and unbounded dependency in generalized phrase structure grammar: some preliminaries. In *Syntax and Semantics. Vol. 20: Discontinuous Constituency.* GJ Huck and AE Ojeda (eds.). Academic Press: New York.

OJEDA AE, (1988). A linear precedence account of cross-serial dependencies. *Linguistics and Philosophy*: **11**; 457–492.

PATEMAN T, (1987). *Language in Mind and Language in Society.* Oxford University Press: Oxford.

PERLMUTTER DM, (1971). *Deep and Surface Structure Constraints in Syntax.* Holt, Rinehart and Winston: New York.

PERLMUTTER DM, (1983). Personal vs impersonal constructions. *Natural Language and Linguistic Theory*: **1**; 141–200.

PERLMUTTER DM (ed.), (1983). *Studies in Relational Grammar* 1. University of Chicago Press: Chicago.

PERLMUTTER DM and PM POSTAL, (1983). Toward a universal definition of the passive. In DM Perlmutter (ed.), (1983).

PERLMUTTER DM and C ROSEN (eds.), (1984). *Studies in Relational Grammar* 2. University of Chicago Press: Chicago.

PESETSKY D, (1982). *Paths and Categories.* Ph.D. dissertation. MIT.

POLLARD C, (1985). Phrase structure grammar without metarules. *Proceedings of the West Coast Conference on Formal Linguistics*: **4**. Stanford Linguistics Association: Stanford.

POLLARD C and I SAG, (1988). *Information-Based Syntax and Semantics. Vol. 1: Fundamentals.* CSLI: Stanford.

POLLARD C and I SAG, (1990). Anaphors in English and the scope of binding theory. Unpublished paper. Carnegie Mellon University and Stanford University.

POLLARD C, and I SAG, (forthcoming). *Information-Based Syntax and Semantics. Vol. 2: Topics in Control and Binding.* CSLI: Stanford.

POLLOCK J-Y, (1989). Verb-movement, universal grammar, and the structure of IP. *Linguistic Inquiry*: **20**; 365–424.

POSTAL PM, (1962). *Some Syntactic Rules of Mohawk.* Ph.D. dissertation. Yale University.

POSTAL PM, (1971). *Crossover Phenomena.* Holt, Rinehart and Winston: New York.

POSTAL PM, (1972). On some rules that are not successive cyclic. *Linguistic Inquiry*: **3**; 211–222.

POSTAL PM, (1974). *On Raising.* MIT Press: Cambridge, Mass.

POSTAL PM, (1986). *Studies of Passive Clauses.* State University of New York Press: Albany.

POSTAL PM and GK PULLUM, (1988). Expletive noun phrases in subcategorized positions. *Linguistic Inquiry*: **19**; 635–670.

POUTSMA H, (1926–29). *A Grammar of Late Modern English.* Noordhoff: Groningen.

PULLUM GK, (1977). Word order universals and grammatical relations. In

Syntax and Semantics 8: Grammatical Relations. P Cole and JM Sadock (eds.). Academic Press: New York.

PULLUM GK, (1980). Syntactic relations and linguistic universals. *Transaction(s) of the Philological Society*; 1–39.

PULLUM GK (1987). Natural language interfaces and strategic computing. *AI and Society*: **1**; 47–58.

PULLUM GK, (1988). Citation etiquette beyond thunderdome. *Natural Language and Linguistic Theory*: **6**; 579–588.

PULLUM GK and D WILSON, (1977). Autonomous syntax and the analysis of auxiliaries. *Language*: **53**; 741–788.

QUIRK R, S GREENBAUM, G LEECH and J SVARTVIK, (1985). *A Comprehensive Grammar of the English Language.* Longman: London.

RADFORD A, (1988). *Transformational Grammar: A First Course.* Cambridge University Press: Cambridge.

REINHART T, (1976). *The Syntactic Domain of Anaphora.* Ph.D. dissertation, MIT.

RIEMSDIJK H VAN, (1978). *A Case Study in Syntactic Markedness: The Binding Nature of Prepositional Phrases.* Foris: Dordrecht.

RIEMSDIJK H VAN and E WILLIAMS, (1981). NP-structure. *The Linguistic Review*: **1**; 171–217.

RIEMSDIJK H VAN and E WILLIAMS, (1986). *Introduction to the Theory of Grammar.* MIT Press: Cambridge, Mass.

RIZZI L, (1982). *Issues in Italian Syntax.* Foris: Dordrecht.

ROSENBAUM PS, (1967). *The Grammar of English Predicate Complement Constructions.* MIT Press: Cambridge. Mass.

ROSS JR, (1967). *Constraints on Variables in Syntax.* Ph.D. dissertation. MIT.

ROSS JR, (1969). Auxiliaries as main verbs. In *Studies in Philosophical Linguistics*: **1**. W Todd (ed.). Great Expectations Press: Evanston.

ROTHSTEIN S, (1983). *The Syntactic Forms of Predication.* Ph.D. dissertation. MIT.

RUDIN C, (1988). On multiple questions and multiple WH fronting. *Natural Language and Linguistic Theory*: **6**; 445–501.

SADOCK JM, (1985). Autolexical syntax: a theory of noun incorporation and similar phenomena. *Natural Language and Linguistic Theory*: **3**; 379–440.

SAFIR K, (1984). Multiple variable binding. *Linguistic Inquiry*: **15**; 603–638.

SAG IA, G GAZDAR, T WASOW and S WEISLER, (1985). 'Coordination and how to distinguish categories', *Natural Language and Linguistic Theory* 3, 117–171.

SAMPSON G, (1975). The single mother condition. *Journal of Linguistics*: **11**; 1–11.

SELLS P, (1985). *Lectures on Contemporary Syntactic Theories: An Introduction to Government-Binding Theory, Generalized Phrase Structure Grammar and Lexical-Functional Grammar.* CSLI: Stanford.

SHIEBER S, (1987). *An Introduction to Unification-Based Approaches to Grammar.* CSLI: Stanford.

SIMPSON J and J BRESNAN, (1983). Control and obviation in Warlpiri. *Natural Language and Linguistic Theory*: **1**; 49–64.

SPENCER A, (1991). *Morphological Theory: An Introduction to Word Structure in Generative Grammar.* Basil Blackwell: Oxford.

SPORTICHE D, (1988). A theory of floating quantifiers and its corollaries for constituent structure. *Linguistic Inquiry*: **19**; 425–449.

STOWELL T, (1978). What was there before *there* was there. *Papers from the Fourteenth Regional meeting of the Chicago Linguistic Society.*

STOWELL T, (1981). *Origins of Phrase Structure.* Ph.D. dissertation. MIT: Cambridge, Mass.

TARALDSEN KT, (1978). The scope of *wh*-movement in Norwegian. *Linguistic Inquiry*: **9**; 623–40.

TESNIERE L, (1959). *Elements de Syntaxe Structurale.* Klincksieck: Paris.

VAN DER AUWERA J, (1985). Relative *that* – a centennial dispute. *Journal of Linguistics*: **21**; 149–179.

WASOW T, (1972). *Anaphoric Relations in English.* Ph.D. dissertation. MIT: Cambridge, Mass.

WASOW T, (1977). Transformations and the lexicon. In *Formal Syntax.* P Culicover, T Wasow and A Akrajian (eds.). Academic Press: New York.

WASOW T, (1980). Major and minor rules in lexical grammar. In *Lexical Grammar.* T Hoekstra, H van der Hulst and M Moortgat (eds.). Foris: Dordrecht.

WILKINS W (ed.), (1988). *Syntax and Semantics, Vol. 21: Thematic Relations.* Academic Press: New York.

WILLIAMS E, (1982). The NP-cycle. *Linguistic Inquiry*: **13**; 277–295.

WILLIAMS E, (1983). Against small clauses. *Linguistic Inquiry*: **14**; 287–308.

WILLIAMS E, (1984a). *There*-insertion. *Linguistic Inquiry*: **15**; 131–153.

WILLIAMS E, (1984b). Grammatical relations. *Linguistic Inquiry*: **15**; 639–673.

WILLIAMS E, (1986). A reassignment of the functions of LF. *Linguistic Inquiry*: **17**; 265–301.

ZWICKY A, (1987). Slashes in the passive. *Linguistics*: **25**; 639–669.

Glossary

This glossary is not exhaustive but it includes the most important terms used in this book. Terms that are used as chapter titles are not included.

A (Adjective)   One of the main lexical categories exemplified by words like *young*, *old*, *angry*, *likely* and *eager*. *See* 2.2, 10.2 and 11.2.

A-bound   A term used in GB. A category is A-bound if it is coindexed with a c-commanding category in an A-position (i.e. subject, object or object of a preposition). A category that is not A-bound is A-free. *See* 9.4.

Acceptability   A sentence is acceptable for a speaker if it is felt to be natural and normal. Unacceptable sentences may be unacceptable because they are ungrammatical or for other reasons. *See* 1.4.

Across-the-board   *See* Coordinate Structure Constraint.

Adjuncts   Optional constituents generally allowed in any phrase of a particular kind whatever its head is. *See* 5.

Adjunction   A movement process assumed within Transformational Grammar, which makes the moved category the sister of some existing category and the daughter of another instance of that category. For example, if NP is adjoined to S, the result is the following:

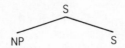

See 7.6.

Adjunct-Island Condition   One of a number of island constraints. It stipulates that a *wh*-dependency cannot cross the boundary of an adverbial expression. It accounts for the ungrammaticality of examples like * *What did he criticize Chomsky without reading*. Within GB it is a consequence of the Subjacency Condition, and within PSG it can be attributed to the SLASH Principle. *See* 13.2–4.

A-free   A term used in GB. A category is A-free if it is not A-bound, i.e. if it is not coindexed with a c-commanding category in an A-position (i.e. subject, object or object of a preposition). *See* 11.3.

Anaphor   A term applied in GB to reflexives, NP-traces and PRO, and to the reciprocal pronoun *each other*. An anaphor is required to be A-bound in its governing category. *See* 9.4.

Antecedent   An expression which determines who or what a pronoun refers to. The restrictions on where the antecedents of various kinds of pronoun can be located have been a major concern of GB. *See* 3.5.

Antecedent government   *See* proper government.

AP   One of the main full phrasal categories. *See* 2.

A-position   A term applied in GB to the positions subject, object and object of a preposition. *See* 9.4.

Ā-position   A term used in GB for a position which is not an A-position. Also known as a non-A-position. The most important Ā-position is the clause initial position in which *wh*-phrases appear in S-structure. *See* 12.

Auxiliary   A verbal item that can appear before the subject in a question. *Be* is an auxiliary given the grammaticality of *Was he singing*, but *stop* is not given the ungrammaticality of * *Stopped he singing*. The main auxiliaries are *be*, modals like *may* and *must* and perfective *have*, the *have* that combines with a past participle. *See* 4.2 and 8.2.

Barrier   A term used in connection with the Subjacency Condition of GB. The Condition blocks movement across the boundary of more than one barrier. *See* 13.3. The term is also used in connection with government.

Binding theory   One of the subtheories of GB. *See* 14.2.

Bounding node   A term used instead of barrier in early formulations of the Subjacency condition. *See* 13.4.

Bounding theory   A term applied to the Subjacency Condition seen as one of the subtheories of GB. *See* 14.2.

Case   Different forms of nouns and pronouns that appear in different contexts are said to be different Case forms. In English, *I*, *he*, *she*, *we* and *they* are nominative forms, while *me*, *him*, *her*, *us* and *them* are accusative or objective forms. *See* 9.4.

Case filter   A GB principle which requires an NP with phonetic content to have Case. It determines which NP positions can be occupied by overt NP's on the surface. It ensures that NP-movement is obligatory in passive and raising structures and that only a PRO subject is possible with certain infinitives. *See* 9.4, 10.3 and 11.3.

Case theory   One of the subtheories of GB. It consists of various Case-marking conventions and the Case filter. *See* 14.2.

Category-neutral rules   Rules which make no reference to specific categories such as NP, VP, etc. Immediate dominance rules are category-neutral in GB and HPSG, though not in GPSG. *See* 5.4 and 5.5.

C-command   A relation between nodes in a tree, which is particularly important in GB. A node X c-commands a node Y if neither dominates the other and the first branching node (node with more than one daughter) above X dominates Y. *See* 3.5.

Chomskyan Phrase Structure Grammar   A term used in the present book to refer to Chomsky's formalization of the descriptive practices of pre-Chomskyan linguists. It is similar in some ways to Phrase Structure Grammar as it developed in the 80's, but there are also some major differences. *See* 1.7, 3.2, 4.1.

Classical Transformational Grammar   The version of Transformational Grammar that was widely assumed in the 60s. Also known as the Standard Theory. *See* 1.7 and 9.4.

Cleft sentences   Sentences like *It is beer that Ben likes*, which provide a way of emphasizing a constituent. They are an important example of a *wh*-dependency construction. *See* 2.2, 2.4 and 12.5.

C (COMP, Complementizer) A category which includes items such as *that*, which introduce a subordinate clause. C has often been seen as combining with an S to form an S'. In recent GB, however, C is analyzed as a head of phrase which takes an S as its complement and has a specifier position which is the landing site for *wh*-movement. *See* 9.4 and 12.3.

Complementizer-gap constraint One of a number of island constraints. It stipulates that a *wh*-dependency gap cannot appear in subject position in a clause introduced by a complementizer. It rules out examples like * *Who do you think that saw Stefan*. Within GB, it is a consequence of the Empty Category Principle. *See* 13.2.

Complements Elements associated with a lexical head which normally appear as its sisters. *See* 5.

Complex-NP-constraint An important island constraint. It stipulates that a *wh*-dependency cannot cross the boundary of a clause and an NP that contains it. It accounts for the ungrammaticality of examples like * *What do you know the man who saw* and * *What do you believe the claim that Stefan saw*. It can be attributed to the Subjacency condition within GB and to the SLASH Principle within PSG. *See* 13.2.

Constituent The constituents of an expression are the words and phrases of which it is composed. In terms of trees, X is a constituent of Y, if Y dominates X. *See* 2.

Controller The NP which is understood as subject of the infinitive in a control sentence. In *Stefan tried to do it*, *Stefan* is the controller, while in *Stefan persuaded Maja to do it*, *Maja* is the controller. *See* 11.1 and 11.2.

Coordinate structure constraint An important island constraint, which stipulates that a *wh*-dependency cannot cross the boundary of a coordinate structure unless it affects every conjunct. It accounts for the ungrammaticality of examples like * *Who do you think that Stefan dislikes and that Maja hates Ben*. The qualification embodied in the *unless* clause allows examples like *Who do you think Stefan likes and Maja hates*, which are known as across-the-board exceptions to the constraint. *See* 13.2.

Coordination The combining of categories with words like *and* and *or*. In general, only constituents can be coordinated. *See* 2.4.

Cross-categorial generalizations Generalizations that affect different lexical categories or different phrasal categories. *See* 4.4.

Daughter A relation between nodes in a tree. A node X is the daughter of another node Y if and only if Y immediately dominates X. *See* 2.3.

Descriptive adequacy An analysis of a construction is said to achieve descriptive adequacy if not only allows all and only the examples of the construction but also captures whatever generalizations can be found in the data. *See* 3.3.

Det (Determiner) A lexical category which includes among others the articles *the* and *a* and the demonstratives *this* and *that*. *See* 2.2.

Discontinuous constituent A constituent whose parts are not all adjacent. *See* 2.3.

Dominance A relation between nodes in a tree. A node X dominates a node Y if there is a purely downward path through the tree from X to Y. *See* 2.3.

Double-object sentences Sentences containing a verb which takes two NP complements, e.g. *Stefan told Maja the truth*. *See* 8.2 and 8.4.

D-structure A term used within Transformational Grammar for the most abstract structure of a sentence from which the ordinary obvious structure of a sentence is derived by a number of transformational processes. *See* 7.6.

Dummy   A pronoun with no semantic function. Also known as an expletive or pleonastic. *It* in *It was raining* is a dummy as shown by the impossibility of asking * *What was raining? See* 6.2.

Echo-question   A question which echoes someone else's statement such as *You saw who* or *He did what. See* 7.4.

E-language   A term used by Chomsky to refer to a language seen as a set of sentences. *See* 1.3.

Empty Category Principle (ECP)   An important principle of GB, which requires a trace to be properly governed. It accounts for the ungrammaticality of sentences like * *Who do you think that annoyed Debbie*, * *Who thought that who did it* and * *What did who do. See* 13.2 and 13.6.

Empty *wh*-element (Empty operator)   An empty category assumed within GB, which undergoes *wh*-movement just like an overt *wh*-expression and accounts for *wh*-dependencies in which there is no overt *wh*-expression. *See* 12.5.

Ergative sentences   *See* unaccusative sentences.

Exceptional clause   A type of clause assumed within GB, in which the predicate is an infinitival expression. A representative example is *Stefan considers Ben to be a fool*. Within PSG, the subject and predicate are analyzed as two separate complements. *See* 5.2.

Expletive   *See* dummy.

Extended projection principle   A term used in GB for the combination of the Projection Principle and the requirement that a predicate has a subject. *See* 6.3.

External   θ-role which is assigned by a lexical head to its subject. It is assumed that some lexical heads have an external θ-role while others do not. Passives, unaccusatives and raising verbs do not have an external θ-role. *See* 6.3, 9.4, 9.6 and 10.3.

Extraposition   A type of movement process assumed in Transformational Grammar which moves part of a phrase to end of the sentence and accounts for examples like *A book has appeared about syntax* and *The news broke that Ben had resigned*. In GB, it has often been suggested that extraposition applies in the mapping from S-structure to PF. *See* 14.2.

Features   The basic building blocks of categories. Every feature has a number of possible values, which may be simple entities such as '+' and '−', or complex entities such as categories. *See* 4.5.

Finite   Finite verbs are verbs which are marked for tense and which vary in form according to the person and number of the subject. A finite clause is a clause whose main verb is finite. A non-finite verb is one which is not marked for tense and does not vary in form. A non-finite clause is one whose main verb is non-finite.

FOOT features   A term applied within PSG to the features SLASH and WH, which unlike other features commonly have the same value in a mother and a non-head daughter. *See* 12.4.

The FOOT Feature Principle   A PSG principle, which governs the distribution of the FOOT features SLASH and WH. *See* 12.4.

Foil phrasal categories   Categories that classify full phrasal expressions.

The main full phrasal categories are NP, VP, AP and PP. S and S′ are also often seen as full phrasal categories. In GB, they are analyzed as IP and CP, respectively.

Gapping   A term used in connection with conjoined sentences the second of which lacks a verb. A typical example is *Stefan likes beer, and Ben wine*. *See* 2.4.

Generalized Phrase Structure Grammar (GPSG)   One of two versions of phrase structure grammar that developed during the 80s. *See* 1.7.

Generate   The set of sentences that are identified as possible by a set of rules and a lexicon is said to be generated by them. *See* 3.3.

Generative   Precise and explicit. *See* 1.5.

Government   A relation between nodes in a tree which plays a major role in GB. All definitions of government entail that a lexical head governs a complement and the subject of an exceptional clause or small clause complement and that the agreement features associated with a finite verb govern its subject. *See* 9.

Government-binding theory (GB)   A version of Transformational Grammar which emerged at the end of the 70s and which was first presented in Chomsky's *Lectures on Government and Binding*. *See* 1.7.

Governing category   A notion employed in GB   conditions on anaphors and pronouns. The governing category of an item is the minimal (i.e. smallest) NP or S containing the item and an item governing it. *See* 9.4.

Grammar   A precise description of the syntax of a language. *See* 1.1.

Grammatical   A sentence is grammatical if it conforms to all relevant linguistic rules. Sentences may be unacceptable because they are ungrammatical, but they may also be unacceptable for other reasons. *See* 1.4.

Grammatical functions   A term applied to notions like subject and object. *See* 8.1.

Head   The central element in a phrase. In a typical NP, the head is the N′ which it immediately dominates or the N which the N′ immediately dominates. Similarly, in a typical AP, the head is the A′ which it immediately dominates or the A which the A′ immediately dominates. *See* 4.3.

Head-driven Phrase Structure Grammar (HPSG)   One of two versions of Phrase Structure Grammar which developed during the 80s. *See* 1.7.

I-language   A term used by Chomsky to refer to a language seen as a set rule and principles in the mind of a speaker. *See* 1.3.

Immediate constituent   A relation between expressions. An expression X is an immediate constituent of another expression Y if and only if Y immediately dominates X. *See* 2.3.

Immediate dominance   A relation between nodes in a tree. A node X immediately dominates a node Y if and only if X dominates Y and there is no node Z such that X dominates Z and Z dominates Y. *See* 2.3.

Immediate dominance rules   Rules which specify what categories a category can immediately dominate but which unlike phrase structure rules say nothing about the order of the categories. *See* 3.4.

I (INFL, INFLECTION)   A category assumed within GB, which incorporates the agreement features and tense information which is associated on the surface with a finite verb. Modals and infinitival *to* are members of this category. It is generally assumed that I is the head of S, which is therefore IP. *See* 9.4, 10.3 and 10.5.

Instantiation   A term used in connection with the relation between categories in rules and the lexicon and categories in trees. Where a category in a rule or the lexicon has a variable as the value of some feature and the corresponding category in a tree has an ordinary value or constant as the value of the same feature, the variable is said to be instantiated. *See* 6.4.

Intermediate phrasal categories   Categories that classify expressions that are potentially larger than a single word but smaller than a full phrase. Intermediate phrasal categories typically combine with a specifier to form the related full phrasal category. *See* 2.5.

Landing site   A term applied to the empty category which is replaced by a moved category in a substitution process. *See* 7.5.

Lexical categories   Categories that classify single words. The main lexical categories are N (noun), V (verb), A (adjective) and P (preposition). Other important lexical categories are Det and C (COMP), and within GB, I (INFL).

Lexical Functional Grammar (LFG)   Alternative to Transformational Grammar which has developed since the late 70s. For LFG, the syntactic structure of a sentence has two components: a constituent structure (or c-structure) and a functional structure (or f-structure).

Lexical rules   Rules which derive lexical entries from lexical entries. They are particularly important in PSG. *See* 9.5.

Lexicon   A list of words assigned to various lexical categories and provided with semantic interpretations. A lexicon may also include various lexical rules. *See* 3.3 and 9.5.

LF (Logical form)   A level of structure assumed within GB which is derived from S-structure by processes rather like *wh*-movement. It is motivated in part by semantic considerations but the main motivation for it involves certain syntactic facts. *See* 13.6.

Linear precedence rules   Rules which impose restrictions on the order in which certain categories can appear. Within PSG, these rules only affect categories that are sisters. Within GB, linear precedence restrictions may affect categories which are not sisters. *See* 3.4 and 14.2.

Linguistic competence   A term used by Chomsky in his writings of the 60s and 70s with essentially the same meaning as I-language. *See* 1.3.

Local trees   A tree consisting of a category and its daughters. Within PSG no grammatical statement refers to anything larger than a local tree, but for GB grammatical statements may refer to larger structures. *See* 3.5 and 14.3.

Maximal projection   Another term for full phrasal category. *See* 4.3.

Modal   A term applied to words like *may*, *must*, *will* and *shall* which are auxiliaries, but which differ from the other auxiliaries, *have* and *be* in having no non-finite forms. Within GB, they are regarded as members of the I category.

Monostratal   A term applied to theories of syntax in which the structure of a sentence is a single tree. The most important example is Phrase Structure Grammar. *See* 7.5.

Mother   A relation between nodes in a tree. A node X is the mother of another node Y if and only if X immediately dominates Y. *See* 2.3.

Move α   The single transformation assumed within GB. It is essentially a license to move anything anywhere, movement being either substitution or adjunction. *See* 9.4.

Multistratal A term applied to theories of syntax in which the structure of a sentence is a number of trees. The most important example is Transformational Grammar. *See* 7.6.

N (Noun) One of the main lexical categories, exemplified by words like *boy*, *girl*, *destruction* and *betrayal*. *See* 2.2 and 9.6.

Node A labelled position in a tree representing the structure of a sentence. *See* 2.3.

Noncanonical complement A constituent which functions as the complement of a lexical head, i.e. satisfies its subcategorization requirements, but is not a sister of the head as complements normally are. *Wh*-questions and passives can involve noncanonical complements. *See* 7.2.

Noncanonical subject A constituent which functions as the subject of a predicate although it is not a sister of the predicate. *Wh*-questions and raising sentences can involve a noncanonical subject. *See* 7.3.

Non-configurational language A language with very free word order. A notable example is the Australian Aboriginal language Warlpiri. *See* 14.5.

Non-finite *See* finite.

Non-local conditions on trees Conditions which affect something larger than a local tree consisting of a node and its daughters. Such conditions play a major role in GB, but are rejected by PSG. *See* 3.5.

NP One of the main full phrasal categories. *See* 2.2.

NP-movement A term used in GB for the movement of an NP to an empty NP position. *See* 9.4 and 10.3.

NP-trace A term used in GB for a trace left by NP-movement. NP-traces are classified as anaphors. *See* 9.4 and 10.3.

Null-subject language A language which allows finite clauses with no overt subject. Such languages are also known as pro-drop languages. *See* 6.3.

Object A complement of a verb which becomes a subject in a passive. *See* 1.2 and 8.

Observational adequacy An analysis of a construction is said to achieve observational adequacy if the rules that it consists of combined with a suitable lexicon will generate all and only the examples of the construction. *See* 3.3.

Of-insertion A process assumed in GB to be involved in examples like the *the Vikings' destruction of the monastery* and *the destruction of the monastery by the Vikings*. The assumption that such examples involve *of*-insertion allows one to assume that deverbal nouns like *destruction* have an NP complement in D-structure just like the related verbs. *See* 9.6.

P (Preposition) One of the main lexical categories exemplified by words like *to*, *for*, *by* and *from*. *See* 2.2.

Parasitic gaps Gaps in *wh*-dependency constructions which are only possible because another 'ordinary' gap is present. In *Which book did he criticize without reading* the gap after *reading* is only possible because there is a gap after *criticize*. This is shown by the ungrammaticality of * *Which book did he criticize Chomsky without reading*, in which the latter is missing. *See* 13.5.

PF (Phonetic Form) A term used within GB for the phonetic representation of a sentence. *See* 14.

Phrasal categories   Categories that classify phrasal expressions. *See* 2.

Phrase Structure Grammar (PSG)   A term applied both to Chomsky's formalization of the descriptive practices of his predecessors and to certain approaches to syntax that were developed during the 80s. *See* 1.7.

Phrase structure rules   Rules which specify what categories a category can immediately dominate and what order they can appear in. *See* 3.2.

Pleonastic   *See* Dummy.

PP   One of the main full phrasal categories. *See* 2.2.

Predicate   An expression which in English and many other languages normally combines with a subject to form a clause. *See* 6 and 8.

Pro   An empty pronoun assumed within GB. It appears in subject position in finite clauses in what are known as null-subject languages. *See* 6.3.

PRO   An empty NP assumed within GB. It is assumed that PRO appears as the subject of controlled infinitives. It is standardly analyzed as both an anaphor and a pronominal. *See* 11.3.

Pronominal   A term applied within GB to ordinary pronouns, *pro* and PRO. *See* 11.3.

Pronoun   A term sometimes applied both to ordinary pronouns like *I*, *you* and *he*, and to reflexive pronouns like *myself*, *yourself* and *himself* and sometimes applied just to ordinary pronouns. It is used in the latter way within GB. *See* 3.5, 4.2 and 11.3.

Projection principle   An important principle in GB, which requires syntactic representations to observe the subcategorization properties of lexical items. *See* 5.4.

Proper government   A notion employed in the Empty Category Principle of GB. α properly governs β if and only if (a) β is a complement to which α assigns a θ-role or (b) β is governed by and coindexed with α. In the first situation, β is said to be θ-governed. In the second, it is said to be antecedent governed. *See* 13.3.

Pseudo-cleft sentences   Sentences like *What Ben likes is beer*, which provide a way of emphasizing a constituent. They are an important example of a *wh*-dependency construction. *See* 2.2, 2.4 and 12.5.

Pseudo-passive   A passive sentence in which the missing constituent is on the face of it not a complement of the verb but a complement of a preposition, e.g. *The bed hasn't been slept in*. *See* 9.6.

Reanalysis   A process assumed within GB which adjoins a preposition to a preceding verb, creating a complex verb. This process gives a second structure for sentences involving a verb followed by a PP, and allows pseudo-passives. *See* 9.6.

Recursion   A set of rules is said to allow recursion if it allows a particular category to dominate itself. Given a suitable lexicon, a set of rules that allows recursion will generate an infinite number of sentences. *See* 3.3.

Reflexive pronouns   Items like *myself*, *yourself* and *himself*. Within GB, these are classified as anaphors. *See* 3.5 and 9.4.

Relational Grammar   The first major alternative to Transformational Grammar, which emerged in the early 70s. Like Transformational Grammar, it is a multistratal framework, but unlike Transformational Grammar, it treats grammatical functions like subject and object as primitives. *See* 1.7 and 8.3.

Relative clause   A type of NP adjunct which involves a *wh*-dependency. In

English, relative clauses may contain an overt *wh*-expression but they need not. *See* 12.5.

R-expressions A term applied within GB to non-pronominal NP's and *wh*-traces. R-expressions are required to be A-free. This accounts for the fact that *he* and *Stefan* in the following cannot be the same person in *He thinks John is clever*. In its application to *wh*-traces, it accounts for the strong crossover phenomenon. *See* 12.3.

Right-node raising A term used in connection with sentences involving conjoined clauses each lacking a final constituent followed by a constituent which functions as the final constituent of both clauses. A typical example is *Ben likes but Debbie hates the man next door*. *See* 2.4.

Sister A relation between nodes in a tree. A node X and another node Y are sisters if and only if they have the same mother. *See* 2.3.

SLASH A feature employed in PSG analyses of *wh*-dependencies. *See* 12.4 and 13.4.

The SLASH Principle A principle of PSG, which governs the distribution of the SLASH feature and accounts for a number of island constraints, notably the Subject Condition, the Complex NP Constraint and the Adjunct island Condition. *See* 13.4.

Small clause A type of clause assumed within GB, in which the predicate is an AP, NP, PP or base VP. Representatives examples are *Stefan considers Ben foolish, Stefan considers Ben a fool, Stefan wanted Ben out of the room* and *Stefan made Ben do it*. Within PSG, the subject and predicate are analyzed as two separate complements. *See* 5.2.

Specifier An expression that combines with an intermediate phrasal category to form the related full phrasal category. Determiners are nominal specifiers, *so* is an adjectival specifier, and measure phrases like *a mile* are prepositional specifiers. *See* 2.5.

S-structure A term used within Transformational Grammar to refer either to the ordinary, obvious structure of a sentence or to something only slightly more abstract. The S-structure of a sentence is derived from its D-structure by various transformational processes. *See* 7.6 and 14.2.

Structural change Part of a transformation of the kind employed in classical TG, which indicates the change that the rule licences. *See* 9.3.

Structural description Part of a transformation of the kind employed in classical TG, which indicates identifies the type of tree to which the rule applies. *See* 9.3.

Strong crossover phenomenon A term used within Transformational Grammar to refer to the impossibility of interpreting the *wh*-word and pronoun as the same person in sentences like *Who does he think did it*. The term reflects the fact that the *wh*-word in such an example has been moved across the pronoun. *See* 12.3.

SUBCAT A feature assumed within HPSG, whose value is a list of categories, often known as a SUBCAT list. It indicates what complements an item takes and in some versions what kind of subject it requires as well. *See* 5.5 and 6.4.

Subcategorization A term used to refer to the subclassification of lexical heads on the basis of what complements that they take. *See* 5.

Subcategorization Principle A principle of HPSG which ensures that a lexical head has the appropriate complements. *See* 5.5.

SUBJ   A feature assumed in some versions of PSG, which indicates what sort of subject an item requires. *See* 6.4.

Subjacency Condition   An important GB principle, which bars movement across the boundary of more than one bounding node or barrier. It accounts for a number of island constraints, especially the Subject Condition, the Complex NP Constraint, the *Wh*-island condition, and the Adjunct Island Condition. *See* 13.3.

Subject   An expression which in English and many other languages normally combines with a predicate to form a clause. *See* 6.

Subject Condition   An important island constraint. It stipulates that a *wh*-dependency cannot cross the boundary of a subject. It rules out examples like* *Who was a picture of on the table* and * *Who is that Stefan saw likely*. In GB it is a consequence of the Subjacency Condition, while in PSG it can be attributed to the SLASH Principle. *See* 13.2.

Substitution   A movement process assumed within Transformational Grammar, which substitutes the moved category for an existing empty category. The empty category is standardly referred to as a 'landing site' for moment. *See* 7.6.

Subsumption   A term used in connection with the relation between categories in rules and the lexicon and categories in trees. A category X subsumes a category Y if and only if Y contains all the feature specifications in X and all instances of a single variable in X are instantiated in the same way in Y. *See* 4.6 and 6.4.

Successive cyclic movement   A term applied within TG to the situation in which a constituent undergoes a specific type of movement more than once. *See* 12.3.

'Tough' sentences   Sentences containing one of a small class of adjectives, including *tough*, which take a complement involving a *wh*-dependency. A typical example is *Stefan is easy to impress*. *See* 12.5.

Trace   An empty category assumed within GB. It is assumed that movement leaves a trace, an empty category coindexed with the moved category. *See* 9.

Transformation   A rule that converts one tree into another tree. *See* 9.3 and 9.4.

Transformational Grammar (TG)   An approach to syntax which assumes that the full structure of a sentence is a sequence of trees. *See* 7.6.

TVP   A label applied to a constituent consisting of a verb and any non-object complement, which combines with an object to form a VP. *See* 8.

θ-government   *See* proper government.

θ-roles   Semantic roles such agent, source, goal and location, which are associated with lexical heads. Within GB, it is assumed that all complements must be assigned a θ-role but that the subject position need not be. *See* 5.6 and 6.3.

θ-theory   One of the subtheories of GB. Its central component is the requirement that no NP can have more than one θ-role. Its main function is to restrict the positions to which movement is possible. *See* 9 and 14.

Unaccusative sentences   Sentences like *The vase smashed* and *The ice melted* in which the subject, like the subject of a typical passive, is interpreted like an object. Also known as ergative sentences. For GB, the subjects originate in object position and undergo NP-movement. *See* 9.6.

V (verb) One of the main lexical categories exemplified by words like *give*, *take*, *seem* and *try*. *See* 2.2, 10.2 and 11.2.

Vacuous movement A term used within Transformational Grammar, for a movement process which changes the structure of the sentence but does not change the linear order of the words it contains. Sentences like *Who saw Stefan* involve vacuous movement within Transformational Grammar. *See* 12.3.

Verb-fronting A process assumed in transformational analyses of sentences in which the verb precedes the associated subject. *See* 8.5.

VP One of the main full phrasal categories. *See* 2.2.

Weak crossover phenomenon A term used within Transformational Grammar to refer to the impossibility of interpreting the *wh*-word and pronoun as the same person in sentences like *Who does his mother love*. As in sentences exemplifying the strong crossover phenomenon, the wh-word has been moved across a pronoun, but the pronoun does not c-command the position from which the *wh*-word has been moved. *See* 13.6.

Wh-dependencies The dependency between a missing complement or subject and a specific type of higher structure often but not always containing a *wh*-element. *Wh*-dependencies are found in *wh*-questions, relative clauses, clefts, pseudo-clefts, and 'tough' sentences, among other constructions. In GB *wh*-dependencies involve *wh*-movement, while in PSG they involve the SLASH feature. *See* 12.

Wh-island condition An island constraint which stipulates that a *wh*-dependency cannot cross the boundary of a subordinate *wh*-question. It rules out examples like * *Who do you wonder what he did to*. It is a consequence of the Subjacency Condition in GB and it can attributed to the SLASH Principle in PSG. *See* 13.2.

Wh-movement A movement process which is responsible within Transformational Grammar for *wh*-dependencies. For recent GB, *wh*-movement is a substitution process, moving a *wh*-phrase into an empty specifier position associated with COMP. *See* 12.3.

Wh-questions Questions which involve a question word (or *wh*-word) of some kind like *who*, *what* or *how*. They are one of a number of *wh*-dependency constructions. *See* 7 and 12.

Wh-trace A trace left by *wh*-movement. *Wh*-traces are grouped together with non-pronominal NP's as a class of 'R-expressions'. This classification permits an account of the strong crossover phenomenon. *See* 12.3.

X-bar theory A body of ideas about constituent structure originating in Chomsky (1970) and developed during the 70s, especially in Jackendoff (1977). The ideas have been absorbed in one way or another into most current theories. In GB, the term is applied to a number of category neutral immediate dominance rules which define the basic types of syntactic structure. *See* 4.3 and 14.2.

Index

235